"Matt Smethurst has researched an impressive amount of content for this book: sermons, books, papers, courses, articles, and unpublished conversations. He found resources even I wasn't familiar with, and he has produced a work of scholarship that will long stand as the most thorough examination of the biblical themes that animated all of Tim's ministry."
Kathy Keller

"Few pastors have demonstrated a multilayered, multifaceted understanding of how the gospel of Jesus Christ transforms everything like Tim Keller did. Matt Smethurst has done a wonderful job organizing Tim's teaching on the gospel in everyday life—in a way that is engaging, practical, and heart and life changing. May this gospel continue to transform us and everything our lives touch. Read and reread this book!"
Paul David Tripp, author, *Everyday Gospel*

"Imagine sitting with Tim Keller in his living room and asking him whatever is on your mind about the Christian life. Well, my friend Matt Smethurst has opened the door to that room in this book. Flip its pages and you'll receive compelling wisdom from this beloved pastor, which will help you practice your faith within your family, job, or community. *Tim Keller on the Christian Life* is particularly timely, as many of us are struggling to make Christ-honoring imprints on our skeptical culture. But by the last chapter of this remarkable work, you'll grasp what it means to truly embody the gospel in all your spheres of influence. Thank you, Matt, for giving us the very best of Tim Keller."
Joni Eareckson Tada, Founder and CEO, Joni and Friends International Disability Center

"The way the ministry of Tim Keller and Redeemer Church penetrated the secularized culture of Manhattan drew the attention of a surprised media. Remarkably, this was based not on an ever-changing pragmatism ('whatever works') but on an intelligent, clearly articulated, and winsomely expounded Christ-centered biblical theology. *Tim Keller on the Christian Life* explores the manifold ways this theology shaped Tim's understanding of how the gospel restores and transforms. Those who heard Tim will be understandably eager to read these pages, and all readers will find a stimulating exploration of the impact of gospel grace. Congratulations and thanks are due to Matt Smethurst for this groundbreaking study."
Sinclair B. Ferguson, Professor of Systematic Theology, Reformed Theological Seminary; author, *The Whole Christ*

"You don't need to agree with everything Tim Keller said to recognize that God gave him uncommon wisdom that can benefit the church and your own discipleship. Matt Smethurst has done an impressive job distilling this wisdom, spread across many books and countless sermons, into ten engaging chapters. Think of it as a 'Keller's Greatest Hits' volume. It's a remarkable and grace-giving work, one that I'll certainly encourage my family members and church members to read."
Jonathan Leeman, Editorial Director, 9Marks

"What a blessing to read a book by a friend, about a friend's wisdom on the Christian life. I got to watch Tim Keller practice what he proclaimed, especially while battling terminal cancer. No matter your familiarity with Tim's body of work, Matt Smethurst's distillation will prove an aid and blessing. He puts his finger on themes and emphases that will enrich your engagement with our brother's enduring ministry. Matt has told me what a spiritually rewarding exercise it was to write this book. You will find it spiritually rewarding to read."

Ligon Duncan, Chancellor and CEO, Reformed Theological Seminary; cohost, *The Everyday Pastor* podcast

"I was eager to open this book to better appreciate Keller's pastoral legacy and to see how Smethurst would tell the story. I found exactly what I'd hoped for: a wise pastor curating the wisdom of another wise pastor. The result is a treasure—a study about our Father's love to us, which awakens our love for him and for others. The beautiful fruit of the heart-transforming gospel."

Tony Reinke, Senior Teacher, Desiring God; author, *Ask Pastor John*

"Tim Keller had a knack for presenting Christ and what it means to follow him in ways that I, as someone who had spent my whole life absorbing Christian teaching, had never heard before. It often stopped me in my tracks. It challenged my deeply ingrained understandings and interpretations. But most importantly, it enabled me to see the beauty, necessity, and sufficiency of Christ in ways that moved and changed me. This book enables those familiar with Keller's teaching to be reminded of its core truths—and those who know little of it to get to its essence in summary fashion."

Nancy Guthrie, author; Bible teacher

"There will never be another Tim Keller—a man uniquely raised up by God to teach a generation of believers to treasure the gospel and to teach a generation of skeptics to consider the gospel. Matt Smethurst takes us into the genius of Tim's ministry, drawing from its breadth to synthesize and distill the key insights for how Jesus Christ changes us from the inside out. This is a deeply edifying read."

Dane Ortlund, Senior Pastor, Naperville Presbyterian Church, Naperville, Illinois; author, *Gentle and Lowly*

"Matt Smethurst has done the church a great service by distilling, in ten insightful chapters, the core convictions that shaped Tim Keller's life and ministry. The reader discovers what made Keller's ministry so impactful: His convictions, along with his humility, were formed in the fires of pastoral work. *Tim Keller on the Christian Life* is a faith-enriching reminder, through the legacy and example of a beloved pastor, that Christianity is far more than a religious idea. It is the most satisfying and beautiful way of life."

Sam Ferguson, Rector, The Falls Church Anglican, Washington, DC

Tim Keller on the Christian Life

Tim Keller on the Christian Life

The Transforming Power of the Gospel

Matt Smethurst

∷ CROSSWAY®

WHEATON, ILLINOIS

Tim Keller on the Christian Life: The Transforming Power of the Gospel

© 2025 by Matt Smethurst

Published by Crossway
        1300 Crescent Street
        Wheaton, Illinois 60187

Cover design: David Fassett

Cover image: Tim Keller 2019 TGC Conference © The Gospel Coalition, other images from Rawpixel

First printing 2025

Printed in the United States of America

Hardcover ISBN: 978-1-4335-9619-3
ePub ISBN: 978-1-4335-9621-6
PDF ISBN: 978-1-4335-9620-9

Library of Congress Cataloging-in-Publication Data

Names: Smethurst, Matt, author.
Title: Tim Keller on the Christian life : the transforming power of the Gospel / Matt Smethurst.
Description: Wheaton, Illinois : Crossway, [2025] | Includes bibliographical references and index.
Identifiers: LCCN 2024045084 (print) | LCCN 2024045085 (ebook) | ISBN 9781433596193 (hardcover) | ISBN 9781433596209 (pdf) | ISBN 9781433596216 (epub)
Subjects: LCSH: Christian life. | Keller, Timothy, 1950-2023.
Classification: LCC BV4501.3 .S6345 2025 (print) | LCC BV4501.3 (ebook) | DDC 248.4—dc23/eng/20241115
LC record available at https://lccn.loc.gov/2024045084
LC ebook record available at https://lccn.loc.gov/2024045085

Crossway is a publishing ministry of Good News Publishers.

LB			34	33	32	31	30	29	28	27	26	25
15	14	13	12	11	10	9	8	7	6	5	4	3	2	1

To Maghan,
mighty helper and dearest friend.
I love you.

Contents

Introduction

HOPEWELL, VIRGINIA, IS EASY TO MISS. Roughly twenty-five miles south of Richmond, and about three hundred fifty miles from New York City, this rural town is where Tim Keller (1950–2023) cut his pastoral teeth from 1975 to 1984. For nearly a decade, Keller prepared three biblical expositions a week—Sunday morning, Sunday evening, and Wednesday night—for his flock at West Hopewell Presbyterian Church. By age thirty-three, he had delivered approximately fourteen hundred expository messages. Like many small-church pastors, his job description seemed endless: doing pastoral visits, caring for the sick, officiating weddings, conducting funerals, even cheering on the church softball team—not to mention leading and loving his family.

This season was so important that we cannot understand Keller's ministry in Manhattan without considering Hopewell. Far from a quick pit stop, his time there provided "the most formative ministry years of his life."[1] Hopewell is where, in Keller's words, "Kathy and I learned for the first time how to walk beside people who were facing grief, loss, death, and darkness."[2] This is why so many sermon illustrations at Redeemer Presbyterian Church came from experiences and counseling moments in his first church.

Keller observed that, generally speaking, in a small town "your pastoring sets up your preaching." That is, people won't respect you as a preacher unless they trust you as their pastor. But in a big city it's often the opposite: "Your preaching sets up your pastoring."[3] People won't trust you as their pastor unless they respect you as a preacher. Keller experienced both dynamics, but his renowned preaching was infused with wisdom gleaned from years of diligent pastoring.

Hopewell was also where Keller honed the art of contextualization, which (rightly practiced) is about clarity and therefore love. In an interview two months before his death, Keller defined this fancy term as simply giving a message in "the most understandable and persuasive way without compromising or changing the message itself." What was his main reason, the interviewer asked, for caring about contextualization? Simple: "I want people to fall in love with Jesus."[4]

A Sketch of His Life

Born on September 23, 1950, to middle-class parents in Allentown, Pennsylvania, Timothy James Keller was the oldest of three children. His parents could hardly have been more different from one another: Bill seemed remote, while Louise could be downright stifling. The family dutifully attended a mainline Lutheran church, but Tim rarely heard the gospel and remained unconverted.[5]

At Bucknell University, though, the Lord invaded his life and captured his heart. After a season of spiritual wrestling, Tim repented of his sin and trusted in Christ in April 1970.[6] "During college the Bible came alive in a way that was hard to describe," Keller later reflected. "The best way I can put it is that, before the change, I pored over the Bible, questioning and analyzing it. But after the change it was as if the Bible, or maybe Someone through the Bible, began poring over me, questioning and analyzing me."[7] Through involvement with Inter-Varsity Christian Fellowship, Keller was introduced to solid Christian literature—including British authors such as J. I. Packer and John Stott, who helped crystallize the gospel and its implications for life.

After college, Keller moved to Massachusetts in the fall of 1972 to attend Gordon-Conwell Theological Seminary. Another first-year student—an acquaintance from western Pennsylvania—would become his closest friend. Collin Hansen writes,

> Even before Kathy Kristy took the name Keller, she would become the most formative intellectual and spiritual influence on Tim Keller's life. When you're writing about Tim, you're really writing about Tim and Kathy, a marriage between intellectual equals who met in seminary over shared commitment to ministry and love for literature, along with serious devotion to theology.[8]

The three years on campus would prove pivotal in their theological formation. They entered with patchwork beliefs and emerged with thought-out convictions: historic Reformed theology, dynamic complementarianism, inward spiritual renewal, gospel-shaped missiology, and so on. Tim and Kathy were married on January 4, 1975, before their final semester. A thirty-six-year-old R. C. Sproul officiated the ceremony.

When Tim stepped into his first pastorate that summer, the Presbyterian Church in America (PCA) was only two years old. Those years in Hopewell, Virginia, were a baptism of fire for the newly minted pastor.[9] From preaching to counseling to hospital visitation to just about anything else that a solo small-town pastor is expected to do, Keller poured his life into the salt-of-the-earth saints the Lord had entrusted to his care. "It didn't take long for Keller to realize he needed to adjust his preaching—to become more concrete, clear, and practical. . . . He realized he needed to listen and learn before he spoke, so that he could persuade."[10] Hansen conveys it well:

> Many have concluded that in Hopewell, Keller learned to "put the cookies on the bottom shelf." . . . Hopewell's blue-collar congregation forced Keller to develop his skill for distilling difficult and complicated concepts in ways that Christians and non-Christians alike can understand. If he would have jumped straight from seminary to a

highly educated congregation, he might never have become a widely popular writer or preacher.[11]

Keller would always look back on the Hopewell years as foundational to his life of ministry.

While pastoring in Virginia, Keller had received a doctor of ministry degree—studying the work of deacons—through Westminster Theological Seminary in Philadelphia. Eventually, after nine years in Hopewell, Westminster hired him to teach practical theology part-time. (Keller also became the first director of mercy ministries for the PCA's Mission to North America.) So the Kellers moved back north, and the pastor became a professor.

While enjoying a fruitful teaching ministry at Westminster in the late 1980s—Keller was one of the school's most popular professors— the PCA asked him to consider planting a church in the heart of New York City. He declined and offered to try to recruit someone else.[12] But in God's providence, he couldn't find a pastor willing to move there. Meanwhile, he was becoming more and more attracted to the challenge himself:

> Keller's friends back in Philadelphia had been praying for Tim for months as he first searched for a different pastor for this calling and then slowly realized he would need to go. Finally, he came to the group and said, "I have to do this myself." Kathy considers that decision "one of the most truly 'manly' things" her husband ever did. The move scared him. But he felt God's call. He had no way of knowing the result would be a dynamic, growing megachurch. He just knew it was the next step of faith, even if the church were to end in failure.[13]

So in the summer of 1989, the Kellers moved to New York, three young sons in tow, with the goal of establishing a new outpost of Christ's kingdom.[14] From a rural town in Virginia to the quiet suburbs of Philadelphia to the city that never sleeps, God had brought the Kellers to the place he had prepared them for.

Redeemer Presbyterian Church was soon born and, almost immediately, experienced revival-like growth. "Everyone who remembers those first three years says they've never seen anything like it," Keller recounts. "We had conversions, a sense of God's presence, changed lives—all the stuff everyone hopes for. . . . It was unusually thick and rich—beyond anything we expected."[15] Or as Kathy has sometimes quipped, "Want to know the secret to planting a successful megachurch? Find out where God is going to send a revival . . . and move there the month before."[16] Redeemer experienced other significant surges in growth over the years, including after the terrorist attacks of September 11, 2001.[17]

Keller was instrumental in developing several ministries that grew out of Redeemer: Hope for New York (an effort to resource local nonprofit groups focused on mercy ministry), the Center for Faith and Work (a resource for believers seeking to bring the gospel to bear on their vocations), Redeemer Counseling (a professional counseling and training center), and Redeemer City to City (a global church-planting network). After retiring as senior pastor of Redeemer Presbyterian Church in 2017, Keller focused much of his time on serving church planters around the world.

Additionally, over lunch at a Manhattan sidewalk cafe in 2002, Keller and Bible scholar Don Carson dreamed up what would eventually become the Gospel Coalition (TGC). From an invite-only pastors' colloquium in 2005 to the organization's first national conference in 2007, TGC was founded to help restore the center of historic, confessional evangelicalism in the broadly Reformed heritage. Some of Keller's most edifying material is found in keynote talks and workshops he delivered at TGC conferences over the course of fifteen years.

Distillation, Not Evaluation

This book is not a biography. With rare exceptions, the focus is not on detailing Keller's life or assessing his legacy. The aim is more modest:

to *synthesize and distill Tim Keller's best teaching on the Christian life.*
For clarity, let's briefly consider these phrases.

Synthesize and distill. This book seeks to *show* more than *tell*, to let
Keller's own voice feature most prominently and ring with coherent
clarity. That word *coherent* represents the book's challenge, and its potential value—not because Keller was unclear but because his body of
work was so expansive and sprawling. How do you summarize nearly
fifty years of pastoral teaching on Christian living? One topic at a
time. In short, by taking key ingredients from the various cupboards
of Keller's wide-ranging work, this book endeavors to serve a nourishing, multicourse meal.

Tim Keller's best teaching. Keller left behind a staggering amount
of material. Many Christians will simply not have time to listen to
thousands of his sermons and read thirty-plus books. But they might
be willing to start with one—which seeks to bring out the "best of"
his teaching and, ideally, whets the appetite for partaking of more from
the well-stocked pantry of Keller's work.

On the Christian life. This book focuses on practical Christian discipleship—rather than, say, Keller's thoughts on more controversial
theological or political matters. Those are worthy topics for another
writing project. In general, the target here is Keller's contribution to
timeless, bread-and-butter aspects of everyday Christian living.

If you're like me, you probably didn't agree with Keller about everything. That's okay. For example, I disagreed with him on baptism
and church polity,[18] on aspects of practical ecclesiology and ministry
philosophy, and on some emphases in the realm of public theology.
Keller was an evangelist at heart, and I believe his genuine desire to
reach the lost convinced him to remain, at times, "above the fray" on
certain social issues, more than perhaps was warranted.

Though my purpose is to distill Keller's best teaching on the Christian
life, rather than evaluate his legacy, I will take the liberty to point out
that he was a three-dimensional voice in a two-dimensional world. To

borrow philosophical categories, Keller combined the *normative* (keen biblical insight) with the *situational* (studied awareness of the cultural moment) with the *existential* (searching heart application).[19] Think Bible teacher meets cultural analyst meets biblical counselor. Most great pastors tend to do two of these well, but Keller excelled at all three. The first and third are where he is probably least appreciated. Some may hear Keller quoting philosophers and *New York Times* columnists and assume his preaching was super scholarly or fancy. But it really wasn't. His illustrations were vivid, and his applications penetrating—precisely because they were down-to-earth.

Reverberating Voice

It's impossible to know whether people will still be reading and listening to Tim Keller in a hundred years. But since his death, numerous people have suggested that his impact will stand the test of time. Whether or not that will happen, it's striking that so many seem to assume it. Keller's voice has found unique resonance around the world. And because he left such an immense body of work, focused mainly on enduring topics of Christian living—the kind we'll be exploring in this book—his voice is primed to reverberate for generations to come.

When the news hit on May 19, 2023, that Keller had gone to be with his Savior, the outpouring of gratitude for his life—from myriad sectors of the church—was remarkable to witness. What accounts for Keller's titanic appeal across typical divides? Why can't Christians (of various stripes) seem to get enough of his teaching? The answer lies not in his sophistication but in his simplicity, in his ability to clarify the complex—a skill he nurtured as a young pastor in rural Virginia. And to do this, he had to listen widely, and well. Hansen is correct:

> Keller's originality comes in his synthesis, how he pulls the sources together for unexpected insights. . . . This God-given ability to integrate disparate sources and then share insights with others has been

observed by just about anyone who has known Keller, going back to his college days. He's the guide to the gurus. You get their best conclusions, with Keller's unique twist.[20]

My aim in this volume is to synthesize the master synthesizer. Drawing from nearly fifty years of sermons, conference messages, interviews, articles, books, and more, I attempt to draw out the best of Keller's teaching where it shines brightest—biblical wisdom for everyday life.

The appetite from Christians is there. The ingredients from Keller are there. Again, my hope is to simply open the various cupboards and deliver a nourishing meal.

1

One Hero

Jesus Christ in All Scripture

WHEN THINKING ABOUT the ongoing relevance of Tim Keller's teaching, it's easy to think of his cultural analysis, his attention to idolatry, his teaching on justice and mercy, or any number of emphases, many of which we'll explore in this book. But no theme can be understood, much less situated in Keller's thought, apart from the topic of this first chapter.

Running through Keller's enormous body of work is a single thread that connects the diverse dots into a coherent whole.[1] Above all, he was enamored with one great reality—the person and work of Jesus Christ—and he spent his life showcasing this treasure.

And learning to read the Bible with eyes for the Lord Jesus—seeing him as not just the main character but the main *point*—could change your life.

Setting the Stage

If you grew up in church, you're likely familiar with well-known Bible stories.[2] You've marveled at Noah's floating zoo, you've faced down giants in your life like David did, and maybe you've even dared to be a

Daniel. And that's just the Old Testament. In the Gospels you learned about Jesus's miracles, and you also likely learned that these stories aren't just intended to amaze; they're meant to make you a better person. See how generous that little boy was with his lunch? Go and do likewise.

Many of our nonbelieving neighbors assume that the Bible is a well-meaning series of morality tales, an anthology of philosophical musings, or an archaic rulebook that should remain confined to hotel-room drawers. Indeed, increasing numbers of people today believe that Scripture is downright dangerous, a tool to oppress the weak and prevent the gullible from being true to themselves.

Contrary to popular belief, though, the Bible is not simply a collection of principles, platitudes, or abstract life lessons. It is a single, unfolding drama, a story of epic proportions that's more thrilling than your favorite fairy tale—because it's true. That's God's word.

If we ever hope to properly handle the stories *in* the Bible, we must first grasp the story *of* the Bible. And that story—one that traverses its way from Genesis to Revelation—though recorded for you, is not ultimately about you.[3] The central focus is higher, and the central figure is better. Given the Bible's breathtaking diversity, the plotline's essential coherence is astonishing:

- sixty-six books of various genres
- over forty authors from various backgrounds and occupations
- over fifteen centuries
- ten civilizations
- three continents
- three languages
- one unified story of redemption

Remarkably, the Bible has one ultimate plan, one ultimate plot, one ultimate champion, one ultimate hero. And from the beginning we can see his silhouette.

Learning from Jesus

Consider what Jesus himself claims regarding his unique place in the pages of Scripture.

In Luke 24, shortly after his resurrection, Jesus appears incognito to two of his followers on a road. Bewildered and breathless, they relay the buzz surrounding the inexplicably empty tomb. It's the *inexplicable* part that prompts Jesus, still unrecognized, to speak: " 'O foolish ones, and slow of heart to believe all that the prophets have spoken! Was it not necessary that the Christ should suffer these things and enter into his glory?' And beginning with Moses and all the Prophets, he interpreted to them in all the Scriptures the things concerning himself" (Luke 24:25–27).[4] After revealing himself to the eleven disciples, he reiterates the same point: " 'These are my words that I spoke to you while I was still with you, that everything written about me in the Law of Moses and the Prophets and the Psalms must be fulfilled.' Then he opened their minds to understand the Scriptures" (Luke 24:44–45).

It wasn't only *after* his resurrection that Jesus spoke this way, however. For example, before his death he had explained to the Pharisees—the Jewish religious establishment, the "Bible experts" of the day—his central place in their great story: "You search the Scriptures because you think that in them you have eternal life; and it is they that bear witness about me, yet you refuse to come to me that you may have life. . . . For if you believed Moses, you would believe me; for he wrote of me" (John 5:39–40, 46).

To put it mildly, such claims were not typically well received.

It has been said that if the New Testament is Jesus Christ *revealed*, the Old Testament is Jesus Christ *concealed*.[5] That is exactly right. To paraphrase the late theologian B. B. Warfield, the Old Testament is like a room full of treasures, but the room is dimly lit.[6] It's filled with prophets that predict him, patterns that preview him, and promises that anticipate him. A sweeping, aerial view of the Bible's topography, focused on Christ, would therefore look something like this:

- **Old Testament:** anticipation
- **Gospels:** manifestation
- **Acts:** proclamation
- **Epistles:** explanation
- **Revelation:** consummation[7]

From beginning to end, the Bible is an epic story about Jesus.

Consider, Keller advises, what it would be like to read a chapter in a great novel without being privy to the surrounding context. Much would be incomprehensible. "If you don't see how the chapter fits into the whole story, you don't understand the chapter."[8] This is akin to reading any portion of God's word without seeing how it connects to God's Son.

Discovering Christ in the Old Testament

In Keller's foreword to Alec Motyer's book *A Christian's Pocket Guide to Loving the Old Testament*, he recounts traveling in the summer of 1972 to R. C. Sproul's Ligonier Valley Study Center. Fresh out of college, Keller was a fairly new Christian for whom the Old Testament was rather "confusing and off-putting."[9] Motyer was visiting from England and fielding questions when someone asked about the relationship between Old Testament Israelites and Christians today. He imparted an illustration that always stayed with Keller. Asking the group to imagine how the Israelites under Moses would have given their "testimony," Motyer suggested it would sound something like this:

We were in a foreign land, in bondage, under the sentence of death. But our mediator—the one who stands between us and God—came to us with the promise of deliverance. We trusted in the promises of

God, took shelter under the blood of the lamb, and he led us out. Now we are on the way to the Promised Land. We are not there yet, of course, but we have the law to guide us, and through blood sacrifice we also have his presence in our midst. So he will stay with us until we get to our true country, our everlasting home.

Motyer's conclusion—that a Christian today could "say the same thing, almost word for word"—left Keller "thunderstruck." The thought experiment brought Keller to an astounding recalculation: not only had the Israelites been saved by grace, not works, but "God's salvation had been by costly atonement . . . all along."[10]

Learning from Paul

We could turn to many places in Scripture for clues about how to read the whole, but consider the apostle Paul's simple statement to the church in Corinth: "For I decided to know nothing among you except Jesus Christ and him crucified" (1 Cor. 2:2). As we begin to unfold Keller's comprehensive teaching, consider his commentary on this pivotal verse:

> At the time Paul was writing, the only Scripture to preach from was what we now call the Old Testament. Yet even when preaching from these texts Paul "knew nothing" but Jesus—who did not appear by name in any of those texts. How could this be? Paul understood that all Scripture ultimately pointed to Jesus and his salvation; that every prophet, priest, and king was shedding light on the ultimate Prophet, Priest, and King. To present the Bible "in its fullness" was to preach Christ as the main theme and substance of the Bible's message.[11]

Yet, you may wonder, won't a relentless focus on Jesus in our Bible study become tiresome? Keller counters, "I can speak from forty years of experience . . . to tell you that the story of this one individual never needs to become repetitious—it contains the whole history of the universe and of humankind alike and is the only resolution of the plotlines of every one of our lives."[12]

Perhaps we could say that the reason seeing Christ is never monotonous is because he is less like an intriguing *Where's Waldo?* answer and more like water for our deepest thirst. He is not a mere ticket to heaven; he is the one for whom we were made, and only a profound sense of his love will reconfigure our hearts.

Vital union with the living Christ, the hero of the biblical story, is the wellspring from which virtually every other Keller teaching flows.[13]

Why Begin Here?

Before we proceed, it's worth clarifying again why we're starting here. Why is *this* the topic of chapter 1? The answer, most basically, is that Keller sees the Bible as the foundation for the Christian life.

Without the sure anchor of revelation, we will always be adrift in speculation. And those are dangerous waters. Until we gladly submit our lives to the supreme authority of God's word, we will remain captives to the clamoring voices of man.[14] Cultural sensibilities, personal preferences, and a hundred other factors will hold sway in our hearts. Keller is blunt: "Contemporary people tend to examine the Bible, looking for things they can't accept, but Christians should reverse that, allowing the Bible to examine *us*, looking for things God can't accept."[15] Or even more simply: "Unless you have an authoritative view of the Bible, you've got a God you created and you're going to be lonely."[16]

Even though this book is for ordinary laypeople, not just professional ministers, the wisdom Keller commends to preachers about getting to the heart of the Scriptures can help *all of us* better read our Bibles "with the Jesus grain," and not against it. Christ-centered interpretation is vital for life transformation, for following Jesus closely.

Everything we will cover in this book, therefore, is built on a Christ-centered reading of God's word.

Careful, Now

Simply naming Jesus, however, doesn't necessarily honor him. We can be so quick to "find" Christ in the Old Testament that we fail to do justice to the original text. Pulling him out of a hat—*voila!*—undercuts the integrity of the Bible and robs us of the benefit of reading it as God intended.

Though Keller is known for "getting to Christ," he warns against treating scriptures as mere springboards. In his book on preaching, which is helpful for any Bible reader, he identifies two common pitfalls. The first is studying a passage—even one about Jesus—without seeing the gospel. The second is getting to Jesus too quickly or carelessly.[17] Before seeing the Savior, Keller notes, we must ensure we've understood the text. We dare not "leapfrog over historical realities" in the Old Testament as though they bore "little significance to the original hearers."[18] So we mustn't make the focus all about Christ while ignoring the text, or make it all about the text while ignoring Christ.

Every now and then, Keller is critiqued for somewhat predictably getting to Christ but failing to apply the force of God's moral demands. In my experience, though, Keller was exemplary at showing how the gospel *transforms* us—how it's not only the last word but also, in a sense, the first word and the foundation of everything else. We shouldn't merely "tell people all the ways they must be moral and good without relating such exhortation to the gospel," he warns. But nor should we merely "tell them over and over that they can be saved only by free grace without showing how salvation changes our lives."[19]

Consider, for example, how Keller explains his typical sermon structure (again, this is relevant not just to those who deliver sermons but to all who listen to them):

- **Intro:** What the problem is; our contemporary cultural context: *Here's what we face.*
- **Early points:** What the Bible says; the original readers' cultural context: *Here's what we must do.*
- **Middle points:** What prevents us; current listeners' inward heart context: *Why we can't do it.*
- **Late points:** How Jesus fulfills the biblical theme and solves the heart issue: *How Jesus did it.*
- **Application:** *How through faith in Jesus you should live now.*[20]

This is not the only way to teach a passage (at least I hope not because I don't exactly follow this template). But notice that when Keller does finally "get to Jesus," the message is not over. With the final movement—moral application—his teaching reaches a summit, and the vista is clear. As a case study, he offers the example of Abraham and Isaac in Genesis 22:

1. **What we must do:** Put God first in every area of life, as Abraham did. (This is unfortunately where many sermons end!)
2. **But we can't:** We can't! We won't! So we deserve to be condemned.
3. **But there was one who did:** On the cross, Jesus put God first. His was the ultimate and perfect act of submission to God. Jesus is the only one to whom God ever said, "Obey me, and as a result I will judge you and condemn you." Jesus obeyed anyway—just for truth's sake, for God's sake. The only perfect act of submission.
4. **Only now can we change:** Only when we see that Jesus obeyed as Abraham did—*for us!*—can we begin to live like Abraham. Let your heart be shaped by this.[21]

Again, the point is not that every faithful sermon will simulate this structure. But a preacher's approach is incomplete if he virtually *never* sounds a "by the mercies of God, live like Abraham" note. Some gospel-centered voices are so allergic to sounding moralistic that they end up, despite good intentions, not sounding much like the Bible. Moral application (good) becomes moralistic application (bad) only when divorced from gospel grace.

Keller didn't shy away from direct moral application; this book, in fact, is a tour of Scripture-derived imperatives: resist idolatry (chap. 2), avoid moralism (chap. 3), be a good friend (chap. 4), work for God's glory (chap. 5), live justly (chap. 6), pray fervently (chap. 7), and suffer courageously (chap. 8). From beginning to end, Keller summons us to life transformation by the power of the Spirit. But we'll lose our footing if we don't start from a robust foundation of grace.[22]

Jesus, the True and Better

The Old Testament presents endless opportunities to discover the manifold wonders of Jesus Christ. We can see his glory in the Bible's every theme,[23] every genre and section,[24] every deliverance storyline,[25] every major image,[26] and, of course, every major figure.[27] As for the latter, it's hard to improve on Keller's classic formulation. (Read slowly—this is not just a rhetorical flourish; it captures the greatest news in the world.)

Jesus is the true and better *Adam*, who *passed* the test in the garden and whose obedience is imputed to us. . . .

Jesus is the true and better *Abel*, who, though innocently slain, has blood that cries out for our acquittal, not our condemnation. . . .

Jesus is the true and better *Abraham*, who answered the call of God to leave the comfortable and familiar and go out into the void, "not knowing whither he went," to create a new people of God.

Jesus is the true and better *Isaac*, who was not just offered up by his father on the mount but was truly sacrificed for us all. God said to

Abraham, "Now I know you love me, because you did not withhold your son, your only son whom you love, from me." [So] we can say to God, "Now *we* know that you love us, because you did not withhold your son, your only son whom you love, from us."

Jesus is the true and better *Jacob*, who wrestled with God and took the blow of justice we deserved so that we, like Jacob, receive only the wounds of grace to wake us up and discipline us.

Jesus is the true and better *Joseph*, who, at the right hand of the king, forgives those who betrayed and sold him and uses his new power to save them.

Jesus is the true and better *Moses*, who stands in the gap between the people and the Lord and who mediates a new covenant. . . .

Jesus is the true and better *rock of Moses*, who, struck with the rod of God's justice, now gives us water in the desert.

Jesus is the true and better *Job*—the *truly* innocent sufferer—who then intercedes for and saves his stupid friends. . . .

Jesus is the true and better *David*, whose victory becomes his people's victory, though they never lifted a stone to accomplish it themselves.

Jesus is the true and better *Esther*, who didn't just risk losing an earthly palace but lost the ultimate heavenly one, who didn't just risk his life but gave his life—to save his people.

Jesus is the true and better *Jonah*, who was cast out into the storm so we could be brought in.[28]

David, Jonah, Esther . . . and Bruce Willis

Again, we can be so quick to "get to the gospel" in our Bible reading that we run roughshod over the text at hand. That's a legitimate danger. Thankfully, though, the instinct for detecting Christ responsibly can be honed. In fact, the experience is a bit like watching the Bruce Willis film *The Sixth Sense*—for the second time. Keller explains,

> That movie has a startling ending that forces you to go back and reinterpret everything you saw before. The second time through, you can't *not* think of the ending as you watch the beginning and middle of the movie. The ending sheds unignorable light on everything that went before. In the same way, once you know how all the lines of all the stories and all the climaxes of all the themes converge on Christ, you simply can't *not* see that every text is ultimately about Jesus.[29]

Keller shows us God's provision on page after page in the Hebrew Scriptures—Adam and Eve's clothing; the promises made to Abraham and the patriarchs; the intricate sacrificial system; persons (e.g., Moses), events (e.g., the exodus), and institutions (e.g., the Day of Atonement) that prefigure Christ; and explicit promises of a coming Messiah. When we say the Bible is about Jesus, therefore, we're observing that the whole thing hums with the music of saving grace. And the all-sufficient work of Christ is the key that unlocks good news from every passage. Keller goes so far as to say that whenever you come to a biblical text, "you are *not finished* unless you [consider] how it shows us that we cannot save ourselves and that only Jesus can."[30]

Keller's approach to the well-known narrative of David and Goliath, for example, goes beyond where many might land as they seek to muster courage and faith to face the "giants" of life. Taking the passage into the Christ-centered realm brings Keller to a more meaningful and complex conclusion: the point is that the Israelites "could not face the giant [by] themselves. . . . [T]hey needed a champion who would fight in their place—a substitute who would face the deadly peril in their stead." Shifting the narrative to spotlight the gospel, Keller thereby quells the temptation we may have to make every Bible story about *us*. Again and again, he recalibrates our thinking to see both our need and heaven's provision. In the case of David and Goliath, Keller asserts that "God used the deliverer's weakness as the very means to bring about the destruction of the laughing, overconfident Goliath. David triumphs through his weakness, and his victory is imputed to his people. And so does Jesus. It is through his suffering, weakness, and death that sin is defeated." Thus, Keller utilizes a story that could easily end up as little more than a morality tale to showcase what it means that "we have died with Christ (Rom. 6:1–4) and are raised up and seated with him (Eph. 2:5–6). Jesus is the ultimate champion . . . who did not merely risk his life for us, but who gave it. And now his victory is our victory, and all he has accomplished is imputed to us."[31]

What about the "sign of Jonah" (Matt. 12:38–42) and how the runaway prophet points us to Christ? The Pharisees were demanding spectacular magic tricks, as it were, to prove Jesus's authority as a teacher and sage. But they had it backward, Keller notes: "Jesus isn't one more teacher, come to tell you how to save yourself and find God. He is God himself, come to save and find you." The Savior is infinitely greater than a sage:

> So the miraculous sign of Jonah isn't so much a display of power as an astonishing display of weakness. Jesus laid aside his divine glory and prerogatives and humbled himself even to the point of death on the cross. Just as Jonah was cast into the water to save the sailors from the wrath of God, so Jesus would be cast into death to bear all the punishment our sins deserve—to save us. And just as Jonah came "back from the dead," so Jesus was raised for our justification. That's the sign of Jonah.[32]

Or consider how Keller teaches the story of Esther. She saved her people through identification and mediation:

> Her people were condemned, but she identified with them and came under that condemnation. She risked her life and said, "If I perish, I perish." Because she identified, she could mediate before the throne of power as no one else could, and because she received favor there, that favor was transferred to her people. . . . Does that remind you of anyone?[33]

Keller reminds us that Esther's bold advocacy for her people was based on a comparatively "vague revelation that God is a god of grace." But our revelation is decidedly not vague: "[Queen Esther] didn't know God was actually going to come to earth himself and do what she was doing on an infinitely greater scale, at an infinitely greater cost, with infinitely greater benefits to humanity. We now know so much more about his grace, our value to him, and our future."[34]

Indeed, Keller uses this Old Testament account—among many others—to hurl us headlong at the feet of our Savior and King. Jesus Christ "lived in the ultimate palace with ultimate beauty and glory, and he voluntarily left them behind." He did not exploit his divine status but emptied himself, identifying with us and bearing our condemnation (Phil. 2:5–11). Marveling at the staggering extent of Christ's sacrifice, Keller characterizes it as both definitive ("He didn't say '*If* I perish, I perish,' but '*When* I perish, I'll perish'") and ultimate ("He didn't do it at the risk of his life but at the *cost* of his life"). Truly, Christ's atonement for us was the "ultimate mediation," and we enjoy the spoils of his victory.[35]

From BC to AD

The "one hero" thread in Scripture is not confined to the pages of the Old Testament. For example, Keller reflects on the beatitudes in Matthew 5:1–12 by pointing a laser beam at the work of Jesus Christ:

Why can we be as rich as kings? Because he became spiritually and
utterly poor.

Why can we be comforted? Because he wept inconsolably and died
in the dark.

Why can we inherit the earth? Because he became meek, like a lamb
before his shearers. He was stripped of everything—they even cast
lots for his garment.

Why can we be filled and satisfied? Because on the cross he cried,
"I thirst."

Why can we obtain mercy? Because he got none—not from Pilate,
not from the crowd, not even from God.

Why can we someday see God? Because he was pure. We can see
God because, on the cross, Jesus could not.[36]

"When you see Jesus Christ being poor in spirit *for you*," says Keller,
"that helps you become poor in spirit before God and say, 'I need your
grace.' And once you get it and you are filled, then you are merciful,
you become a peacemaker. . . . The beatitudes, like nearly everything
else in Scripture, point us to Jesus far more than we think."[37]

Self-Substitutionary Love

In our cultural moment, it is vital to grasp that Jesus didn't merely die
to boost our self-esteem or to set a moral example.[38] Such a perspective, however well-meaning, domesticates what he did. He stooped to
take our place on the cross because we scramble to take his place on
the throne. Indeed, so much of Keller's teaching about Jesus Christ,
our mighty Champion and King, focused on his sacrificial *substitution*.
When Redeemer was less than a year old, he invoked beautiful words
from John Stott:

The concept of substitution may be said, then, to lie at the heart of
both sin and salvation. For the essence of sin is man substituting

himself for God, while the essence of salvation is God substituting himself for man. Man asserts himself against God and puts himself where only God deserves to be; God sacrifices himself for man and puts himself where only man deserves to be. Man claims prerogatives that belong to God alone; God accepts penalties that belong to man alone.[39]

Consider again the example of Jonah, hurled into a raging storm of judgment so that undeserving men might live. Does that sound familiar?

This is why Jesus couldn't have perished, say, with his disciples on a storm-tossed boat (Mark 4:35–41). He couldn't have died in that storm because he had come to face down a greater one. And that's what he did—willingly pinned to a Roman cross, plunged into the waters of God's wrath so that fugitives like us could be saved. Jonah was a prophet thrown overboard for his own sin; Jesus, the final prophet, was thrown overboard for ours. We all deserve the floodwaters of divine justice. But God so loved the world that he gave his only begotten Son, to perish in our place, that whoever believes in him might have eternal life. Here's how Keller puts it:

> A God who [in Christ] suffers pain, injustice, and death for us is a God worthy of our worship. In a world of pain and oppression, how could we give our highest allegiance to someone who was immune to all that? This is a God who knows what storms are like because he came into the world and dove straight into the greatest pain and suffering. Because of his self-substitution, we can have life.[40]

Or consider Jesus the good shepherd's promise: "I lay down my life for the sheep" (John 10:15). "Have you ever known," asks Keller, "the glorious release of realizing your shepherd knows you to the bottom and yet loves you to the skies?" He wasn't merely willing to take our place; he delighted to (Heb. 12:2). "He glories in his substitution for us," declares Keller, as if Jesus is saying, "I die in the dark so they can live in the light. I take their cross so they can have my crown. I take their punishment so they can have my reward. I die instead of them."[41]

When Redeemer was less than two years old, Keller pressed home that robust theology, once internalized, makes all the practical difference in the world:

> You, my dear friends, have to realize there is no way you will ever have a loving, Christian lifestyle unless you're continually coming back to this doctrine. To the degree that you have grasped the doctrine of the substitutionary, vicarious death of Jesus Christ on the cross, you will walk in love. If you don't walk in love, you haven't grasped the doctrine.[42]

From beginning to end, Keller's teaching is suffused with the good news of Christ's self-giving love as he absorbs—for our sins—God's righteous judgment in our place.[43]

Ultimately about You—or Him?

In the final analysis, says Keller, there are two ways to read the Bible: as if it's all about you, or all about him. They are "radically different" approaches:

> Yes, you [should] obey the things the Bible says. But if you read it as all about you and something you have to do to live up to God, that will just crush you into compliance. But if you read it as salvation by grace through Jesus Christ, it'll melt your heart into *wanting* to obey those things.
>
> Every other culture, every other religion, every other philosophy gives you an identity based on your performance. It's an *achieved* identity, so it's fragile. But only Christianity gives you a *received*

identity, so it's stronger than heaven and earth. It's "I love you. You know you're my beloved child, in whom I'm well pleased, because of what Jesus Christ has done." Only when you read the Bible like that does [it] become a life-changing story instead of just a millstone around your neck.[44]

We miss out on the breathtaking beauty of the Bible when we reduce it to *only* a textbook or *only* a devotional book or *only* a morality book. Above all, the word of God is a Jesus book.

Don't lose sight of his glory, majesty, and beauty as you turn the pages. Christ is all.[45]

2

Excavating Sin

A Tale of Disordered Loves

IT HAS DECIMATED EMPIRES and devastated families. It brings utter ruin to relationships. As you read these words, it is wreaking havoc not just in your nation but in your neighborhood, not just in your home but in your heart. Perhaps you're wading through its wreckage even now.

What is this persistent, pervasive disrupter of everything we hold dear? What has corrupted God's creation and spoiled his good world?

The answer, of course, is sin. Sin has caused all this mess. Sin is what's wrong with the world. Sin is what's wrong with our hearts. Welcome, class, to Christianity 101.

But it is precisely because sin is basic that its true dimensions are rarely seen. For too many Christians, being aware of sin is like knowing of a termite problem out back in the shed—annoying but manageable. In reality, meanwhile, the foundations of the house have rotted out.

Our thin view of sin is captured in our analogies. We say that it's an old archery term: "sin" simply means "missing the mark." And we all *have* missed the mark—arrows whizzing past the target altogether— because we've flouted heaven's commands. What about this archery analogy could possibly be wrong? Isn't the Bible clear that sin is lawlessness (1 John 3:4) and that we've all fallen short of God's glory (Rom. 3:23)? Sin makes us break his rules, spurn his laws, sail right past his target. Why complicate a simple truth?

The archery analogy misses the mark not because it's unbiblical but because it's insufficient. The danger lies in what it leaves unsaid. When we explain sin *only* as missing a target, or violating heaven's laws, we risk reducing a cosmic emergency to a knuckleheaded lapse.

Sin is not less than missing the Ten Commandment bullseye, but it is considerably more. In fact, Keller shows, it is considerably *worse*.

Deepening Sin

One of the most pronounced features of Tim Keller's teaching is that the problem of sin is, at bottom, a problem of worship. We may not prostrate ourselves before physical idols—we're sophisticated modern people, after all—but we're by no means immune to more insidious forms. Our hearts are like little houses with idols set up in every room.

Where did this notion of "heart idolatry" originate? Certainly not in twentieth-century Manhattan. Look at God's charge against Israel's leaders, through the prophet Ezekiel, more than twenty-five hundred years ago:

> And the word of the LORD came to me: "Son of man, these men have *taken their idols into their hearts,* and set the stumbling block of their iniquity before their faces. . . . Therefore speak to them and say to them, Thus says the Lord GOD: Any one of the house of Israel who *takes his idols into his heart* and sets the stumbling block of his iniquity before his face, and yet comes to the prophet, I the LORD will answer him as he comes with *the multitude of his idols,* that I may lay hold of the *hearts* of the house of Israel, who are all estranged from me *through their idols.*" (Ezek. 14:2–5)

I used to wonder whether Keller's teaching on idolatry had the effect, however unintentionally, of sidestepping the severity of sin. The idea of "counterfeit gods," after all, sounded more clever than offensive.[1] But sin is the most offensive reality in the universe! We should never get cute with the horror of human wretchedness. In short, I assumed Keller's description of sin—clothed in the urbane language of idolatry—was a bit simplistic.

As I kept interacting with his material, though, an uneasy realization set in: *my* perspective was simplistic. Sure, Keller's teaching on idolatry is sophisticated,[2] but it doesn't make sin more palatable—it makes it more pronounced. Viewing sin as a *worship* problem is like being shown a three-dimensional object after having access to only a stick figure. And this is no easy sight—to unearth a counterfeit god is to be shown a clearer, and more hideous, picture of yourself. "You have not believed the gospel of our salvation," Keller warned in a 1992 sermon, "until you see your sin as idolatry and deserving of the wrath of God."[3]

Finding a message in which Keller touched on idolatry is like finding a game in which Michael Jordan scored forty points; it isn't difficult. A 1998 sermon titled "Enslaved to Non-Gods" is characteristic.[4] Our idols are ubiquitous and far from innocuous—they are a direct assault on grace. This means not just that the gospel is the only alternative to idolatry but also, in the deepest sense, that idolatry is "the only alternative to the gospel." Nobody is truly an unbeliever. Either you trust the real God or you're enslaved to something you *treat* as a god.

Awakening to Idolatry

Interestingly, Keller didn't always see idolatry as "one of the main themes of the Bible," or at least didn't emphasize it as such. By the time he moved to Manhattan in 1989, he'd already preached over fourteen hundred messages—a remarkable figure—at his small church in rural Virginia.[5] Those talks didn't hum with this theme. But when he began to hear Scripture's accent on idolatry, it changed his life. "It changed my preaching, my counseling, everything. It really only dawned on me a number of years ago, right around the time I was getting Redeemer started"[6]—that is, in the late 1980s.

This awakening came about, in part, through a Martyn Lloyd-Jones sermon. Reflecting on the final verse of John's first letter—"Little children, keep yourselves from idols" (1 John 5:21)—the twentieth-century Welsh preacher said,

> The greatest danger confronting us all is not a matter of deeds or of actions, but of idolatry. That may sound strange to some. They may think that above all we need to be warned not to *do* certain things. . . . [But] our deeds and actions are always the outcome of our attitudes and our thoughts. . . . The greatest danger in the spiritual life is idolatry, and it comes into all our activities.[7]

"When I read that," Keller recalled, "it hit me like a ton of bricks." The idea—that misplaced worship is the essence of sin—became a "revolutionary principle" for him. "I began to make changes in my life once I figured that out [and] began to, in my counseling and my preaching, help people a lot more than I was before." The newly minted church planter was exploring terrain beneath our behaviors. *Why* do we commit particular sins? The answer is not flattering: "Something besides God has taken functional title to your heart. Something besides God is your beauty. Something besides God is your highest good. Idolatry is under every sin . . . always."[8] In one of Keller's earliest sermons at Redeemer, with a newly sharpened understanding of idolatry, he observed we all have "little lords, little gods, pseudo-gods . . . , things we worship—and we're bound by those things. They control our lives. We're co-conspirators in our own kidnapping."[9] Within the first three months, he'd already preached a sermon titled "Removing Idols of the Heart."[10]

But Keller kept learning, and in the early 1990s he experienced another breakthrough, courtesy of an insightful essay by his friend David Powlison. Among other things, "Idols of the Heart and 'Vanity Fair'" plunged Keller deeper into the Puritans. Decades later he would credit Powlison's seminal essay with being a "major influence" on his ministry in New York, even inspiring his book *Counterfeit Gods*.[11]

Augustinian Roots

Fifteen centuries before Keller set foot in Manhattan—and a thousand years before the Protestant Reformation—Augustine (AD 354–430) had described sin as a problem of disordered loves. Keller often referenced the North African bishop, including on September 9, 2001—forty-eight hours before New York's most fateful day: "Augustine was always saying it. The essence of sin is . . . wrongly ordered loves. It's loving something too much in relationship to God. It's mortgaging yourself to it so you can get a sense of self—which you desperately need if you're not getting affirmation from him."[12] Elsewhere he writes,

> I [have] often referred to Augustine's description of sin in his *Confessions* as a disorder of love. So, for example, if we love our own reputation more than the truth, it's likely that we'll lie. Or if we love making money more than our family, we'll neglect our children for our career. Disordered love always leads to misery and breakdown. The only way to "reorder" our loves is to love God supremely.[13]

No wonder Martin Luther, who was trained as an Augustinian monk, described the human heart as hopelessly "curved in" on itself.[14] According to Keller, no one grasped better than Luther that idolatry lurks behind every sin. Why do the Ten Commandments begin with a prohibition against it ("You shall have no other gods before me"; Ex. 20:3)?

Because, relaying Luther's thought, "the fundamental motivation behind lawbreaking is idolatry. We never break the other commandments without breaking the first one."[15] Keller elaborates,

> We do not lie, commit adultery, or steal unless we first make something else more fundamental to our hope and joy and identity than God. When we lie, for example, our reputation (or money or whatever) is at that moment more foundational to our sense of self and happiness than the love of Christ. If we cheat on our income tax form, then money and possessions—and the status or comfort from having more of them—have become more important to our heart's sense of significance and security than our identity in Christ. Idolatry, then, is also *the root of our other sins and problems*.[16]

This brings us to the white-hot center of how people change. How can we find the power to live a godly life? The best solution is not to scare ourselves into doing the right thing but to "apply the gospel to our hearts' idols, which are always an alternate form of self-salvation apart from Jesus. . . . We will never change unless we come to grips with the particular, characteristic ways our hearts resist the gospel and continue their self-salvation projects through idolatry."[17]

Another Protestant Reformer, John Calvin, famously likened the human heart to "a perpetual factory of idols."[18] Substitute gods aren't just mass-produced; they also come in a variety of forms. To make this point in his first year at Redeemer, Keller contrasted himself and his wife, Kathy.[19] Though gentle and kind, Kathy is more naturally direct because she "doesn't mind if somebody is offended." Meanwhile, Keller admitted, "my [idol] is approval. I don't mind if somebody is bothering me and creating pain as long as they're not unhappy with me."

But despite diverse expressions, idolatry is a singular problem. It's not just one sin among many; it's our fundamental plight.[20] The first chapter of Romans is bracing in its clarity: misplaced worship (1:21–23) is the soil from which other sins spring (1:24–32). Channeling the apostle Paul, Keller puts it categorically: *idolatry is always the reason we ever do anything wrong.*[21]

Good Things versus Ultimate Things

Idols are almost always good things in themselves. This makes intuitive sense once we recognize that the greater the good, the more likely we are to expect it to satisfy our deepest hopes. Anything can serve as a counterfeit god—"especially the very best things in life."[22]

One of Keller's favorite diagnostics encourages us to consider the difference between sorrow and despair. One way to know whether a good thing in your life has been inflated into an ultimate thing—an idol—is to assess how you respond when it's threatened or lost. Christians are not Stoics; it is natural and right to express deep sorrow. But the presence of despair suggests a deeper chokehold:

> Sorrow is pain for which there are sources of consolation. Sorrow comes from losing one good thing among others, so that, if you experience a career reversal, you can find comfort in your family to get you through it. Despair, however, is inconsolable, because it comes from losing an *ultimate* thing. When you lose the ultimate source of your meaning or hope, there are no alternative sources to turn to. It breaks your spirit.[23]

But what happens when your spirit *is* broken, when your idols have begun to crumble and leave you disillusioned? There are, Keller concludes, four basic responses. First, you can *blame the idols* and move on to better ones, but this is the way of "continued idolatry and spiritual addiction." Second, you can *blame yourself,* but this is mere "self-loathing and shame." Third, you can *blame the world*—"Curses on the entire opposite sex!"—but this is silly. Thankfully, there is another option: resist blaming and "reorient the entire focus of your life toward God."[24]

How, though, can we discern idols in the first place? Begin by examining four particular things: (1) your imagination,[25] (2) how you spend money,[26] (3) how you respond to unanswered prayers and frustrated hopes,[27] and (4) your most uncontrollable emotions.[28] Regarding the latter, pose a series of questions to yourself. If you're angry, ask, *Is there something I must have at all costs?* Do the same with debilitating fear: *Is something being threatened that I think is a necessity when it's not?* If you're battling despair or guilt, ask, *Have I lost or failed at something that I think is a necessity when it's not?* If you're overworking, driving yourself into the ground with frantic activity, ask, *Do I feel I must have this thing to be significant and fulfilled?* In one of his earliest Redeemer sermons, Keller is blunt: If you cannot live without a certain thing, then you're not prepared to live with it. Why? Because anything added to Jesus as a "requirement for being happy" is a rival god that will sap you and fail you.[29]

If you wish to know what's stifling peace and joy in your life, pull your emotions up by the roots. You will often find your idols clinging to them.[30]

Idolatry also cripples our ability to forgive. Keller recounts a story from early in his ministry:

As a pastor at my first church in Hopewell, Virginia, I found myself counseling two different women, both of whom were married, both of whom had husbands who were poor fathers, and both of whom had teenage sons who were beginning to get into trouble in school and with the law. Both of the women were angry at their husbands. I advised them and talked (among other things) about the problems of unresolved bitterness and the importance of forgiveness. Both women agreed and sought to forgive. However, the woman who had the worst husband and who was the least religious was able to forgive. The other woman was not. This puzzled me for months until one day the unforgiving woman blurted out, "Well, if my son goes down the drain then my whole life will have been a failure!" She had centered her life on her son's happiness and success. That was why she couldn't forgive.[31]

And what about the now-fashionable concept of self-forgiveness? This too is often indicative of idolatry. Again, Keller doesn't mince words: "When people say, 'I know God forgives me, but I can't forgive myself,' they mean that they have failed an idol, whose approval is more important to them than God's."[32]

It's a recipe for misery to build your life on any created thing.[33]

Love, Trust, Obey

When Christians hear the words *love*, *trust*, and *obey*, we tend to think of how we're supposed to relate to the Lord. But, Keller points out, they are also biblical metaphors for how we relate to idols.[34] For example, Scripture regularly describes idolatry in *relational* terms (e.g., Isa. 54:5–8; 62:5; Jer. 2:1–4:4; Ezek. 16:1–63; Hos. 1–4). The Lord is a perfect spouse, but we rendezvous with false lovers instead:

> Idols capture our imagination, and we can locate them *by looking at our daydreams*. What do we enjoy imagining? What are our fondest dreams? We look to our idols to love us, to provide us with value and a sense of beauty, significance, and worth.[35]

The Bible also talks about idolatry in *religious* terms (e.g., Deut. 32:37–38; Judg. 10:13–14; Isa. 45:20; Jer. 2:28). Though "salvation belongs to the LORD" (Jonah 2:9), we look to success or money to give us the security we need:

> Idols give us a sense of being in control, and we can locate them *by looking at our nightmares*. What do we fear the most? What, if we lost it, would make life not worth living? We make "sacrifices"

to appease and please our gods, who we believe will protect us. We look to our idols to provide us with a sense of confidence and safety.[36]

Scripture also casts idolatry in *ruling* terms (e.g., Judg. 8:23; 1 Sam. 8:6–8; 12:12). Though God is our Master and Lord, whatever we love (relational metaphor) and trust (religious metaphor) we also serve (ruling metaphor):

> In this paradigm, we can locate idols *by looking at our most unyielding emotions*. What makes us uncontrollably angry, anxious, or despondent? What racks us with a guilt we can't shake? Idols control us, since we feel we must have them or life is meaningless.[37]

Love, trust, obey. Until we reckon with this multifront war for our souls, we will remain impotent in the face of idolatry's allure.

Surface Idols versus Deep Idols

One of Keller's shrewdest contributions is the distinction between visible "surface idols" and the invisible "deep idols" that power them. The heart's idolatry structure is complex because counterfeit gods tend to come in clusters; therefore, our analysis will remain superficial without this distinction.[38] Surface idols are things, such as money or work or children or sex, "through which our deep idols seek fulfillment."[39] Deep idols, meanwhile, are things such as approval, power, comfort, or control. Our deep idols are propelling the surface idols we serve.

Here's how it works. Sin is expressed differently because it *infects* us differently. And the difference is decided in our deepest motivations. Consider the contrast, for example, between one person driven by a deep idol of approval and another by a deep idol of power. The first person is willing to lose power in order to gain approval, whereas the second is willing to lose approval in order to gain power. Every deep idol—whether approval, power, comfort, or control—nurtures a "different set" of hopes and fears.[40]

All the while, surface idols are like the vehicles our deep idols are driving. The solution is not to try out a new car—it's to replace the driver. Otherwise we'll just toggle between surface idols without ever addressing the real problem. Keller offers the example of how one surface idol (say, money) can simultaneously be feeding different foundational impulses or deep idols. Imagine a fearful person who wants lots of money in order to feel secure. They save carefully and live frugally. Meanwhile, their neighbor wants lots of money to climb the social ladder. The same surface idol (money) is serving different deep idols (control in the first case; approval in the second). And not surprisingly, someone using money to attain control will feel superior to someone using it to attain approval—and vice versa.[41]

If we merely fixate on surface idols, our treatment plans will remain superficial.

The N-U-R Strategy

In one section of a 1994 sermon, "The Freedom of Service," Keller introduces a practical strategy for destroying idols. While nonbelievers exchange truth for lies (Rom. 1:25), Christians must learn to reverse that instinct—exchanging lies for truth. To weaken an idol's grip, Keller proposes an acronym: N-U-R.[42]

First and foremost, we *name*. We look underneath the surface of our hearts—where God replacements lurk—and acknowledge the misplaced worship we find. Why is this step one? Because we cannot dismantle what we haven't diagnosed. Keller's challenge is clear:

> There is nothing wrong with psychological analysis as long as you finally go to theological analysis—and call it what it is. Name the thing. Admit why it's so important to you. Admit the reason you're happy

is because you're compromising the salvation of Jesus. You're saying, "Jesus is nice, but I have to have *this* too if I'm going to be [happy]."[43]

Then we *unmask*. Just as Eve saw the forbidden tree was "good for food," a "delight to the eyes," and "to be desired to make one wise" (Gen. 3:6), so we are allured by idols—which is why we must unmask their true danger. The idols in your life are slave traders disguised as abolitionists.[44] There comes a point, Keller says, when you must look at an idol and say, "I see what you are. You've had your hands around my throat for years. You've been jerking me around for years. You've had me on a leash for years. I won't have it anymore." In short, we must see idols—and loathe them—for what they are: wannabe gods.

Finally, *rejoice*. We think idols will deliver joy, but instead they dismantle it. Looking to a created thing for what only God can give is a well-trodden path to pain. Only he is big enough to bear the weight of our deepest hopes and fears. This means we must train our hearts to derive joy from him—from the real God—more than from rival gods. According to Keller, we need to look up from an idol and say, "Jesus, you are my justifier, not this. You are my peace, not this. You are my master, not this. You are my Savior, not this." The exercise is not cold or clinical; it's a drama of omnipotent love. "Haven't you cared for somebody so much and seen that person in love with somebody who is abusing them?" Keller asks. "That's how God sees you. He sees you in the arms of the idols." No wonder Scripture often describes God as jealous. He loves us too much to be anything less. His jealousy is not insecurity; it's *protecting* us from what will never fulfill us. And so, to the degree your heart rests in—revels in—God's jealous love, the iron grip of your idols will weaken.

Getting Traction Today

Focusing on idolatry doesn't deny that sin is lawlessness (1 John 3:4), but it does add color and texture to the diagnosis. As we've seen, Augustine and Luther and Calvin and Lloyd-Jones convinced Keller the approach was biblical. In Manhattan, he discovered it was effective. "I found that I got the most traction with people when I turned to the Bible's extensive teaching on idolatry," Keller reflected after a quarter century in the city.[45]

Getting cultural traction doesn't necessarily mean you're selling out; it could just mean you're making sense. This is especially the case if a society's "conditions of belief" have shifted.[46] To be sure, there has never been a time (since Genesis 3) when people wanted to submit their lives to God, when the gospel message wasn't offensive, when conversion required anything less than a sovereign invasion in a dead heart. The good news applies to every society because the bad news is relevant to every sinner. Amen and amen. But there are different kinds of cultural weather. And in the late-modern West, we are facing some unprecedented headwinds. Keller offers one example:

> Former generations in Western society believed it was most important for someone to be a *good* person. Today in the West, our values have shifted, and our cultural narrative tells us it is most important to be a *free* person. The biblical theme of idolatry challenges contemporary people precisely at that point. It shows them that, paradoxically, if they don't serve God, they are not, and can never be, as free as they aspire to be.[47]

If this is true, then we have the opportunity to *connect* with our neighbors through one claim ("you were created to be free") in order to more effectively *confront* them with another ("you are a sinner before God"). If we always lead with the latter, we may feel valiant, but are we communicating to be understood? Are we really courageous if we're not clear? Unless we take time to climb into our neighbors' ways of seeing and inhabiting the world, we may be throwing about terms—even biblical ones—that will only be misconstrued. We may just be adding static to the air.

But is all this "idolatry" talk a clever tactic for softening sin for late-modern people? Again, no. "The biblical message of heart idolatry adapts the message to their cultural sensibilities," Keller admits, "but it's far from telling them what they want to hear. It convicts them and makes sin *more* personal. Making an idol out of something means giving it the *love* you should be giving to your Creator and Sustainer."[48]

In sum, accentuating idolatry is one of the most important ways, biblically and practically, to show people how sin has deformed their hearts and disordered their loves. And it can uniquely unveil the depth of their slavery and their farness from the freedom of gospel grace.[49]

This is why it's so imperative for Christian communicators to address the heart:

> What the heart most wants, the mind finds reasonable, the emotions find valuable, and the will finds doable. . . . What makes people into what they are is the order of their loves—what they love most, more, less, and least. That is more fundamental to who you are than even the beliefs to which you mentally subscribe. Your loves show what you actually believe in. . . . [So growth] requires nothing *less* than changing your thinking, but it entails much more.
>
>   . . . Change happens not just by giving the mind new arguments but also by feeding the imagination new beauties.[50]

What Keller means by "new beauties" is essentially what Thomas Chalmers advocated two hundred years ago.

Mowing versus Weeding

In his classic sermon *The Expulsive Power of a New Affection*, the nineteenth-century Scottish pastor observed, "It is seldom that any of our tastes are made to disappear by a mere process of natural extinction [or] mental determination. But . . . one taste may be made to *give way to another*, and to lose its power entirely as the reigning affection of the [heart]."[51]

The secret to destroying idols is not just to remove them; it's to *replace* them. Idols are like weeds. You don't deal with weeds by wheeling out the lawnmower; you kneel in the dirt and uproot them, one by one by one. But you can't just uproot an idol and walk away. It will grow back. You must plant something else—a superior love—in its place.

Channeling Chalmers, Keller writes, "The human heart's desire for a particular valuable object may be conquered, but its need to have *some* such object is unconquerable."[52] And you will be released from an idol's grip only when your heart melts under a sense of God's love. Elsewhere Keller observes,

> An ultimate love cannot be displaced—it can only be *re*placed with a more powerful one. It is only as you inflame the heart with love for Christ through meditation on him as he is revealed in the Word and gospel that you can get freedom from enslaving idols.
>
> . . . If our self-worth is based on being a good person rather than on Christ, then we will . . . not be able to admit our flaws or sins. The more we know Christ's love, the easier it will be to confess our sin, and the more we confess our sin, the more precious and wonderful the grace of Jesus will become.[53]

This is no academic exercise; nor is it just for the hyperspiritual. All Christians wake up each morning to new mercies (Lam. 3:23)—and new weeds. Unless you uproot your idols and plant Christ's love in their place, day after day, you "cannot have life and peace."[54] The stakes are that high.

Audio versus Video

Switching metaphors, consider the difference between merely hearing a movie and actually watching it. It's easy to overhear and roughly discern a plot while doing stuff around the house, but to watch a story unfold before your eyes is absorbing. It fills your vision. Likewise, it's possible to know about Christ's love with your head but not your heart.

This insight came home to Keller through, of all people, an insecure teenager at his small Virginia church in the 1970s. One day she blurted out her frustration with the *felt inadequacy* of Christian truth: "I know God loves me," she said, "but what good is that if I can't get any dates?" Keller recounted this story numerous times over the years because it affected him so much. "My life has been impacted by [her statement]. I will never forget it as long as I live."[55]

His big takeaway: It's dangerously easy for the gospel to remain abstract. *God loves me* and *boys won't date me* were both facts, but one was "on audio" in the girl's heart while the other was "on video." In other words, since sin is an "infection of the imagination,"[56] the only way for Christ's love to "go on video" is to dynamically encounter his grace. Nothing less can truly melt and start to restructure our prone-to-wander hearts.[57]

When Idols Pervade Culture

In an incisive 2009 conference address, "The Grand Demythologizer: The Gospel and Idolatry,"[58] Keller lists three idol categories we must discern and expose. *Personal* idols are the most intuitive; they include things like money, romance, and children. *Religious* idols are subtler, including things like truth, gifts, and morality. We've already considered both forms. But we are also beset, whether or not we realize it, by *cultural* idols—pervasive tendencies among an entire population. These can include things like human reasoning, traditionalism or individualism, and politics.

Consider Paul's strategy of going after a culture's gods. Far from a one-off tactic, this was his consistent approach—from Lystra (Acts 14) to Philippi (Acts 16) to Athens (Acts 17) to Ephesus (Acts 19). What did he proclaim, for instance, to everyday Ephesians on the street? A local nonbeliever gives us a shrink-wrapped synopsis: "This Paul . . . [is] saying that gods made with hands are not gods" (Acts 19:26). Remember, an idol is not a bad thing but a good thing made into an ultimate thing. So when beauty was deified in the ancient world, you didn't have just beauty—you had Aphrodite. When reason was deified, you didn't just have reason—you had Athena. When money was deified, you didn't just have money—you had Artemis.

And the modern world is no less idol riddled; the only difference is that ours are harder to spot. Any society "not dominated by the glory and grace of God" will be built on "the deification of something else." It's inevitable. Survey the history of civilization. (Just be sure to look down, lest you trip over the ruins of failed gods.)

But idolatrous expressions across time are no match for the timeless truth of Jesus Christ. Regardless of cultural location, the gospel has always possessed "supernatural versatility to address the particular hopes, fears, and idols" of any people.[59] As an example, Keller points out that when Paul wrote to the Corinthians, he took one approach with pagan Greeks but a different one with religious Jews. What was the difference based on? Their respective idols:

> For Jews demand signs and Greeks seek wisdom, but we preach Christ crucified, a stumbling block to Jews and folly to Gentiles, but to those who are called, both Jews and Greeks, Christ the power of God and the wisdom of God. For the foolishness of God is wiser than men, and the weakness of God is stronger than men. (1 Cor. 1:22–25)

Paul's strategy wasn't simply to "rail against the Greeks' love of intellect and the Jews' love of power," Keller observes—it was to show them that they were "pursuing these things in a self-defeating way."[60] It's good to value strength, but without Jesus, the pursuit yields only weakness. And yet his apparent weakness brings true power. *This is what the Jews needed to hear.* Likewise, it's good to value wisdom, but without Jesus, the pursuit yields only foolishness. And yet his bloody corpse displays true wisdom. *This is what the Greeks needed to hear.* Notice, Keller says, that Paul doesn't simply "dismiss a culture's aspirations; rather, he both affirms and confronts, revealing the inner contradictions in people's understanding."[61] This is the art of subversive fulfillment.[62] And this is why the church, at her best, has always been decidedly countercultural:

> In Jesus's day the message of the kingdom contradicted all the world's categories. In our time the Christian faith is seen as something traditional rather than radical and disruptive. Nothing could be further from the truth. Properly understood, the message of God's kingdom will subvert the dominant beliefs of our own culture.[63]

If you're trying to communicate the gospel, it's immensely helpful to know someone's personal and cultural idols. Why? Because while the gospel says, "You're justified by grace," the idols disagree: "No, you're justified by something else."[64] So if we boldly announce that our neighbor can be saved by grace, not works, but fail to explain different forms of works-based righteousness—different substitute saviors—we risk muting the depth of their slavery, the horror of their sin, and the wonder of God's grace.

Whether personal, religious, or cultural in form, idols are shape-shifting and ever-present threats to being joyfully satisfied in Jesus Christ. When something in your heart becomes a deity, it's only a matter of time before it becomes a demon.[65]

Known to the Bottom, Loved to the Skies

Counterfeit gods demand levels of allegiance that should be reserved for God alone. Beckoning us to love, trust, and obey them, the battle for our souls is multifront. It's also multidirectional.

When idolatry intersects with the *past*—when we've failed an idol—it often leads to debilitating guilt. When idolatry intersects with the *present*—when an idol is blocked or removed by circumstances—it tends to roil us with anger and despair. And when idolatry intersects with the *future*—when an idol is threatened—it can spark paralyzing anxiety and fear.[66] What comfort and hope is there amid such danger? Even when false gods morph and assault us on every side, the Son of God remains the same yesterday, today, and forever (Heb. 13:8).

And our Savior is not just unchanging in character; he's also unequaled in power to reorder our loves.[67] Every substitute god is a taskmaster that will enslave you. But not him. Jesus is the only master who will free you. And while your idols demand and disappoint and crush you into the ground, only he arrives and says, "I'll be crushed for you."

Until we see Jesus as supremely beautiful—the one for whom all things were created (Col. 1:16)—we will remain a slave to something he has made. But he loves us enough to forgive us, fulfill us, free us. And where, specifically, does this good news intersect with an idolatrous heart? At the point of substitution. We have substituted so many things for Jesus. But in astonishing grace, he substituted himself for us.

Here's how Keller put it in a 2012 address to students at the Oxford Town Hall in England:

> If you build your life on your career, or your spouse, or your money, or your morality, and it fails, there is no hope for you. Do you know why? Because every other savior but Jesus Christ is not really a savior. If your career fails, it won't forgive you. It can only punish you with self-loathing and shame. Jesus is the only savior who if you gain him will satisfy you, and if you fail him will forgive you.[68]

Anything else you serve will "abandon you in the end."[69] It certainly won't die for your sins. Indeed, nothing less than the self-giving love of Christ—not an abstract belief, but a moving, dynamic encounter in the heart—will help us see things in proper perspective. Reflecting on how Jonah's story anticipates Jesus's sacrifice, Keller offers a personal word:

> When I struggle with my idols, I think of Jesus, voluntarily bowing his head into that ultimate storm, taking it on frontally, for me. He

sank in that storm of terror so I would not fear any other storm in my life. If he did that for me, then I can know my value, confidence, and mission in life all rest in him. Storms here on earth can take away many things, even my physical life, but not my Life.[70]

This greater-to-lesser logic has been enormously helpful in my own life. Because Jesus faced down the ultimate darkness for me, I can trust him in smaller moments—even if they don't *feel* small—when the sky goes black (2 Cor. 4:17). The beauty of this truth has proven power to galvanize. It is a source of deep consolation for sufferers and strugglers in a fallen world.

The greatest problem you face each day doesn't reside outside you; it resides within. Your sin is your most towering foe. More specifically, though, what rattles around in the dungeon of your heart are idols—good things that have become ultimate things, undeserved gifts promoted to nonnegotiables, whatever you feel you *need* to be happy. And that—not your sin in general, but that thing in particular—has you in shackles and is standing between you and freedom, between you and peace, between you and life abundant, perhaps even between you and life eternal.[71] Because it stands between you and Jesus Christ.

No wonder John closes his first letter with one simple charge: "Little children, keep yourselves from idols" (1 John 5:21).

3

Three Ways to Live

Why Religion Needs Grace

THE GOSPEL TRACT *Two Ways to Live*[1] is superb. The concept is simple: When it comes to Jesus Christ, there is no middle ground. You are either for or against him.

This kind of fork-in-the-road framing rings true because it's reminiscent of God's word. Consider, for example, the prophet Elijah's charge to the Israelites: "How long will you go limping between two different opinions? If the LORD is God, follow him; but if Baal, then follow him" (1 Kings 18:21). Or the contrast between the righteous and the wicked that pervades Psalm 1. Or Christ's forthright declaration: "Whoever is not with me is against me, and whoever does not gather with me scatters" (Matt. 12:30). And of course, we may recall the sharp contrasts in the Sermon on the Mount: two gates, two trees, two paths, two houses (Matt. 7:13–27).

Scripture could scarcely be clearer that there are two ways to live—no more. Right?

Two or Three Ways?

Keller's sermons regularly feature—far more than one might assume, given his gentle demeanor—this kind of in-your-face, choose-ye-this-day directness. This is not surprising when you consider the voices who influenced him. At one point early in his ministry, Kathy joked that if he didn't stop reading so many George Whitefield sermons, he might accidentally say "methinks" from the pulpit.[2] Keller also devoured hundreds of sermons from the no-nonsense Welsh preacher Martyn Lloyd-Jones. And of course, no writer shaped his apologetic style more than C. S. Lewis, a master at deploying razor-sharp logic to bring readers to a point of decision. (Lewis once wrote, "Christianity . . . if false, is of no importance, and if true, of infinite importance. The one thing it cannot be is moderately important.")[3] Listen to a few Keller sermons and you will soon discover he was not averse to dichotomous—*this way or that*—language, especially with an evangelistic edge. In fact, he relished it.

And yet, given how the human heart tends to operate, Keller came to realize such framing can be reductionistic. Are "God's way" and "man's way" the only two options we face each day? Technically, yes— but what *is* man's way? What does it look like to reject God and live for self? Does presenting two ways to live, in other words, capture the complexity presented in the Bible? Not exactly.

Three Ways in Romans

Consider Paul's argument at the outset of Romans. Before describing what it looks like to live for God, he graphically depicts what it looks like *not* to. The opening chapters are a blistering indictment against the rebellion in our hearts. But how specifically does human rebellion express itself? Here's where conceiving of "man's way" as a monolithic category can obscure more than illumine. Paul in fact shows there are two general ways, not one, that humans tend to resist and reject God's loving authority.

The first is obvious: unapologetic idolatry (Rom. 1:18–32). *I live for myself, and I'm proud of it.* The second way, though, is more subtle: religious hypocrisy (Rom. 2:1–29). *I live for myself, and nobody can find out.* In other words, you can avoid God through immorality, but you can also avoid God through performative morality. The first option is common sense; the second is cancerous.

So what's the danger in reducing "man's way" to outright rebellion? It risks leaving *religious* rebels comfortable in their sin. Paul's Jewish readers no doubt loved Romans 1:18–32. *Get those pagans, Paul.* But when he pivoted to make eye contact with *them*, I imagine the mood changed. According to the apostle, then, there are three ways to live: one way to be reconciled to God, but two ways to reject him.

As Keller's ministry matured, he came to see the effectiveness of leaning into the Bible's threefold texture.[4]

Back to History's Most Famous Sermon

Even if Romans teaches there are *three* ways to live—one way to embrace Christ and two to avoid him—what are we to make of those dichotomous warnings at the end of the Sermon on the Mount? "Enter by the narrow gate," Jesus implores. "For the gate is wide and the way is easy that leads to destruction, and those who enter by it are many. For the gate is narrow and the way is hard that leads to life, and those who find it are few" (Matt. 7:13–14).[5] He also proceeds to contrast two trees (7:15–20) and two houses (7:24–27).[6] The message is straightforward: there is no middle ground.

Could our Lord be any clearer that there are only two ways to live? Shouldn't we think and teach accordingly? Keller used to think so—until he encountered a fascinating observation from the Anglican pastor Dick Lucas.[7] The conclusion of the Sermon on the Mount, Lucas observed, is likely a summary—which means we should look back through the whole message to find two ways contrasted. Sure enough, Jesus does this repeatedly. *But which two ways does he contrast?* The answer is not simply God's way versus man's way; it's God's way versus *the Pharisees'* way. "Beware of practicing your righteousness before other people in order to be seen by them," Jesus warns, "for then you will have no reward from your Father who is in heaven" (Matt. 6:1). So when you give to the needy (6:2–4) or pray (6:5–6) or fast (6:16–18), don't do it to appear superspiritual. And don't look down on others in the process (7:1–4).

In short, the Sermon on the Mount is a warning against rebellion dressed up as religion. The path of blatant immorality isn't in view at all. Jesus is simply contrasting the intuitive path of moralism from the radical path of kingdom life.

Two Lost Sons

The Bible's most potent depiction of this truth—that there's more than one way to be lost—is crystallized in Luke 15:11–32. The broad outline of the parable is familiar: a father has two sons, the younger of whom demands his share of the inheritance and then moves to a far country, where he squanders it on wild living. Eventually, after coming to his senses, the prodigal returns home empty-handed and broken; he simply hopes his father will take him back as a hired servant. But seeing his wayward son from a long way off, the father runs to meet him and requests a party thrown in his honor.

Many people tend to stop there, at least in terms of emphasis, which is why it's known to history as the parable of the prodigal son—singular. But the returning son isn't the only prodigal. That's actually the whole point. Jesus is not addressing the wayward but is aiming the story, like a heat-seeking missile, at the religiously devout. Note the context of the chapter:

> Now the tax collectors and sinners were all drawing near to hear [Jesus]. And the Pharisees and the scribes grumbled, saying, "This man receives sinners and eats with them." So he told them this parable. . . . (Luke 15:1–3)

In light of the audience, then, we dare not overlook the dramatic final scene:

Now [the father's] older son was in the field, and as he came and drew near to the house, he heard music and dancing. And he called one of the servants and asked what these things meant. And he said to him, "Your brother has come, and your father has killed the fattened calf, because he has received him back safe and sound." But he was angry and refused to go in. His father came out and entreated him, but he answered his father, "Look, these many years I have served you, and I never disobeyed your command, yet you never gave me a young goat, that I might celebrate with my friends. But when this son of yours came, who has devoured your property with prostitutes, you killed the fattened calf for him!" And he said to him, "Son, you are always with me, and all that is mine is yours. It was fitting to celebrate and be glad, for this your brother was dead, and is alive; he was lost, and is found." (Luke 15:25–32)

On September 11, 2005, Keller preached a sermon titled "The Prodigal Sons"—plural—which became the genesis of his 2008 best-seller *The Prodigal God: Recovering the Heart of the Christian Faith*. This book captures the most distilled essence of Keller's teaching regarding the heart. Near the beginning he credits a sermon on Luke 15 by his mentor, Ed Clowney, that altered his understanding:

Listening to that sermon changed the way I understood Christianity. I almost felt I had discovered the secret heart of Christianity. Over the years I have often returned to teach and counsel from the parable. I have seen more people encouraged, enlightened, and helped by this passage, when I explained the true meaning of it, than by any other text.[8]

That last sentence is a remarkable statement. What about the parable is so powerful? If you compare the teaching of Jesus to a lake, Keller says, this parable is "one of the clearest spots where we can see all the way to the bottom."[9] And that's because what Jesus says about the elder brother is one of Scripture's most vital teachings.[10] We impoverish ourselves, therefore, when we fixate on the younger brother:

> The first time I heard the parable, I imagined Jesus's original listeners' eyes welling with tears as they heard how God will always love and welcome them, no matter what they've done. We sentimentalize this parable if we do that. The targets of this story are not "wayward sinners" but religious people who [think they] do everything the Bible requires. Jesus is pleading not so much with immoral outsiders as with moral insiders. He wants to show them their blindness, narrowness, and self-righteousness, and how these things are destroying both their own souls and the lives of the people around them. It is a mistake, then, to think that Jesus tells this story primarily to assure younger brothers of his unconditional love.[11]

Apart from Jesus Christ, flagrant lawbreaking *and* fastidious rule keeping are dead ends. In Keller's words: "Jesus's purpose is not to warm our hearts but to shatter our categories."[12]

Each brother in the parable represents "a different way to be alienated from God"[13]—and both ways are strikingly resonant with the late-modern West. Keller dubs the approaches "the way of *moral conformity* and the way of *self-discovery*."[14] In fact, he observes, Western culture is "so deeply divided between these two approaches"[15] that it's difficult to imagine an alternative option:

> If you criticize or distance yourself from one, everyone assumes you have chosen to follow the other, because each of these approaches tends to divide the whole world into two basic groups. The moral conformists say: "The immoral people—the people who 'do their own thing'—are the problem with the world, and moral people are the solution." The advocates of self-discovery say: "The bigoted people—the people who say, 'We have the Truth'—are the problem with the world, and progressive

people are the solution." Each side says: "Our way is the way the world will be put to rights, and if you are not with us, you are against us."[16]

But King Jesus is not kind to false dichotomies. Nor is he beholden to natural expectations:

> So we have two sons, one "bad" by conventional standards and one "good," yet both are alienated from the father. The father has to go out and invite each of them to come into the feast of his love. . . .
>
> But Act 2 comes to an unthinkable conclusion. Jesus the storyteller deliberately leaves the elder brother in his alienated state. The bad son enters the father's feast but the good son will not. The lover of prostitutes is saved, but the man of moral rectitude is still lost. We can almost hear the Pharisees gasp as the story ends. It was the complete reversal of everything they had ever been taught.[17]

Both sons are lost, but only one knows it. *You* are lost, Jesus is saying, but you refuse to know it.

Self-Salvation Projects

It's sobering to notice that when the older son protests, "Look, these many years I have served you, and I never disobeyed your command" (Luke 15:29), the father doesn't disagree! His firstborn *has* been obedient; he *has* done everything "right." And ironically, it's keeping him from the feast. His outward goodness—and resultant pride—has erected a barrier between him and the father's love.

An elder-brother mindset can haunt us all. Keller offers an example:

> I knew a woman who had worked for many years in Christian ministry. When chronic illness overtook her in middle age, it threw her into despair. Eventually she realized that deep in her heart she had felt that God owed her a better life, after all she had done for him.

That assumption made it extremely difficult for her to climb out of her pit, though climb she did. The key to her improvement, however, was to recognize the elder-brother mindset within.

Elder brothers obey God to get things. They don't obey God to get God himself—in order to resemble him, love him, know him, and delight him. So religious and moral people can be avoiding Jesus as Savior and Lord as much as the younger brothers who say they don't believe in God and define right and wrong for themselves.[18]

The stakes are that high. If you think God should accept you because you're good, "then Jesus may be your helper, your example, even your inspiration, but he is not your Savior." How could he be? *You* are occupying that role.[19] Keller concludes,

> At the end of the story, the elder brother has an opportunity to truly delight the father by going into the feast. But his resentful refusal shows that the father's happiness had never been his goal. . . . If, like the elder brother, you seek to control God through your obedience, then all your morality is just a way to use God to make him give you the things in life you really want.[20]

So there are two ways, not one, to be your own Savior and Lord: you can break all the moral rules and chart your own course, or you can try keeping all the external moral rules and seek to earn heaven's favor. Both are strategies for avoiding God. Apart from Jesus Christ, every person is "dedicated to a project of self-salvation, to using God and others in order to get power and control for themselves. We are just going about it in different ways."[21]

Equally Wrong, Not Equally Dangerous

By the end of Jesus's parable, only one son has been reconciled to his father. Why conclude like this? Why not show us a redemptive arc for both brothers? The reason certainly isn't that elder brothers are hopeless; if they were, the father wouldn't have gone into the field and pleaded at all. We can't know for sure, of course, but perhaps Jesus is conveying that while "both forms of the self-salvation project are equally wrong," they are not "equally dangerous."[22] The younger brother's rebellion is obvious; the elder brother's is not. And therein lies the danger:

> He would have been horribly offended by the suggestion that he was rebelling against the father's authority and love, but he was, deeply. Because the elder brother is more blind to what is going on, being an elder-brother Pharisee is a more spiritually desperate condition. "How dare you say that?" is how religious people respond if you suggest their relationship with God isn't right. "I'm there every time the church doors are open." Jesus says, in effect, "That doesn't matter."[23]

The takeaway, Keller says, is shocking: "Careful obedience to God's law may serve as a strategy for rebelling against God."[24] He often returned to an image of two people sitting side by side in the same pew—hearing the same sermons, singing the same songs, engaging in the same spiritual activities—but for utterly different reasons. One does it all to please God; the other does it to justify self.

And yet on the outside, they look exactly the same.[25]

Nonidentical Twins from the Same Womb

Such similarities in appearance aren't that surprising, though, when we consider their similar roots. Younger brothers and elder brothers—and the ways of life they represent—are much more alike than they first appear. Keller explains,

> Underneath the brothers' sharply different patterns of behavior is the same motivation and aim. Both are using the father in different ways to get the things on which their hearts are really fixed. It was

the wealth, not the love of the father, that they believed would make them happy and fulfilled.[26]

In his foreword to Sinclair Ferguson's brilliant book *The Whole Christ*, Keller writes, "It is a fatal pastoral mistake to think of legalism [trying to earn God's love through law keeping] and antinomianism [rejecting God's love through law breaking] as complete opposites. Sinclair says that, rather, they are 'nonidentical twins from the same womb.' "[27] In other words, lawbreaker and legalist alike are in thrall to the "Edenic poison"[28]—Satan's ancient lie that our Maker cannot be trusted. He slithered in to convince our first parents, Adam and Eve, that God is stingy—a withholder of good—and that they needed to fend for themselves. And so, distrusting his character, they took what wasn't theirs.

Both the legalist and the antinomian, notes Keller, participate in "the same incomprehension of the joy of obedience—they see obedience as something imposed on us by a God whose love is conditional and who is unwilling to give us blessing unless we do quite a lot of work. The only difference is that the legalist wearily assumes the burden, while the antinomian refuses it and casts it off."[29]

To be sure, obedience should not be mistaken for legalism. The first is beautiful; the second is deadly. Legalism creeps in when obeying God's good commands becomes a means, rather than a response, to his love.

Evangelistic Value

Why did Keller preach so forcefully against legalism in New York City? It's not exactly known for attracting elder-brother types. There are two answers. First, he was convinced that self-justification, commonly associated with legalism, is the default mode of every human heart.[30] But the second reason was simple: he wanted younger brothers to comprehend the real gospel.

Most non-Christians, particularly irreligious ones, do not grasp the good news. In fact, most lost persons we meet have never rejected the gospel. *That's because they've never heard it.* Sure, they've rejected what they *think* is the gospel. But ask the average person on the street to explain it; you're not going to hear Ephesians 2:8–9 with its rich declaration of salvation by grace. You're probably going to get some version of moralism, some version of "I've been a decent person."[31]

In other words, though elder-brother lostness and Christianity are not the same thing, many younger brothers assume they are. We serve them, therefore, by clarifying that we aren't simply asking them to become better people.[32] John Piper has shared how this simple insight had a revolutionary effect on him:

[Tim said something] years ago that just walloped me and has made a significant impact upon the way I think about preaching to unbelievers in our day. He said that if you're going to preach to libertines—people who are basically lawless; they do what they want and don't care about anybody's rules—you need to preach *against* legalism in the process.

And I thought, *What? Legalism is not their problem.* He explained that . . . if you can persuade a libertine that they're building their life on sand—but you don't give them a gospel alternative for how to live—their default alternative is law, right? . . . He said so insightfully: "Look, if you're going to help a libertine out of his lawlessness into gospel, Holy-Spirit living, you've got to warn against the other side—namely, the [legalistic] alternative."

That was, to me, absolute gold. . . . It made a huge difference. I'm thankful for it to this day.[33]

The True Elder Brother

When it comes to pleasing God, both the rebellious path and the religious path are dead ends. But Jesus shows us a more excellent way. It is not a comfortable middle option between earthly extremes, for his gospel occupies a transcendent plane.[34]

In the parable, the older son should have gone into the far country in pursuit of his wayward brother. He should have rejoiced at his return. He should have gladly relinquished part of his inheritance in order to reinstate his brother's. He should have joined the party. But, as Keller observes, "By putting a flawed elder brother in the story, Jesus is inviting us to imagine and yearn for a true one."[35]

Jesus Christ is the ultimate elder brother who didn't just travel to a far country; he descended from heaven to earth to seek and save the lost. "Who is the *true* elder brother?" Keller asked in a funeral sermon for his own younger brother Billy. "Who is the one who *truly* obeyed the Father completely? Who *truly* has lost his robe so he [could] put it on us? Jesus!"[36] He is the "God of Great Expenditure,"[37] who, at infinite cost to himself, paid our debt and now binds our wounds and brings us home to the Father.

This message is true, but it's not tame. The process of reckoning with it is disruptive to idol-ridden hearts. Keller recounts a time when a woman coming to Redeemer was hearing, for the first time, that she could be accepted not on the basis of her behavior but by God's sheer grace. Keller was intrigued by her response: "*That* is a scary idea! Oh, it's good scary, but still scary." When he asked what was so scary about unmerited free grace, she replied,

> If I was saved by my good works—then there would be a limit to what God could ask of me or put me through. I would be like a taxpayer with rights. I would have done my duty and now I would deserve a certain quality of life. But if it is really true that I am a sinner saved by sheer grace—at God's infinite cost—then there's nothing he cannot ask of me.

Keller comments,

> She could see . . . the wonderful-beyond-belief teaching of salvation by sheer grace had two edges to it. On the one hand it cut away

slavish fear. God loves us freely, despite our flaws and failures. Yet she also knew that if Jesus really had done this for her—she was not her own. She was bought with a price.[38]

As we wait in hope for the ultimate feast and eternal party, may we never get over what it cost to bring us home.

In December 1662, a Scottish minister named David Dickson lay dying when a close friend of over fifty years arrived to inquire how he was. The eighty-year-old man replied, "I have taken all my good deeds, and all my bad deeds, and have cast them together in a heap before the Lord, and have fled from both to Jesus Christ, and in him I have sweet peace."[39]

That is the message of the gospel, and it is the message Tim Keller loved to communicate. Don't just flee your bad works. Flee your "good" works, too. Flee them both and collapse into the open arms of Jesus Christ.

4

Friends on Purpose

How the Gospel Transforms Relationships

WE ARE THE LONELIEST PEOPLE in the history of the world.

That may sound dramatic, but it's true. The statistics are in, and they're disturbing. The late-modern West is in a relational state of emergency. So bad are the health effects that loneliness has become, quite literally, an epidemic.[1]

Forging friendships has never been easy. But surely it's never been more difficult than it is today.

Though it's not often mentioned, friendship was one of the most pronounced themes in Tim Keller's ministry. No doubt this was generated, in part, by his pastoral context: the dizzying transience of urban life isn't exactly a greenhouse for deep friendships—hence the emphasis. We could identify other factors too, not least the influence of C. S. Lewis's *The Four Loves* and Tim's remarkable friendship with Kathy that spanned more than fifty years.[2]

Above all, though, it was God's own words in Scripture that convinced Keller of the importance and weight of friendship—and the dangers of neglecting it. In the final analysis, friendship should matter to us because it matters so deeply to God.

We might say that friendship is not just a gift; it is also a mirror—not just a divine creation but also a divine reflection. From all eternity the persons of the Trinity—Father, Son, and Spirit—have mutually known and delighted in each other.[3] Here's how Keller explained it in an early sermon: "Friendship was never created. There was never a time in which friendship was not, because from all eternity, the Father, the Son, and the Holy Spirit were knowing and loving and delighting in each other. . . . Friendship is at the roots of reality."[4]

This suggests why, even in a world without sin, something was still "not good" (Gen. 2:18). Adam was alone. He needed a helper, a partner, a friend—and so do we. The primordial need for companionship is a feature, not a bug, of being created in God's image.[5]

Learning from Frankenstein

It's no surprise, then, that there is a humanizing power to friendship. One of Keller's go-to illustrations for this came from a rather unlikely place: James Whale's 1935 horror film *The Bride of Frankenstein*. Keller recounts a particularly poignant scene:

> The monster stumbles into a blind man's cottage deep in the forest. The blind man, of course, can't see the hideousness of the monster, but he perceives the monster can't speak. He says, "Are you afflicted as I? I cannot see, and you cannot speak. Maybe we can help each other. We can be friends!" The poor blind man gets down on his knees, and he says, "I thank you, gracious Lord, for you have heard my relentless prayers, and you have sent me a friend in my terrible loneliness."
>
> The monster lives in the blind man's cottage for a few days, and the blind man plays songs on his violin. He also teaches the monster to speak a few words—words like "good" and "food" and "more" and, most importantly, "friend." The only humanity he develops, he

develops in that cottage—in the spot where a person grabs him by the hand and calls him *friend.*

The scene ends when a group of hunters arrive, see the monster, try to attack, and, in the process, burn down the cottage. The last thing you see is the monster groping back out into the cold wilderness, alone, saying, "Friend? Friend? Friend?"[6]

It's a touching scene with a profound point: even Frankenstein's monster started to become human under the influence of somebody who loved him. There are few things that dehumanize us more than loneliness—and few things that bring life to us more than friendship.

The unprecedented loneliness of modern society, then, is a deadly serious problem.

It hasn't always been this way. Keller notes that the ancients lauded friendship as the most virtuous of *all* the loves—largely because it's the most deliberate. Other kinds of love "push" themselves on you, in a sense. Family love comes to you involuntarily, and romantic love often arrives unbidden, but friendship love is fundamentally a choice. Keller cites Lewis's words:

Few value [friendship] because few experience it. And the possibility of going through life without the experience is rooted in that fact which separates friendship so sharply from . . . the other loves. Friendship is—in a sense not at all derogatory to it—the least *natural* of loves; the least instinctive, organic, biological, gregarious, and necessary. It has least commerce with our nerves; there is nothing throaty about it; nothing that quickens the pulse or turns you red and pale.[7]

And because friendship is not "helped along" by natural affection or heart-pounding emotion—because it is utterly deliberate—the ancients viewed it as the purest, noblest form of love.[8]

It Takes a Community to Know Him

Thankfully, the Lord Jesus has not made his opinion on friendship ambiguous, nor has he left us all by ourselves to figure out where to find friends. Though God saves us as individuals, he doesn't leave us to chart our own spiritual course; he saves us *into* community. Your relationship with the Lord will suffer if you try to know him apart from others who also know him.

To illustrate the principle, Keller relates a counterintuitive lesson about friendship that C. S. Lewis learned the hard way. Lewis, who was called "Jack" by his friends, was very close with two men, Charles (Williams) and Ronald (J. R. R. Tolkien). Eventually Charles died, leaving Jack heartbroken. His only consolation, quite naturally, was that Charles's absence would enable him to have "more of Ronald." But oddly, the opposite happened. He had *less* of Ronald. Why? Because Charles had been able to bring something out of Ronald that Jack himself, given his different personality and strengths, never could. And so, Jack essentially concludes: "When I lost Charles, I actually lost part of Ronald too."[9] Lewis explains,

> In each of my friends there is something that only some other friend can fully bring out. By myself I am not large enough to call the whole man into activity; I [need] other lights than my own to show all his facets. Now that Charles is dead, I shall never again see Ronald's reaction to a specifically Caroline joke. Far from having more of Ronald, having him "to myself" now that Charles is away, I have less of Ronald.[10]

Here's Keller's takeaway: if it takes a varied community to know an ordinary person, how much more to know the living God? "You will never know the multidimensional glory and beauty of your Savior," he warns, "unless you know him in community. You need a whole pile of other people who also know Jesus well, who are different than you, and you've got to know them to know *him*."[11]

No biblical discussion of friendship is complete without recognizing the importance of the local church. It's not enough, in other words, to simply hang around the margins of Christian community. Keller was straightforward:

> The busy New York Christian thing is, *I'm very busy with my career . . . and you're lucky I'm even coming to church*. But I'm sorry, that's not good enough. . . . You have to join, you have to be a member of a church, you've got to commit yourself to brothers and sisters. . . . Without knowing Jesus, you would never know these people; [and] without knowing these people very well, you will never know Jesus—at least you won't know the full, multidimensional beauty and glory of your Savior.[12]

The local church is "the only human institution Jesus started" and "the only one inhabited by the Spirit and glory of God."[13] Indeed, divine glory is available to you in the church in a way it's not available anywhere else.[14] This is why every Christian must belong—meaningfully belong—to a healthy church. Keller went so far as to say that "you are not an obedient Christian if you are not a member of a church. You can't obey [Hebrews 13:17] without membership."[15] It's nothing less than an implication of the gospel.[16]

None of this means God's people should be insular. The local church exists not for itself but for the good of those who don't yet know Jesus Christ. We're meant to shine like "a city set on a hill," visible for miles in the dark (Matt. 5:14). But to be radiant, we must be distinct. As Keller often said, the church is designed to be an "alternate city" within every city, an "alternate society" within every society. Becoming a Christian, then, is less like "joining a club" and more like "changing your culture."[17] You're stepping into a whole new way of being. And so, Keller warned, if "the world around looks at Redeemer . . . and doesn't see us living any differently than the rest of the people of New York when it comes to sex, money, or power, we're not light. We're not up on the lampstand. We're not a city on a hill."[18]

In his fifth sermon at Redeemer in 1989, Keller underscored this foundational point: "The church is not just a lecture hall [or] a social club. It's a counterculture. It's a pilot plant of what humanity would be in every area under the lordship of Christ."[19] A decade later, he was still pressing the question home: "Redeemer, are we a social club or are we a colony, a pilot plant of a new humanity? Are we a weekly Christian show, or are we a counterculture?"[20] The community that is "created by the cross," therefore, is not just a "warm family" or "aggregation of people giving one another emotional support."[21] It is an alternate society with different habits, different customs, different loves. It is a "foretaste" of the heavenly city to come.[22]

Or to think of it another way, a church community should be like a thick tapestry showcasing God's brilliant design (Eph. 3:10). Keller explains,

> Our human lives are as fragile as threads, but if you take thousands of threads and really interweave them so they are deeply interdependent, they become a piece of fabric that is enormously strong and very often beautiful. Jesus says, "When you enter into a relationship with me, I will weave you into a human community deeper and more beautiful than you can imagine."[23]

We will become a counterculture for the common good, simultaneously repellent and attractive to the world, only if we are distinct from the world (1 Pet. 2:11–12). There must be "something different about every single part" of our lives.[24] Otherwise we may avoid offense, but we will be faithless and frankly redundant.[25]

But through service and sacrifice, transparency and generosity, hospitality and evangelism, churches can shine as contrast communities in a dark and broken world.

Three Ingredients

Keller defined friendship, in his first message on the topic at Redeemer, as "deep oneness that comes through a mutual journey to the same horizon."[26] But probably his favorite description was that a true friend "always lets you in and never lets you down." That simple phrase became a touchpoint for his teaching on the subject.[27]

But what is the recipe for a good friendship? Synthesizing Keller's teaching, we can identify three basic ingredients.

The first is *sympathy* (literally *sym-pathos*, "common passion"). This is based on some kind of connection point that is discovered, often with sudden delight.[28] Keller loved to quote Lewis here:

> Friendship arises . . . when two or more of the companions discover that they have in common some insight or interest or even taste which the others do not share and which, till that moment, each believed to be his own unique treasure (or burden). The typical expression of opening friendship would be something like, "What? You too? I thought I was the only one." . . . It is when two such persons discover one another, when, whether with immense difficulties and semi-articulate fumblings or with what would seem to us amazing and elliptical speed, they share their vision—it is then that friendship is born.[29]

And this means, simply, that friendship must not exist for its own sake. Lewis observes,

> The very condition of having friends is that we should want something else besides friends. Where the truthful answer to the question *Do you see the same truth?* would be "I see nothing and I don't care about the truth; I only want a friend," no friendship can arise. . . . There would be nothing for the friendship to be *about*. . . . Those who have nothing can share nothing; those who are going nowhere can have no fellow travelers.[30]

Friendship, in other words, is always about something besides friendship. Keller often invoked the observation that whereas the profile of romantic love is face to face, friendship love is shoulder to shoulder. Why? Because you're staring at the same thing.[31]

Perhaps we could say that friendship without basis in some commonality is like a house without a foundation. But friendship that features *only* commonality resembles a foundation without a house. We therefore need a second ingredient: *transparency*. Indeed, no friendship is worth the name without it. Authentic friendship will be forged only to the degree that each person is willing to be vulnerable—truly open and honest. This requires risk, even faith. But friendship should be one of the chief places where pretense goes to die.

On occasion, transparency requires speaking truth, though in a manner that doesn't deny love, as we encounter in Proverbs 27:5–6:

> Better is open rebuke
>   than hidden love.
> Faithful are the wounds of a friend;
>   profuse are the kisses of an enemy.

True friends gently rebuke each other when necessary. Though it may be painful, we must be honest enough to tell a friend what he or she needs to hear. Indeed, "If you are too afraid to say what needs to be said, you are really an enemy of your friend's soul."[32]

Have you ever listened to a recording of yourself and thought, *I don't sound like that*? But yes, you do—you can't hear from within your body what your voice really sounds like outside. And without the perspective of others, we will never know our strengths and weaknesses. If you have a measure of status in the world, or if you have chosen friends poorly, you may just be surrounded by flatterers ([Prov.] 29:5). Transparency is scary, but we need it.[33]

Expounding on the importance of transparency, the Kellers draw from both Proverbs 27:9 (a friend gives "earnest counsel") and 27:17 ("Iron sharpens iron, / and one man sharpens another"). Real friendship involves "constructive clashes" through which there is significant sharpening, as both friends challenge each other to grow. A friendship differs dramatically, then, from a therapist-client or a supervisor-employee relationship. Indeed, "the mutuality of the deep counsel that friends can give is rare and something everyone needs. . . . You're never going to become the person you need to be, or that you can be, without it."[34]

In a sermon simply titled "Friendship," Keller explains this dynamic as the balance between carefulness and candor. We must listen to our friend and speak with both sensitivity *and* conviction, tears *and* truth. Things go astray—sometimes with disastrous consequences—when one of these elements smothers the other.[35]

Do you have any such friends in your life—who love you enough to tell you what you may not wish to hear? Have you had the courage to deputize anyone with a warrant, a "hunting license," to point out your most serious flaws? Everyone claims they want community and friendship, Keller notes, but mention "accountability" or "commitment," and people run the other way.[36]

The poverty of modern friendship won't be understood unless we've reckoned with the ways that *autonomy* erodes community. Asked in 2013 about an exodus of millennials from the church, Keller was blunt: "You are the generation most afraid of real community because it inevitably limits freedom and choice. Get over your fear."[37] (And if that's true of millennials, how much more their kids and grandkids.) Keller often warned against the "god of independence," which manifests in an inability to *commit* to things. But in refusing to commit, in refusing to lay down our autonomy, we rob ourselves of the possibilities of real love.[38]

Third, healthy friendships require *constancy*. This is the spirit of Proverbs 17:17 ("A friend loves at all times, / and a brother is born for adversity") and Proverbs 18:24 ("A man of many companions may come to ruin, / but there is a friend who sticks closer than a brother").[39] You simply will not be a good friend to others without availability—and without a certain measure of tenacity. Putting these verses into everyday context, Keller points out that so many friendships form around a certain *usefulness* people provide for one another. Perhaps a person you're drawn to is fun to be with, has similar goals, or is helpful for connecting with others. But a real friend "goes to the mat" for you. A real friend remains—stays with you—even in your darkest valleys, where there is a *cost* to friendship, since he has "deliberately made you not a means to an end but an end in yourself."[40]

For Keller, friendship was not just a teaching topic; it was a vital means of encouragement and endurance in his own life. Tim and Kathy dedicated *The Meaning of Marriage* to a set of five "couple friends" from seminary who stayed in good touch over the years.[41] Tim was especially close with one of the men, David Midwood, a longtime pastor in Massachusetts who went to be with Christ in 2014 after succumbing to colon cancer. According to Collin Hansen, David's wife, Louise, still keeps a birthday card Tim once sent to David. "We have no greater friends than the Midwoods," Tim wrote, "and I have no greater friend than you. And friends are up there with life's greatest blessings."[42]

These ingredients—sympathy, transparency, and constancy—are wise, even essential, principles for forging friendships. But astute readers will notice it's not a *distinctively* Christian list. At least not yet. We will never unlock the true riches of friendship until we know the one "in whom are hidden all the treasures of wisdom and knowledge" (Col. 2:3). If we merely resolve to white-knuckle our way to deeper friendships—even with Bible verses pinned to the dashboard—we will only be spinning our wheels.

To become a great friend to others, we must encounter the ultimate Friend to us.

He Calls Us Friends

Shortly before his death, Jesus Christ instructed his disciples one final time. As you read his words, bear in mind this astonishing fact: he *knew* they were about to abandon him.

> Greater love has no one than this, that someone lay down his life for his friends. You are my friends if you do what I command you. No longer do I call you servants, for the servant does not know what his master is doing; but I have called you friends, for all that I have heard from my Father I have made known to you. (John 15:13–15)

Keller returned often to this passage when teaching on friendship. Recall his favorite description of a true friend: one who lets you in and doesn't let you down. Jesus Christ fulfills both features. On the one hand, Keller writes, Jesus is effectively saying, "You are not a servant but a friend, because I tell you my business. *I let you in.*" On the other, "I give my life for you. *I don't let you down.*"[43] The gospel is the most radical act of friendship in the history of the world.[44]

Reflecting on the biblical admonition to "bear one another's burdens, and so fulfill the law of Christ" (Gal. 6:2), Keller points out that good friends don't remain safely aloof—they get close enough to let some of your suffering "slide onto them."[45] But Jesus Christ didn't just get close to us; he *became* one of us. And then he took our greatest burden—the judgment of God—so that through faith in his sacrifice we could be declared righteous and free.

Doesn't a real friend let you in? Look at Calvary, Keller preached. How much more open could Jesus be? His arms aren't just stretched open to you—they're nailed open.

And a real friend won't let you down, right? Keep staring at Calvary. *There* is the ultimate friend who loves at all times (Prov. 17:17), who sticks closer than a brother (18:24), whose wounds are faithful (27:6). Only in this case, Keller observes, these aren't wounds the friend *inflicts*; these are wounds the friend *bears*—for you and me.[46]

The cross is the pinnacle of burden bearing—and the burden crushed him to death because he's the ultimate Friend.

He Calls Us to One Another

We've already considered three ingredients for any healthy friendship—sympathy, transparency, and constancy. But what makes friendship distinctly *Christian* is when it is an arena for being transformed by gospel grace. Spiritually deliberate friends "share the same Savior, share an experience of amazing grace, love the same Scripture, and hold each other accountable to grow into Christ (Heb. 3:13) and into a profound knowledge of his Word (2 Pet. 3:18)."[47]

The implications of this are staggering—and thrilling. Natural barriers have no power to prevent a friendship between two persons who share the Holy Spirit.[48] "For believers in Christ, despite enormous differences in class, temperament, culture, race, sensibility, and personal history, there is a commonality," Keller insists, "that is more powerful than them all. This is not so much a 'thread' as an indestructible steel cable."[49] Practically, this means that as a Christian you have more in common with a poor migrant worker in another hemisphere who loves Jesus than you do with your own family members who don't.

The biblical picture of Christian friendship is remarkable, Keller says. It is "not simply about going to concerts together or enjoying the same sporting event. It is the deep oneness that develops as two people journey together toward the same destination, helping one another through the dangers and challenges along the way."[50]

Soaring Vision

And what is that destination, that horizon? Ultimately, it is our glorious future as God's redeemed people in the new heavens and new earth.

In friendship we are simply helping one another toward that dazzling day. Teaching on marriage, Keller illumined this principle of friendship by turning to Ephesians 4:22–24 and depicting the "new self" as a wondrous, majestic mountain peak that is often obscured by the clouds and rain of the "old self." As we develop friendships with other Christians, our view of their virtues may at times be hampered—even concealed—by their besetting sins and character flaws. But the beauty of who they are *in Christ* remains fixed:

> The new self is still you, but you liberated from all your sins and flaws. . . . It is a glimpse of where you are going.
>
> [A friend says], "I see who God is making you, and it excites me! I want to be part of that. I want to partner with you and God in the journey you are taking to his throne. And when we get there, I will look at your magnificence and say, 'I always knew you could be like this. I got glimpses of it on earth, but now look at you!'"

Keller then referenced words about marriage from Kathy, which likewise apply to Christian friendship:

> Most people, when they are looking for a spouse, are looking for a finished statue when they should be looking for a wonderful block of marble. Not so you can create the person *you* want, but rather because you see what kind of person Jesus is making.[51]

In gospel friendship, we get the privilege of watching the Great Sculptor chisel away at his masterpieces—beginning with ourselves.

Tenacity and Trust

It is difficult to overestimate the influence, for good or ill, of our friends. They are constantly rubbing off on us, which is why Scripture so frequently warns against bad ones (see Ex. 23:2; Ps. 1:1;

Prov. 13:20; 22:24–25; 1 Cor. 15:33). Though early in life we're shaped most by our family, the rest of the time we're most shaped by our friends. We become like those we are around. "You can't live without friendship," Keller observes. "But remember how *deliberate* friendship must be. Erotic attraction and family relationships push themselves on you in various ways, but friendship will not. It must be carefully, intentionally cultivated through face-to-face time spent together. And in a busy culture like ours, it is one thing that is often squeezed out."[52]

Building rich relationships requires patient determination and deliberate love. And yet, it is not finally our wherewithal, our strategizing, our *doing* that brings about the magic of friendship. Lewis puts it memorably:

> In friendship . . . we think we have chosen our peers. In reality a few years' difference in the dates of our births, a few more miles between certain houses, the choice of one university instead of another . . . the accident of a topic being raised or not raised at a first meeting—any of these chances might have kept us apart. But, for a Christian, there are, strictly speaking, no chances. A secret Master of the Ceremonies has been at work. Christ, who said to the disciples, "Ye have not chosen me, but I have chosen you," can truly say to every group of Christian friends, "Ye have not chosen one another but I have chosen you for one another." The friendship is not a reward for our discriminating and good taste in finding one another out. It is the instrument by which God reveals to each of us the beauties of others. . . . At this feast, it is he who has spread the board, and it is he who has chosen the guests.[53]

As we give ourselves to the great work of forging friendships, the road will not be easy. It will require tenacity and fortitude, staying power and sustaining grace so that, as Keller puts it, we let people in without letting them down. But placed in the sure hands of the Master of the Ceremonies, friendship has the power not just to spur our sanctification and to enhance the lives of others but to reflect the Friend of Sinners himself.

When Faith Goes to Work

Serving God and Others in Your Job

DOES MONDAY MORNING EXCITE YOU? If so, that's great, but that's not how many of us feel.

Our jobs challenge us, exhaust us, and sometimes threaten to consume us. So what does devotion to Jesus Christ look like in our workplace environments—whether they be cutthroat or mundane?

From small-town Virginia to the hustle of New York City, Tim Keller spent his life ministering to believers struggling with work. As he discovered and taught, how we work (and why) reveals our deepest values and dearest treasures.

According to Keller, work is not merely a way to earn money or a strategy for self-advancement or a necessary evil to fund *truly* important things like ministry. Work is a divine calling through which we honor our heavenly Master and love our neighbor in tangible ways.

Not long after Keller planted Redeemer, a soap-opera actor got converted and came to his new pastor asking, "What roles should—and shouldn't—I take? I assume stories don't have to be religious to be good for people, but how do I know which stories are good and which are bad?" He also wondered, "How should I think about method acting?

This is where you don't just act angry; you *get* angry. You tap into something within yourself and really live it. What's your advice?" Though Keller had the wherewithal to reply to the second question by saying, "That doesn't sound like a good idea," he knew he was out of his depth. Despite years of formal theological training and ministry experience, he sensed a gap in his ability to form Christians for daily work. He knew how to encourage deeper involvement in church activities, but here was a young Christian wanting to be discipled for his *public* life. Years later, Keller would point to this interaction as an "epiphany" that propelled him to think more seriously about the integration of faith and work.[1]

Situating Your Job in a Story

Your vocation will make little sense to you unless you've situated it in a significantly larger story. *What's the purpose of my job?* is too small a question to start with. We must first ask, *What's the purpose of my life?* and, more fundamentally, *What's the purpose of the universe?*

Only when we've surveyed God's ultimate plan for the world, as revealed in his word, will we duly grasp the implications for our work. This sweeping story unfolds in the major plot points of creation, fall, redemption, and restoration. Or, Keller notes, we can distill it in four chapters:[2]

Chapter 1	Where did we come from?	From God: the One and the relational
Chapter 2	Why did things go so wrong?	Because of sin: bondage and condemnation
Chapter 3	What will put things right?	Christ: incarnation, substitution, restoration
Chapter 4	How can I be put right?	Through faith: grace and trust

The Bible's storyline presents an unfolding drama that powerfully resonates with our jobs:

- Work was created good.
- Work became corrupted by sin.
- Work is being *partly* redeemed through the Holy Spirit.
- Work will be *fully* redeemed when Jesus Christ makes all things new.

Work Is Created

The Bible begins with the most productive workweek of all time.[3] That's how we're meant to think of it. Note the repetition:

> And on the seventh day God finished his *work* that he had done, and he rested on the seventh day from all his *work* that he had done. So God blessed the seventh day and made it holy, because on it God rested from all his *work* that he had done in creation. (Gen. 2:2–3)

The narrative then rewinds to focus on the sixth day. Though God was exceedingly pleased with his universe (Gen. 1:31), something was lacking: "There was no man to work the ground" (Gen. 2:5). So the Creator knelt down, as it were, to solve the problem:

> Then the LORD God formed the man of dust from the ground and breathed into his nostrils the breath of life, and the man became a living creature. And the LORD God planted a garden in Eden, in the east, and there he put the man whom he had formed. (Gen. 2:7–8)

Behold the King of glory, with his hands in the dirt.

No wonder the first image bearer was given a similar occupation: Adam was put "in the garden of Eden to work it and keep it" (Gen. 2:15). And the job was too much for Adam to handle by himself: "Then

the LORD God said, 'It is not good that the man should be alone; I will
make him a helper fit for him'" (Gen. 2:18). Keller aptly contends,
"We see God not only working, but commissioning workers to carry
on his work. . . . Though [everything] was good, it was still to a great
degree undeveloped. God left creation with deep untapped potential
for cultivation that people were to unlock through their labor."[4]

Could the Bible begin with a more exalted view of work?

Work Is Cursed

Yet by the time we finish the next chapter in Genesis, the story has
become a tragedy. Following Adam and Eve's rebellion, God pronounces
a series of curses, including this:

And to Adam he said,

"Because you have listened to the voice of your wife
    and have eaten of the tree
of which I commanded you,
    'You shall not eat of it,'
cursed is the ground because of you;
    in pain you shall eat of it all the days of your life;
thorns and thistles it shall bring forth for you;
    and you shall eat the plants of the field.
By the sweat of your face
    you shall eat bread,
till you return to the ground,
    for out of it you were taken;
for you are dust,
    and to dust you shall return." (Gen. 3:17–19)

Yet even after banishment from Eden—the original exile—Adam
retains his vocation: "The LORD God sent him out from the garden of

Eden to work the ground from which he was taken" (Gen. 3:23). But work has now become toil. As the father of Noah says, looking at his newborn son, "Out of the ground that the LORD has cursed, this one shall bring us relief from our work and from the painful toil of our hands" (Gen. 5:29).

In one sense, the whole ensuing story of the Bible is about the promise of a royal deliverer who will end the exile and heal the world, bringing relief to our toil and everlasting rest to our souls. But what about the meantime? The curse remains. The exile persists. Thorns and thistles threaten to sabotage even our best efforts. Even though the kingdom of God has made a personal appearance on earth in the person of Jesus Christ, we still await the renewal and restoration of all things—including the gift of work.[5]

The iconic words of Isaac Watts may put you in the Christmas spirit, but they are actually about the joy to come at the King's return:

> No more let sins and sorrows grow,
> Nor thorns infest the ground;
> He comes to make his blessings flow
> Far as the curse is found,
> Far as the curse is found,
> Far as, far as the curse is found.[6]

Dignity of All Work

On the topic of work, Keller invoked no one more often than Martin Luther. The sixteenth-century Protestant Reformer, having reclaimed the biblical truth of the priesthood of all believers, loved to highlight the nobility of all human work—no matter how menial:

> [Luther] mounted a polemic against the view of vocation prevalent
> in the medieval church. The church at that time understood itself
> as the entirety of God's kingdom on earth, and therefore only work

in and for the church could qualify as God's work. This meant that the only way to be called by God into service was as a monk, priest, or nun. . . . [Secular labor was] akin to the demeaning necessity that the Greeks saw in manual labor. Luther attacked this idea forcefully.[7]

Indeed, in his expositions of the Psalms, Luther observed that God cares for his creation not directly but indirectly—through our work. Consider, for example, Psalm 145:

> The eyes of all look to you,
>   and you give them their food in due season.
> You open your hand;
>   you satisfy the desire of every living thing. (Ps. 145:15–16)

But how does God feed us? It is not as if heavenly manna plops onto our plates. No, he works *through* human workers—farmers, drivers, bakers, grocers, and countless others along the way—to provide the food that now sits in your refrigerator or pantry.[8] We pray, "Give us this day our daily bread" (Matt. 6:11), and God answers by dispatching people to their jobs.

Even in the smallest tasks, the Lord Almighty is working through our work. The implications of this teaching, once they sink in, are explosive. Keller reflects,

> Not only are the most modest jobs—like plowing a field or digging a ditch—the "masks" through which God cares for us, but so are the most basic social roles and tasks, such as voting, participating in public institutions, and being a father or mother. These are all God's callings, all ways of doing God's work in the world, all ways through which God distributes his gifts to us. Even the humblest farm girl is fulfilling God's calling. As Luther preached, "God milks the cows through the vocation of the milkmaids."[9]

In one of his first sermons at Redeemer, Keller explained it like this:

> The glorious teaching of the Bible is you can be a person on an assembly line, you can be just turning a screw, you can be somebody who's just sweeping a floor—but if you see it as part of the whole complex way God has enabled us to bring the potential out of his creation—then you can do it with joy. Paul was writing to slaves [in Ephesians 6:5–8], and if this theology can work for *slaves*—if he can say, "Slaves, the menial work you do, you do it for the Lord"—[then you too can] see it as part of everything God made work to be, [and] you can do it with joy.[10]

Though today we tend to think of *vocation* and *job* as synonyms, the former word is far richer. Based on the Latin *vocare* ("to call"), it means nothing less than a calling—an assignment to serve others—whether you work on one side of the political aisle or in the produce aisle.

And these assignments come ultimately from the sovereign throne of a working God. What could possibly infuse more nobility into an ordinary job? "In Genesis we see God as a gardener, and in the New Testament we see him as a carpenter. No task is too small a vessel to hold the immense dignity of work given by God."[11]

Two Ditches

Any treatment of faith and work must reckon with two perennial pitfalls: underwork and overwork. To borrow language from a helpful book by Sebastian Traeger and Greg Gilbert, some are tempted to be *idle* at work, while others are tempted to make an *idol* of work.[12]

Keller pastored both kinds of people. At his first church in rural Virginia, the pews were filled with many blue-collar workers for whom work may have sometimes felt mundane. Every Sunday at Redeemer, however, Keller looked out on many ambitious professionals scrambling to climb the corporate ladder. In fact, in his first sermon in Manhattan on work, Keller sounded two notes. First, *work is not a curse; it's a calling.* Second, *work is not for yourself; it's for God.* He was offering biblical antidotes to both ditches. He even highlighted the difference between his two pastoral communities: "When I was in a blue-collar town, [many] said, 'It's just a paycheck. I hate my job, but that's alright; everybody else I know hates their job too.' And that particular view of work choked them." He went on to tell his New York congregants, "I don't know that that's as much a problem for you" as using work for self-advancement.[13]

Regarding the temptation to *underwork*, or to see it as a necessary evil, Keller is emphatic that work has *been* cursed but is not itself a curse. In light of Paul's charge to bondservants to "serve wholeheartedly, as if you were serving the Lord, not people" (Eph. 6:7 NIV), Keller is clear: "Look at God in the eye when you're working. Say, 'Lord, I'm going to do a good job because you're watching me. I don't care what everybody else thinks. I'm going to do [this with] excellence.'"[14]

As for the second ditch, *idolatrous overwork*, Keller spent nearly thirty years laying rumble strips to keep Manhattanites from swerving into it. When work becomes an identity—a way to make a name for oneself (Gen. 11:4)—everything is turned upside down: God and people become expendable as self-interest rises to occupy the throne. Keller often invoked the words of Martyn Lloyd-Jones, who was a physician before becoming a pastor. In a lecture to medical students and doctors, Lloyd-Jones quipped: "I have had the privilege of meeting [many] whose tombstones might well bear the grim epitaph, 'Born a man. Died a doctor.'"[15]

This can happen to the best of us—and it's dangerous because it doesn't happen overnight. No Christian wakes up one day and thinks, *Well, time to start idolizing my work and living for my glory.* But it happens. How easy it is to know our deepest identity should be in Christ—but to still have a heart functioning as if it's grounded in our work. Keller warns,

Work becomes no longer a way to create and bring out the wonders of the created order, as Calvin would say, or to be an instrument of God's providence, serving the basic needs of our neighbor, as Luther would say. Instead it becomes a way to distinguish myself from my neighbor, to show the world and prove to myself that I'm special.[16]

Here's the tragic irony: when you invest everything—even your identity—in your job, you will eventually do *worse* work. You won't be able to live with inconveniences. Ordinary mistakes from others will infuriate you. Healthy competition will become an unhealthy obsession to win at all costs. And as you become increasingly absorbed in your work, you will likely become increasingly obnoxious to those who slow you down.

And this possibility is something we should be mindful of when choosing a career.

Where (and How) Should I Then Work?

When it comes to choosing a career, Keller points out there are at least two kinds of motivating questions: (1) What will make me the most money and give me the most status? or (2) How, with my existing abilities and opportunities, can I be of greatest service to others, knowing what I do of God's will and human need?[17] Notice something counterintuitive, though, about these two questions:

It is the *latter* that will lead [to] a more sustainable motivation for discipline and excellence at work. If the point of work is to serve and exalt ourselves, then our work inevitably becomes less about the work and more about us. Our aggressiveness will eventually become abuse, our drive will become burnout, and our self-sufficiency will become self-loathing. But if the purpose of work is to serve and exalt something *beyond* ourselves, then we actually have a better reason to deploy our talent, ambition, and entrepreneurial vigor—and we are more likely to be successful in the long run, even by the world's definition.[18]

Assuming that the profession is morally permissible, there is no one-size-fits-all way to choose a career. Adapting categories from John Newton, Keller identifies three factors that often constitute a "call":[19]

- Affinity: *Do you enjoy it?*
- Ability: *Do others think you can do the job well?*
- Opportunity: *Is there an open door?*

Ideally all three are present; in some vocations, they really *must* be.[20] But in a culture that encourages us to look within and "discover ourselves," we should be careful not to overestimate the importance of *passion* for a particular vocation. It's a bit like marriage, Keller suggests: The passion ebbs and flows. It's not what keeps you going. What keeps you going is commitment and hope.[21] Elsewhere Keller reflects,

> As products of the Depression and two world wars, my parents' and grandparents' generations were grateful to have work of any kind because it helped them and their family survive. But members of my children's generation are utterly dissimilar. They insist that work be fulfilling and fruitful, that it fully fit their talents and their dreams, and that it "do something amazing for the world," as one Google executive described his company's mission. . . . While the circumstances shaping my parents' generation perhaps gave them a *lower* view of work than the one found in the Bible's description of creation, so my children's generation has a more *naïve and utopian* view of work than [the Bible's] description of [this fallen world].[22]

Nevertheless, God does wire us in certain ways and entrust us with certain skills. One of Keller's favorite examples of this comes from the film *Chariots of Fire*, based on the true story of Olympic runner Eric Liddell.[23] In one scene, Liddell has a confrontation with his sister, Jennie. She's concerned because she believes his hard work and striving after athletic prowess is getting in the way of his preparation for the mission field, since he was preparing to be a missionary to China. Finally, he says, "Jennie . . . I believe that God made me for . . . China. But he also made me fast, and when I run, I feel his pleasure."

Meanwhile, another runner, Harold Abrahams, remarks to his trainer, "I'm twenty-four and I've never known [contentment]. I'm forever in pursuit, and I don't even know what I am chasing."

Do you see the contrast? Abrahams is enslaved to deriving satisfaction and life from a running track. No wonder he remarks to his coach, shortly before the hundred-yard dash, "I have ten seconds to justify my existence." But Liddell is free. He's not enslaved to the sport—as evidenced by his willingness to miss a likely gold medal due to his conviction that he shouldn't run on Sundays.

Both characters are strikingly similar—same passion, same sport, same event, same training, same opportunity—yet with a profound difference: Abrahams *had* to win. His sense of worth was riding on it. Liddell, meanwhile, could miss the race altogether if conscience demanded it. To the cheering crowds they looked so similar, but for Abrahams it was a sprint for salvation; for Liddell it was an act of worship. As Keller puts it, "Abrahams was weary even when he rested. Liddell was rested even when he [ran]."[24]

Again, apart from a biblical perspective on our jobs, we will be tempted either to *underwork*, reducing it to mere drudgery, or to *overwork*, elevating it to an identity. The danger in both cases is that our jobs become all about us. Like Harold Abrahams, we become enslaved to what Keller calls the "work under the work"—whether it's the exhausting scramble to eke out a sense of self-worth or the fight against disenchantment and despair. Ultimately, the solution to the "work under the work" is a quality of rest that no number of vacations can provide, for only in Jesus do we find "rest under the rest"[25]:

> He is the only boss who will not drive you into the ground, the only audience that does not need your best performance in order to be satisfied with you. Why is this? Because his work for you is finished. In fact, the very definition of a Christian is someone who not only admires Jesus, emulates Jesus, and obeys Jesus, but who "rests in the finished work of Christ" instead of his or her own. Remember, God was able to rest [Gen. 2:1–3] only because his creative work was finished. And a Christian is able to rest only because God's redemptive work is likewise finished in Christ.[26]

So when choosing a vocation, don't make passion the ultimate factor—but don't assume it's unimportant either. What experiences and skills have you been given? What kind of work will bring benefit to others? What will enable you to feel God's pleasure? Keller advises,

> If you have to choose between work that benefits more people and work that pays you more, you should seriously consider the job that pays less and helps more—particularly if you can be great at it. . . . All jobs—not merely so-called helping professions—are fundamentally ways of loving your neighbor. Christians do not have to do direct ministry or nonprofit charitable work in order to love others through their jobs.[27]

Along these lines, Keller shares an illustration from one of his favorite British preachers, Dick Lucas:

> If you were to go to a book table at a church and see a biography titled *The Man God Uses* or *The Woman God Uses*, you would think

it must be the story of a missionary, minister, or specialist in some sort of spiritual work, wouldn't you? That's because the church conditioned you to think this way. But what you have [in the story of Joseph] is a highly successful secular leader. In fact, in some ways being a preacher, missionary, or Bible study leader is easier. There's a certain spiritual glamour to it. But it's much harder to get Christians to see that God is willing to greatly use men and women in every sphere of life—in medicine, in law, in business, in the arts. This is the great shortfall today.[28]

God deploys people into all kinds of jobs for the good of the world. Whether you're thriving or struggling in a vocation—or trying to choose one—know that God is infinitely sovereign and wise. As the apostle Paul writes, "Only let each person lead the life that the Lord has assigned to him, and to which God has called him. This is my rule in all the churches" (1 Cor. 7:17).

What's Your Plot of Dirt?

Keller suggests that the work of a gardener is, in a sense, emblematic for all work. How? "It is creative and assertive. It is rearranging the raw material of God's creation in such a way that it helps the world in general, and people in particular, thrive and flourish."[29] This vision applies not only to ambitious endeavors but also to commonplace ones. Even a young mother, daily pushing back chaos in her home, is reflecting the Divine Gardener, whose image she bears. The question is not whether you will have opportunity to shape an entire society—you probably won't. Very few do. But you *have* been entrusted with some domain, some plot of dirt, to faithfully tend.

Don't underestimate, therefore, what Keller simply calls the ministry of competence: "If God's purpose for your job is that you serve the human community, then the way to serve God best is to do the job as well as it can be done."[30] Excellent work is a form of love.

In a fallen world, though, you will constantly be fighting back thorns and thistles in the soil. Just because you can't realize your highest aspirations at work doesn't mean you've chosen wrongly or aren't called to your profession. It certainly doesn't mean you should start looking for a frustration-free career. Keller says you should "expect to be regularly frustrated in your work even though you may be in exactly the right vocation."[31]

It's unwise to put too much stock in popular words like *impact*. In an era of breathless calls to "change the world," Keller advises a restrained perspective not based on immediately observable metrics. Here's how he phrased it in a conference panel discussion:

> It's very hard to know how God is going to use you. [That's what worries me] about the idea that you can "calculate." You can go into [vocational] ministry, by the way, and God [might] just decide to put you in a difficult spot where you see very little fruit over the years. And if the fruit is one or two changed lives for Jesus in a fifteen-year ministry, that's God's will for you. . . . "I want impact"—that's such an American thing. It's saying, "I'm going to calculate return on investment," basically. That's fine in the business world, but when it comes to how many [you're] going to help . . . you have to leave that to God.[32]

Keller also cautioned against overphilosophizing vocational discourse in a way that smacks of elitism. Having cut his pastoral teeth in a rural context, he was sensitive to this danger:

> [Beware of privileging] white-collar work over blue-collar work. Writers and managers have the opportunity to think out the influence of Christian beliefs in their work. But how relevant is this to the assembly-line worker or the craftsman or technician, whose worldview may not make an obvious difference to their daily tasks?

. . . And so to think of work only in [philosophical] worldview terms, and not in terms of God's providence and love, can subtly imply that the Bible's view of work is less relevant to those of the working classes.[33]

As he bluntly told his urbanite congregation, "We live in a city in which the kind of work we valorize . . . is high paying [and has] lots of talent and technical skills required. We don't want a job unless it's changing the world. And yet if your theology is screwed on straight, all that class snobbery, all that 'I have an educated professional job, and this person just has a blue-collar job'—it should be absolutely gone."[34]

Don't Blend In

Just because you're a Christian doesn't mean you must clumsily insert your faith into your next workplace conversation. Obnoxiousness is not a spiritual gift. It's possible to herald truth and feel valiant in the moment—*I am not ashamed of the gospel!*—but lack relational sensitivity, yielding a counterproductive effect.

Keller identifies two temptations that Christians commonly face when interacting with colleagues. One is to shrink from identifying openly as a Christian, choosing instead to blend in. Another is to broadcast one's faith but treat others with disdain. All the while, Christians who can stay clear of these two workplace contrasts will be "striking an unusual and healthy balance."[35]

Still, it's imperative that Christians stand out in their jobs. How could we not? We are "animated by different virtues, lifted by a different view of humanity, guided by a different source of wisdom, and perform for a different audience."[36] Biblical Christian faith, Keller insists, gives us "significant resources not present in other worldviews, which, if lived out, will differentiate believers in the workplace."[37]

Even wisdom should be a workplace distinctive. For clarity, this does not mean that the Holy Spirit "[makes] us wise in some magical kind of way"—for example, "giving us little nudges and insider tips to help us always choose the best stock to invest in." But Keller does point to occupational wisdom as a work of the Spirit in our lives, "transforming our character, giving us new inner poise, clarity, humility, boldness, contentment, and courage." By God's grace, wisdom grows within us, leading to "better and better professional and personal decisions."[38]

Keller tells of a young woman whose life was changed by the counter-cultural actions of her supervisor. When he could've rightfully laid the blame for a significant mistake on her alone, he "took the fall" instead. She was stunned—and inquired why he had done this:

> Finally he told her, "I am a Christian. That means among other things that God accepts me because Jesus Christ took the blame for things that I have done wrong. He did that on the cross. That is why I have the desire and sometimes the ability to take the blame for others." She stared at him for a long moment and asked, "Where do you go to church?" He suggested she go to Redeemer, and so she did. His character had been shaped by his experience of grace in the gospel, and it made his behavior as a manager attractive and strikingly different from that of others. This lack of self-interest and ruthlessness on the part of her supervisor was eventually life-transforming to her.[39]

Another way Christians can stand out, particularly in a competitive work environment, is by simply resting well. Indeed, one sign the gospel is transforming the way you work, particularly if it's a job you love, is that you are able to take breaks. But the job has perhaps become an idol when days off seem like obstacles rather than joys.

In the ancient Near East, the fourth commandment—to honor the Sabbath (Ex. 20:8–11; Deut. 5:12–15)—was a radical idea. It implied that work and profit taking have limits, like a river that must not burst its banks. Regardless of your perspective on how Christians in the new covenant are meant to apply this law, the principle endures: practicing a form of Sabbath is both an act of trust and a celebration of our design. It is also, notes Keller, a declaration of our freedom. Despite what your culture or boss tells you, "you are not a slave."[40]

Again, no matter how we apply the Sabbath command today, all Christians can agree with Keller on the underlying principle: it points beyond itself to the deeper "Sabbath rest" of the gospel in which we learn to rest in Christ, rather than our works, for salvation.[41] And this deeper rest—what Keller elsewhere dubs the "REM of the soul"[42]—should be reflected in the way we approach both work and rest.

The Bible's perspective on work is unusual and explosive. It has the power to change not only the mindset with which you approach your job but also how your nonbelieving colleagues view the faith you profess.[43]

Leaf by Niggle

When we are frustrated and demoralized in our work—an inevitability in a fallen world—what will keep us going? What hope will propel us to endure through the difficulty? No discussion of Keller's teaching on work would be complete without one of his favorite illustrations, drawn from a rather obscure short story.

At one point while composing *The Lord of the Rings* during World War II, the great J. R. R. Tolkien stalled out. It was a classic case of writer's block—though particularly demoralizing because he'd been working on the saga for decades. One morning Tolkien woke with another story idea, to which he turned his attention. (Sure enough, after finishing it, the clouds parted, and he resumed work on what became the classic trilogy.)

The lesser-known story is about an unappreciated artist named Niggle. In his mind he sees a massive tree—beautiful and breathtaking—and labors to paint it on a huge canvas. He works on it every day, with painstaking attention to detail. The weeks turn into months, and the months into years, and yet he manages to paint only one leaf.

After he dies, Niggle is put on a train to the heavenly country where, along the way, he looks out the window and essentially says, "Stop the train!" He gets out and runs over, and there it is. The tree. *His* tree, with leaves opening and branches bending in the wind, in all its breathtaking beauty. Gazing upward with lifted arms, he cries, "It's a gift!" In this moment, Niggle realizes that the tree he had toiled so unsuccessfully to paint was, it turns out, a glimpse of reality—and a metaphor for his earthly limitations.[44]

Welcome to work in a fallen world. All of us, like Niggle, are incapable of reaching the heights of our vocational dreams. Despite our best efforts, we likely won't get out more than a leaf or two in our lifetime. But one day, in the new heavens and new earth, we will encounter what our hearts longed for. Keller urges us to consider the stakes:

> If this life is all there is, then everything will eventually burn up in the death of the sun and no one will even be around to remember anything that has ever happened. Everyone will be forgotten, nothing we do will make any difference, and all good endeavors, even the best, will come to naught.
>
> Unless there is a God. If the God of the Bible exists, and there is a True Reality beneath and behind this one, and this life is not the only life, then every good endeavor—even the simplest ones, pursued in response to God's calling—can matter forever. That is what the Christian faith promises.[45]

Whether you're a disheartened city planner who can never quite achieve the city of your dreams or a discouraged lawyer whose quest for justice continually falls short, there remains a hope for you—and for *all* of us in our vocational pursuits:

> There really is a tree. Whatever you are seeking in your work—the city of justice and peace, the world of brilliance and beauty, the story,

the order, the healing—it is *there*. There is a God, there is a future healed world that he will bring about, and your work is showing it (in part) to others. . . . If you know all this, you won't be despondent because you can get only a leaf or two out in this life. You will work with satisfaction and joy.[46]

An Identity That Works

The average person will spend approximately ninety thousand hours at work—more time than anywhere else in his or her waking life.[47] That's pretty remarkable to ponder. What a tragedy, then, when Christians are not taught how Sunday worship connects with Monday work—when we're left unequipped to be distinct witnesses in a dark world.[48]

But in Keller we find a penetrating perspective that brings the gospel story to bear on our vocational lives. He demonstrates that work is a wonderful servant but a terrible lord.[49] No matter how successful you are, your career cannot give you a durable identity. It cannot satisfy your soul. It certainly cannot die for your sins.

Only an identity grounded in the love of Jesus Christ can guard you from drifting into overwork or underwork, from succumbing to utopianism or despair. As Keller cautions, "If you make work your identity and you succeed, it will go to your head. If you fail, it will go to your heart."[50]

But when the miracle of grace happens—when your status and joy are no longer tethered to a vocation—you can experience freedom both *from* your work and *in* your work. Your job is simply an assignment from the King to serve others. So labor diligently for his glory—even if you manage to squeeze out only one or two "leaves" in this life.

6

Do Justice, Love Mercy

Embodying the Compassion of the King

IN A TENSE SCENE at the end of *To Kill a Mockingbird*, Harper Lee's classic novel set in 1930s Alabama, defense attorney Atticus Finch closes his case with an impassioned plea to the jury:

> A court is only as sound as its jury, and a jury is only as sound as the men who make it up. I am confident that you gentlemen will review without passion the evidence you have heard, come to a decision, and restore this defendant to his family. In the name of God, do your duty.[1]

After deliberating, the jury comes back: *guilty, guilty, guilty* on all counts. Unanimously they condemn a man known full well to be innocent. As Finch later reflects, "The one place where a man ought to get a square deal is in a courtroom, be he any color of the rainbow, but people have a way of carrying their resentments right into a jury box."[2]

As shown in classic novels, notorious trials, harrowing documentaries, true-crime podcasts, campus protests, and social-media feeds, our culture is enamored with justice. We won't tolerate bad people getting away with bigotry and crimes. Nor will we tolerate the suffering of the innocent and marginalized. This passion is owing to many factors, of course, but not least because it taps into something primal in us. Our consciences—our very natures—cry out for justice to be served.

Now, astute readers may have noticed an uncareful statement in the preceding paragraph: "our culture is enamored with justice." That's not quite true, is it? What we're enamored with is the *idea* of justice. We seem to understand little about the real thing.[3]

Keller's Journey with Justice

Caring about justice didn't come naturally to Tim Keller. "Growing up," he recalled, "I shunned the only child I knew well who was poor—Jeffrey, a boy in my elementary and middle-school classes who lived 'under the Eighth Street Bridge.'"[4] He continued,

> In my school's tightly ordered social system, there were the Insiders and Uncool Outsiders. Then there was Jeffrey, in a category by himself. His clothes were ill-fitting thrift store garments, and he smelled bad. He was mocked mercilessly, excluded from games and conversations, and penalized in classwork, since few wanted to cooperate with him on assignments and projects. I confess that I avoided him most of the time because I was one of the Uncool Outsiders and was hoping to improve my social status. Instead of identifying with Jeffrey and recognizing the injustice of how he was being treated, I turned on the only kid who was more of a social outsider than I was.[5]

This would haunt Keller for years. Another milestone occurred two decades later, when Keller was pastoring in rural Virginia and enrolled in a doctoral program at Westminster Theological Seminary in Philadelphia. "Work on deacons," his advisor told him. "No one knows how important that office is anymore."[6] The assignment proved transformative as he grappled with Scripture's teaching on justice and mercy.[7] Keller later became director of mercy ministries for the Presbyterian Church in America (PCA) in the denomination's formative years, which yielded his first two books in 1985 and 1989.[8] And while serving as professor of practical theology at Westminster in the late 1980s, he and Kathy served on the board of Tenth Presbyterian Church's ministry to AIDS victims.[9]

The Lord used these experiences, along with Kathy's influence,[10] to prepare him to live and minister in a place like Manhattan. When Tim and Kathy arrived with their three young sons in 1989, the city was far more dangerous than cool.[11] Indeed, the realities of the city impelled the Kellers to mine for a deeper understanding of biblical justice.

Justification and Justice

Thankfully, God's word contains numerous resources for navigating life in a world riddled with poverty and distress. Keller often returned to the theme of biblical justice, examining it from various angles, but his basic thesis remained simple: A life poured out in deeds of justice and mercy, especially for the poor, is an inevitable sign of saving faith. The grace that justifies—once it sinks in—cannot help but cultivate a life that is just. Reflecting on his two pastoral environments, Keller concluded,

> There are many great differences between the southern town of Hopewell, Virginia, and the giant metropolis of New York. But there was one thing that was exactly the same. To my surprise, there is a direct relationship between a person's grasp and experience of God's grace, and his or her heart for justice and the poor. In both settings, as I preached the classic message that God does *not* give us justice but saves us by free grace, I discovered that those most affected by the message became the most sensitive to the social inequities around them.[12]

One of Keller's go-to examples was a Hopewell man in the 1970s named Easley Shelton. Having internalized the good news of saving grace, he repented and believed and immediately began to change.

"You know," he remarked to Keller one day, "I've been a racist all my life." Keller was startled, since he hadn't yet taught on the subject of racism. What was happening? The Lord was using the power of gospel grace, unfolded through simple expository preaching, to open this man's eyes to his sin.[13]

It's no secret that professing Christians who are passionate about justice can be wary about justification, and those passionate about justification can be wary about justice.[14] The latter danger is something Keller both lamented and understood. Justice talk *has* often been co-opted by theological liberals who've left the gospel behind. That's a tragedy and a danger. But the solution isn't to avoid the subject altogether. Because Scripture is clear about God's love for justice, we don't have to reengineer orthodoxy in order to value it.

But *how* does grasping justification—God's declaration that a sinner is righteous before him, through faith alone—naturally lead to justice? There are a few ways. First, rightly understanding justification brings about an awareness of the lengths to which Jesus Christ went to rescue you. God's character is so holy—his law so righteous and pure—that nothing less than the death of his incarnate Son was sufficient to save you from his just wrath. That's how soaring the standard is. Justification, therefore, presupposes an enormously high view of *God's* commitment to justice—which will inevitably affect our own.

Second, grasping justification changes our attitude toward the needy. "Blessed are the poor in spirit," Jesus promised, "for theirs is the kingdom of heaven" (Matt. 5:3). Spiritual poverty and material poverty are not identical; the former spans economic classes since it's about humility rather than money. Nonetheless, there is a connection—hence Jesus's comparison. The spiritually poor have, like many of the materially poor, exhausted their own resources. They know they're bankrupt.

Poverty of spirit, in other words, is the death knell of condescension. Even if you are financially stable, the gospel moves you to admit that when you're looking at a destitute person, you're looking at a spiritual mirror.

So beware, warned Keller, of being "middle-class in spirit." As a pastor, he found that "those who are middle-class in spirit tend to be indifferent to the poor, but [those] who come to grasp the gospel of grace and become spiritually poor find their hearts gravitating toward the materially poor."[15]

Finally, God's justifying grace has the explosive power to change not just our attitude *toward* the poor but also the attitude *of* the poor. The Lord Jesus came, in fulfillment of Isaiah's scroll, proclaiming good news to the poor (Luke 4:18; cf. Isa. 61:1). While that doesn't mean his gospel is irrelevant to the rich, it's good news only to those who have come to the end of themselves. Think about the logic of James 1:9–10: "Let the lowly brother boast in his exaltation, and the rich in his humiliation, because like a flower of the grass he will pass away." The statement is startlingly paradoxical. Keller observes,

> James proposes that the well-off person who becomes a believer would spiritually benefit by especially thinking about her sinfulness before God, since out in the world she gets nothing but acclaim. On the other hand, the poor person who becomes a believer would spiritually benefit by especially thinking about her new high spiritual status, since out in the world she gets nothing but disdain.[16]

The gospel of Jesus Christ contains incomparable power to dignify those the world ignores. The last thing the disadvantaged need is a press release that reads, "Behold, I bring you good news of great joy that will be for all the people: God helps those who help themselves!" The gospel is infinitely better news. As Keller remarked at a conference, "Give the self-help thing to the poor, and you're going to destroy them. Give the gospel to the poor, and you're going to transform them."[17] No wonder widows, slaves, and the poor—the scum of Roman society—flocked to Christianity. They'd never heard a message like it.

As surely as justification precedes sanctification, God's great intention is to declare us *just*—and then make us so. Operating as if justification has little to do with justice, then, is like operating as if faith has little to do with deeds.[18] Such logic was inconceivable to the biblical authors.

Evangelism and Social Action

In a section of *Generous Justice* titled "Doing Justice and Preaching Grace," Keller deploys characteristic nuance to shed light on this discussion—particularly the relationship between word ministry (evangelism) and deed ministry (justice and mercy).

He first warns against conflating the two: "Doing justice can indeed lead people to give the message of gospel grace a hearing, but to consider deeds of mercy and justice to be identical to gospel proclamation is a fatal confusion." Keller instead exhorts us to see them as existing in an "asymmetrical, inseparable relationship."[19] The phrase is clunky but careful.

Evangelism and justice are biblically *inseparable*—that's what much of this chapter is about. The gospel produces genuine concern for the poor, and deeds of justice can open the door for the gospel message. The relationship is symbiotic: "Justification by faith leads to doing justice, and doing justice can make many seek to be justified by faith."[20] But what about the *asymmetrical* part? Keller explains that while both aspects are important, even necessary, they are not so in the same way. There is a unique priority on evangelism given its eternal significance: "Evangelism is the most basic and radical ministry possible to a human being," he contends.

> This is true not because the spiritual is more important than the physical, but because the eternal is more important than the temporal. . . . If there is a God, and if life with him for eternity is based on having a saving relationship with him, then the most loving thing anyone can do for [their] neighbor is help him or her to a saving faith in that God.[21]

After providing several scriptural examples, Keller challenges us to grasp the balance he carefully holds in tension:

If we confuse evangelism and social justice, we lose what is *the single most unique service* that Christians can offer the world. Others, alongside believers, can feed the hungry. But Christians have the gospel of Jesus by which men and women can be born again into the certain hope of eternal life. No one else can make such an invitation. However, many Christians who care intensely about evangelism see the work of doing justice as a distraction for Christians that detracts from the mission of evangelism. That is also a grave error.[22]

Differences in theology, temperament, and experience mean that potentially every Christian—and even every congregation—will be prone to one of these errors more than the other. None of us is perfectly balanced. Some might tend toward a heart for evangelism at the expense of justice, and others toward a heart for justice at the expense of evangelism.

Keller's message here is twofold. First, we shouldn't separate what God has joined together, as if we know better.[23] You aren't more sensitive to a given danger than God is (though it's possible you're more paranoid). But second, we must remember: Not all dangers are equally harmful since not all doctrines are equally weighted. If you've been missing the importance of justice, sound doctrine is right there to correct you. But if you lose sound doctrine, what you're calling *justice* is likely unworthy of the name.[24] This is why evangelism must remain the leading partner in the inseparable union.[25]

In 1992, three years after its first gathering, Redeemer Presbyterian launched Hope for New York to mobilize funding and volunteers for organizations meeting physical needs in the city. "The world isn't accustomed to a church that cares just as much about expositional preaching as it does about justice for the poor," notes Collin Hansen. But from the outset at Redeemer, those goals were "theologically inseparable."[26] Far from viewing mercy ministry as a distraction, Keller knew it would help skeptical neighbors see the good news of Jesus as plausible. "Conversion growth looks like accruing power," explains Hansen, "unless those converts sacrifice to meet the needs of their neighbors, regardless of whether they share faith in Jesus."[27] Yet even while seeking a balanced approach, Keller kept the priority on proclamation.[28] This, of course, bears significant implications for discussions about the mission of the church.[29]

Three Components of Biblical Justice

Acknowledging the priority of gospel proclamation, what does a just life look like according to God's word?

Keller defines justice, most basically, as "giving people their due."[30] Synthesizing his teaching on the topic, we can identify three consistent components in Scripture's view of justice. (It's worth noting that Keller was more interested in providing general principles than specific prescriptions here. One must carefully discern—in prayer, study, and conversation with mature friends and pastors—how to implement such principles with situational wisdom.)

1. Universal Dignity

The starting point for any conversation about biblical justice must be the righteous character of God, and the infinite dignity inherent to all who bear his image (Gen. 1:26–27). Every person—regardless of culture, class, ethnicity, developmental stage, mental capacity, or any other factor—has intrinsic and equal value.

The image of God isn't some tacked-on extra, as if we're just slightly upgraded mammals. It's about who we are fundamentally, not just about a few attributes we might possess. Besides being an adopted son or daughter of the King, there is no greater honor in the world than being made in his image. And this has all kinds of practical implications for the way we're meant to treat each other. Because without this awareness—that everyone you encounter bears the image of the living God—you simply won't find lasting motivation to love them.

Just think of common reasons people might have for loving others. *Because they contribute to society. Because it's what works best. Because we're obligated to. Because we identify with them.* But recognizing God's image in literally every human being levels the ground before a common Creator and insists that none of us is inherently superior—or inferior—to anyone else. If we truly love the Lord, we will love what he loves. And what does he love? Those who bear his image.

Regardless of record or character, observes Keller, "all human beings have an irreducible glory and significance to them, because God loves them."[31] He invokes an illustration from Nicholas Wolterstorff that calls us to imagine a foreigner being puzzled by why the Mount Vernon estate in Virginia is so revered as having great worth, considering its relatively modest eighteenth-century architecture and simplicity:

> We would respond that this was the house of George Washington, the founder of our country, and that explains it. The internal merits and quality of the house are irrelevant. Because we treasure the owner, we honor his house. Because it was precious to him, and we revere him, it is precious to us.[32]

Recognizing and treasuring the image of God in one another, especially the least and the last, is the first great motivation for a biblically just life.[33]

2. Deliberate Care

Gratefully, most Christians today will nod along with everything in the previous point. Or at least *almost* everything. But what about that word "especially" in the final sentence? If I had written "even," there would be no concern. But surely "especially" tilts us too far in the direction of special treatment—sinful partiality—right? The Bible's answer seems to be both yes and no.

On the one hand, God's word couldn't be clearer: "You shall do no injustice in court. You shall not be partial to the poor or defer to the great, but in righteousness shall you judge your neighbor" (Lev. 19:15; cf. Deut. 1:16–17). Modern people expect prohibitions against favoring the rich, but this verse also forbids courtrooms that favor the poor. The wealthy deserve a fair shake too, not least because they bear the image of God. Principles of legal justice—including due process and presumption of innocence—must not be deployed in favor of one class or race over another.

On the other hand, while we are to treat all equally and not show partiality to any, Scripture insists that we show special concern for the poor, the weak, and the powerless.[34] So, which is it? Equal treatment for all, or special concern for the poor? The Bible answers with a resounding yes.

We are to show special concern for the poor because that's what our God does. "The Bible says that God is the defender of the poor; it never says he is the defender of the rich," notes Keller. "And while some texts call for justice for members of the well-off classes as well, the calls to render justice to the poor outnumber such passages *by a hundred to one*."[35] Why is this? It's not because God loves the rich less, nor because they aren't susceptible to unjust treatment. But it's a simple fact that injustice is so often "easier to perform against people without the money or social status to defend themselves. . . . In short, since most of the people who are downtrodden by abusive power are those who had little power to begin with, God gives them particular attention and has a special place in his heart for them."[36] No wonder the New Testament's major denunciation of partiality is in the context of favoring the rich (James 2:1–13). This accords with a dizzying number of passages, such as Proverbs 22:22–23:

> Do not rob the poor, because he is poor,
>   or crush the afflicted at the gate,
> for the LORD will plead their cause
>   and rob of life those who rob them.

Or Proverbs 31:8–9:

> Open your mouth for the mute,
>> for the rights of all who are destitute.
> Open your mouth, judge righteously,
>> defend the rights of the poor and needy.

We hear similar admonitions from Moses: "Cursed be anyone who perverts the justice due to the sojourner, the fatherless, and the widow" (Deut. 27:19). And from Jeremiah: "Thus says the LORD: Do justice and righteousness, and deliver from the hand of the oppressor him who has been robbed. And do no wrong or violence to the resident alien, the fatherless, and the widow, nor shed innocent blood in this place" (Jer. 22:3). And from Zechariah: "Do not oppress the widow, the fatherless, the sojourner, or the poor, and let none of you devise evil against another in your heart" (Zech. 7:10). And on and on.

Most strikingly, God identifies with impoverished image bearers such that the way we treat them is often, in a sense, how we are treating *him*:

> Whoever oppresses a poor man insults his Maker,
>> but he who is generous to the needy honors him. (Prov. 14:31)

> Whoever is generous to the poor lends to the LORD,
>> and he will repay him for his deed. (Prov. 19:17)

When we turn to the New Testament, these principles are reinforced—arguably in even stronger terms. Jesus skewers religious leaders who "like to walk around in long robes and like greetings in the marketplaces and have the best seats in the synagogues and the places of honor at feasts, who devour widows' houses and for a pretense make long prayers. They will receive the greater condemnation" (Mark 12:38–40). The Pharisees were so fastidious that they were even tithing out of their spice racks, yet Jesus looks at their lives and isn't impressed, for they "neglect justice and the love of God" (Luke 11:42). Likewise in the parable of the sheep and the goats: Jesus predicts that many who claim his name will be judged forever (Matt. 25:31–46). Keller summarizes,

> [Jesus's] true sheep . . . have a heart for "the least of these my breth-ren," which Jesus defined as the hungry, the stranger, the "naked," the sick, and the imprisoned (verses 35–36). If we assume that Jesus was using the term "brethren" in his usual way, to refer to believers, then he was teaching that genuine disciples of Christ will create a new community that does not exclude the poor, the members of other races, or the powerless.[37]

The message is startling, for Jesus essentially says, "If you don't have any compassion for believers who are downtrodden, distressed, or destitute, you don't have a relationship with me."

Again, consider the book of James. After sounding a warning against favoring the rich (2:1–7), James insists that faith without works is dead (2:17).[38] That's provocative—deliberately so. Now, what *damnably missing* works does he have in mind? Look at the immediate context:

> If a brother or sister is poorly clothed and lacking in daily food, and one of you says to them, "Go in peace, be warmed and filled," without giving them the things needed for the body, what good is that? (James 2:15–16; cf. 1 John 3:17–18)

God's word is clear: Showing practical concern for poor believers doesn't grant you spiritual life. But it may prove your faith isn't a corpse. We could keep multiplying examples.[39]

When people asked Keller how he'd like to be publicly introduced, he usually proposed something like, "This is Tim Keller, minister at Redeemer Presbyterian Church in New York City." Why? It reflected the main thing he did in public life. Likewise, the inspired biblical writers introduce God as a "father of the fatherless and protector of widows" (Ps. 68:5). Why? It's one of the main aspects of who he is.[40]

There's no escaping Scripture's pervasive message of justice and its bracing implications for believers.

3. Radical Generosity

Many modern people reduce generosity to an issue of charity, observes Keller, but in the Bible it is an issue of justice (hence the book title *Generous Justice*). We may not like to hear it, but according to Scripture, to be ungenerous is to be unjust. Consider, for example, Proverbs 3:27–28:

> Do not withhold good from those to whom it is due,
>> when it is in your power to do it.
> Do not say to your neighbor, "Go, and come again,
>> tomorrow I will give it"—when you have it with you.

Or consider the life of righteous Job:

> I delivered the poor who cried for help,
>> and the fatherless who had none to help him.
> The blessing of him who was about to perish came upon me,
>> and I caused the widow's heart to sing for joy.
> I put on righteousness, and it clothed me;
>> my justice was like a robe and a turban.
> I was eyes to the blind
>> and feet to the lame.
> I was a father to the needy,
>> and I searched out the cause of him whom I did not know.
> I broke the fangs of the unrighteous
>> and made him drop his prey from his teeth. (Job 29:12–17)

Job later declares,

> If I have withheld anything that the poor desired,
>   or have caused the eyes of the widow to fail,
> or have eaten my morsel alone,
>   and the fatherless has not eaten of it
> (for from my youth the fatherless grew up with me as with a father,
>   and from my mother's womb I guided the widow),
> if I have seen anyone perish for lack of clothing,
>   or the needy without covering,
> if his body has not blessed me,
>   and if he was not warmed with the fleece of my sheep,
> if I have raised my hand against the fatherless,
>   because I saw my help in the gate,
> then let my shoulder blade fall from my shoulder,
>   and let my arm be broken from its socket. . . .
> this also would be an *iniquity* to be punished by the judges,
>   for I would have been *false to God above*. (Job 31:16–22, 28)

Do you see the logic? Failing to be generous to the poor offends the God in whose image we are all made. When the Bible speaks of the "righteous" and "wicked," we think it simply means the personally "moral" and "immoral." That's only partly right, observes Keller, since the Hebrew words for "righteous"—*tsedaqah* and *mishpat*—are irreducibly social. On this point he often cites Bruce Waltke's pithy summary: "The righteous are willing to disadvantage themselves to advantage the community; the wicked are willing to disadvantage the community to advantage themselves."[41] In other words, concludes Keller,

> The righteous say, "Much of what I have belongs to the people around me, because it all comes from God and he wants me to love my neighbor." The wicked say, "I can do what I want with my

things." Go through Proverbs, reading "righteous" and "wicked" . . . with this fuller definition in mind, and it will become like a whole new book.[42]

Everything we possess is a gift—not from the state but from the Lord himself. Keller observes that a secular person can look at what they've amassed and think, *This is all mine.* At least it's consistent with their worldview. But a Christian should never think that. Everything we possess is a gift from a generous God who calls us to deploy his gifts, with sacrificial love, for the good of others.

This is humbling, even unsettling. What about all those biblical passages that denounce laziness and commend diligence (e.g., Prov. 6:9–11; 10:4; 12:27; 2 Thess. 3:10–12)? Make no mistake: These form a crucial part of the picture. Industriousness often *does* lead to material success.[43] Nonetheless, Scripture insists that the fruit of our labor is ultimately heaven's gift (1 Chron. 29:14; Isa. 26:12; John 3:27; 1 Cor. 4:7; James 1:17).[44]

Doing justice, then, must never be simply relegated to practicing charity. Instead, it means giving image bearers of God—especially those who can't defend themselves—their astonishing biblical due.

Pushing the Button

It's easy to shame believers who aren't generous, but Keller knew that wasn't effective—or biblical. Notice, he loved to observe, *how* Paul encourages the Corinthians to give sacrificially. The apostle neither manipulates their emotions ("Think about all those poor starving kids in Macedonia") nor manipulates their wills ("I'm an apostle! Give because I tell you"). His approach differs altogether:

> For you know the grace of our Lord Jesus Christ, that though he was rich, yet for your sake he became poor, so that you by his poverty might become rich. (2 Cor. 8:9)

That's it. No browbeating, no guilt-tripping. Just a simple summons: *ponder the unfathomable generosity of your King.* Jesus Christ didn't merely "tithe his blood"[45]; he spilled it all—even for the stingiest of sinners. So if you wish to grow in the grace of giving, urges Keller, "don't sit down with a calculator; sit down with a cross."[46]

Keller believed that any true Christian, indwelt by God's Spirit, would be moved by radical grace—even if the *how* of faithful implementation will vary from person to person and situation to situation. It's as if a heart for the poor "sleeps" down in every Christian's soul until it's awakened. And what does that? What "pushes the button"? When a believer sees justice for the poor not as an emotional appeal or a coercive command—much less a political agenda—but as an inescapably beautiful entailment of Christ's self-giving love.[47]

Surely the most striking example of generous justice in the New Testament—and arguably the whole Bible—is Jesus's parable of the good Samaritan. The details are familiar. A Jewish man is beaten, robbed, and left for dead on a roadside. A priest comes along and sees him writhing in pain, but instead of helping he passes by on the other side. Another religious figure, a Levite, does the same. But eventually a Samaritan—a despised cultural enemy—approaches and does what the religious leaders should have: He kneels down, binds up the man's wounds, and carries him to a first-century hospital—at great expense to himself. After finishing the parable, Jesus turns the question on the law expert who had tried to test Jesus and justify himself:

> "Which of these three, do you think, proved to be a neighbor to the man who fell among the robbers?" He said, "The one who showed him mercy." And Jesus said to him, "You go, and do likewise." (Luke 10:36–37)

According to the Bible, then, acts of mercy and justice are expressions of love. Love is at the blazing center of our obligations to fellow image bearers, and though not every act of love is an act of justice, justice is always rooted in love. And what is the character of neighbor love? Jesus answers by showing a person "meeting material, physical, and economic needs through deeds," Keller explains, even at enormous risk and expense. But our Lord doesn't only refuse to let us limit *how* we love. He also, Keller notes, refuses to limit *whom*:

> We [tend to exert ourselves] for people like us, and for people whom we like. Jesus will have none of that. By depicting a Samaritan helping a Jew, Jesus could not have found a more forceful way to say that anyone at all in need—regardless of race, politics, class, and religion—is your neighbor. Not everyone is your brother or sister in the faith, but everyone is your neighbor, and you must love your neighbor.[48]

Of course, the parable is not just an extraordinary challenge; it also conveys the sobering truth that we're all like the dying man on the side of the road—spiritually "dead in our trespasses" (Eph. 2:5). Keller expounds with perception,

> When Jesus came into our dangerous world, he came down our road. And though we had been his enemies, he was moved with compassion by our plight (Rom. 5:10). He came to us and saved us, not merely at the risk of his life, as in the case of the Samaritan, but at the cost of his life. On the cross he paid a debt we could never have paid ourselves. Jesus is the Great Samaritan to whom the Good Samaritan points.[49]

We too are called to offer profoundly costly love—but, notes Keller, we cannot give what we haven't received. Only when we see that we've been rescued by one who owed us the opposite will we go into the world looking to help those in need.

Keller teaches that the causes of poverty are enormously complex and defy easy sloganeering.[50] "There are valid reasons," he admits, "why many become concerned when they hear Christians talk about 'doing justice.' Often that term is just a slogan being used to recruit listeners to jump on some political bandwagon."[51] This isn't to say we must always remain apolitical, lest we end up approving of a wicked status quo.[52] Nonetheless, if we wish to align ourselves with the word of God, its call to justice will sometimes defy easy categorization.

What's incredible—and startling—is that Scripture's most thundering denunciations toward injustice are leveled not against pagans or the profane but against those who appear exceptionally pious. In the scroll of the prophet Isaiah, God wastes no time calling his chosen people to account:

Wash yourselves; make yourselves clean;
    remove the evil of your deeds from before my eyes;
cease to do evil,
    learn to do good;
seek justice,
    correct oppression;
bring justice to the fatherless,
    plead the widow's cause. (Isa. 1:16–17)

By the end of the book, God takes on people so religious they're literally starving themselves to honor him. He is not addressing the obviously wayward but those seen as pillars of righteousness. They register an objection:

"Why have we fasted, and you see it not?
    Why have we humbled ourselves, and you take no knowledge
        of it?" (Isa. 58:3)

Yet notice God's response. What's his *very first* example?

"Behold, in the day of your fast you seek your own pleasure,
and oppress all your workers." (Isa. 58:3)

God continues,

"Is not this the fast that I choose:
to loose the bonds of wickedness,
to undo the straps of the yoke,
to let the oppressed go free,
and to break every yoke?
Is it not to share your bread with the hungry
and bring the homeless poor into your house;
when you see the naked, to cover him,
and not to hide yourself from your own flesh?" (Isa. 58:6–7;
see also 58:10)

That final verse is staggering. In a patriarchal culture in which blood ties were everything, God insists that the poor and destitute are "your own flesh"—your own family.[53]

Foundation and Fabric

God loves _____. How would you fill in the blank? Maybe you'd insert "his glory" or "his creation" or "his only begotten Son" or "wretched sinners like us." Each would be gloriously true! And yet the exercise would be incomplete without an additional word. The Bible is explicit: "For I the LORD love justice" (Isa. 61:8). Justice is not incidental to the divine résumé; it's at the heart of it.

God calls us to lives of justice because he loves justice—and us. To the extent we heed his call, we come to know his heart. After all, Christians know how far God actually went to identify with the poor. In the incarnation he "left the wealthiest neighborhood in the universe"[54] to become a helpless baby in an obscure place:

Seek not in courts or palaces,
Nor royal curtains draw;
But search the stable, see your God
Extended on the straw.[55]

There was nothing remotely extravagant about the circumstances of Christ's life on earth. Born in a stable, placed in a feeding trough, raised in a poor family, homeless with no place to lay his head, riding a borrowed donkey, eating his last meal in a borrowed room, buried in a borrowed tomb—not to mention all his earthly possessions being divvied up among a few Roman guards. But he didn't just know poverty; he knew oppression too. His trial on the last night of his life was an elaborate miscarriage of justice.

All this gives new meaning to that great future question on judgment day: "Lord, when did we see you hungry or thirsty or a stranger or naked or sick or in prison?" (Matt. 25:44). The ultimate answer, says Keller, is *on the cross*, where Jesus died destitute among slaves and thieves. "No wonder Paul could say that once you see Jesus becoming poor for us, you will never look at the poor the same way again."[56]

The nature of justice is inseparably tied to the nature of God. It is not simply a sweet sentiment, or a political talking point, or a modern fad. It is the veritable foundation of God's throne (Ps. 89:14). And therefore, it must be woven deeply into the fabric of our lives.

Answering Heaven

How Prayer Unlocks Intimacy with God

IN 2014, KELLER WAS ASKED what had been his hardest book to write. His answer: "The book I just finished, because it was on prayer."[1]

Prayer was not just a challenging topic to write about; it was also a discipline of great personal struggle for Keller, as it is for countless believers. Over the course of his adult life, though, the great struggle yielded unimaginable reward.

In fact, not long before his death, Keller was asked if, looking back on nearly fifty years of ministry, there's anything that he would have done differently.

"Absolutely," he replied. "I should have prayed more."[2]

Timely Illustration

It's not as if Keller was ever indifferent to prayer. Like any good minister, he taught on it often. But something was still missing, still lacking in the vibrancy of his own friendship with Christ. He opened his 2014 book on the topic with these words: "In the second half of my adult life, I discovered prayer. I had to."

While teaching a Bible study course on the Psalms in the fall of 1999, Keller became keenly aware that his prayer life was nowhere near what God's word indicated it should be. Within a couple years, he faced the harsh realities of ministry to New Yorkers in the wake of 9/11. Compounding this dark time were his own personal weights, as Kathy suffered the effects of Crohn's disease and soon after he received a diagnosis of thyroid cancer. Indeed, Keller's experience with prayer was taking a dramatic turn. Perhaps most formative for him during this season was Kathy's urging to simply and faithfully join her *every night* to pray. She used an illustration that Keller later recounted, which placed prayer in its proper light:

> "Imagine you were diagnosed with such a lethal condition that the doctor told you that you would die within hours unless you took a particular medicine—a pill every night before going to sleep. Imagine that you were told that you could never miss it or you would die. Would you forget? Would you not get around to it some nights? No—it would be so crucial that you wouldn't forget, you would never miss. Well, if we don't pray together to God, we're not going to make it because of all we are facing. I'm certainly not. We *have* to pray; we can't let it just slip our minds." . . .
>
> For both of us the penny dropped; we realized the seriousness of the issue, and we admitted that anything that was truly a non-negotiable necessity was something we could do. . . . [Since then] Kathy and I can't remember missing a single evening of praying together, at least by phone, even when we've been apart in different hemispheres.[3]

Tim and Kathy Keller maintained this unbroken streak night after night for more than twenty years—all the way through until the end of his life.[4]

A Church Prayed into Being

The Kellers did not want to move to New York City. They were enjoying a fruitful ministry and a comfortable life with three young children in the suburbs of Philadelphia. Manhattan, meanwhile, was expensive and dangerous—a lonely destination for gospel ministry. No obvious factor represented the chief obstacle, though. "What held Keller back more than anything else," recounts Collin Hansen, "was the realization that his prayer and spiritual life couldn't handle the scope of this project."[5] He wrestled with the Lord. He tried, in vain, to convince others to go. What ultimately brought Keller to embrace the direction God was taking him was a confrontation with his own cowardice, as he pondered the words of the Puritan William Gurnall: "It requires more prowess and greatness of spirit to obey God faithfully, than to command an army of men; to be a Christian, than to be a captain."[6] As he relinquished his fears and made the consequential decision to move to New York, Keller noted an immediate turning point in his prayer life.

But it wasn't just prayer *from* the Kellers but *for* them that likely made the greatest difference. The Women in the Church of the PCA contributed a third of the funds raised for the church plant; they also formed an army of prayer support. The Kellers could feel the women of over four hundred churches praying for them! Kathy marvels that, despite her "[whiny], most self-pitying prayer letters," the faithful intercession of these warriors moved the heart and hand of God and had an immeasurable impact on the Kellers' ministry beginnings in New York. "They prayed up a storm," Kathy said. "It's like we couldn't make a bad decision in those early years. I'm convinced there was never a church plant, even going back to the apostle Paul and the first-century church, that had so many people, especially women, praying for it."[7] Doubtless, such prayer support was a major factor in the revival-like character of Redeemer's early years.[8]

From the outset of his ministry in Manhattan, Keller's teaching on personal prayer fizzed with candor. He shot straight with his young church:

> Your prayer life is *the* litmus test for your relationship with God. How do you know if you're really a Christian? How do you know? That's a hard question, but I'll tell you this. Your prayer life is the best way to find out. Don't look at whether you witness day and night on the street corner. Don't look at whether you're a moral person. Don't look at whether you go to church. Don't look at even how much you know your Bible. Because, you realize, other people see [those things]—and so it's possible to be motivated out of a desire to look good. It's possible to have an external kind of religion and be motivated by environmental factors. But only God sees you when you pray. As a result, it's your prayer life that tells you what you're really made of spiritually.[9]

Yet despite weekly pastoral prayers and multiple sermon series on the subject, Keller admitted in 2014, "I don't believe I've been particularly good at teaching my church to pray."[10] Even at the age of sixty-nine, he confessed, "I've always sought to have a time of devotion and prayer each morning. And like most other believers, I have found it a struggle to be consistent."[11] Nurturing a rich prayer life, both in himself and in those he served, was a lifelong pursuit.

Theology Drives Intimacy

It wasn't just nightly prayer with Kathy, though, that revolutionized Keller's prayer life. He also began reading and studying, searching for help. Yearning for richer communion with God, he devoured the works of respected Christian thinkers from the past. His quest ultimately yielded a newfound appreciation for, and deeper engagement with, his own theological heritage.[12]

From Augustine in the fifth century all the way to Martin Luther and John Calvin in the sixteenth, John Owen in the seventeenth, John Newton and Jonathan Edwards in the eighteenth, Charles Spurgeon in the nineteenth, and Martyn Lloyd-Jones in the twentieth—and many others in between—Keller realized anew that he didn't have to choose between robust theology and vibrant experience. His own tradition featured both.

As he put it, "I was not being called to leave behind my theology and launch out to look for 'something more,' for experience. Rather, I was meant to ask the Holy Spirit to help me experience my theology."[13]

Think Out, Work In, Pray Up

Perhaps we could say that if experience without theology eventually leads to heresy, theology without experience often results in hypocrisy. Both are serious threats. Prayer, though, is the key that can "turn theology into experience."[14] When Keller was asked to explain this dynamic, he sketched out three simple steps:

- First, *think out* your theology. Know what you believe and why.
- Second, *work in* your theology. It requires honesty to wrestle down a restless heart. "Why are you cast down, O my soul?" the psalmist cried (Ps. 42:5). It also requires uncomfortable questions: How would I be different if I took this theological truth seriously? How would it change my attitudes and actions if I really believed this from the bottom of my heart?
- Third, *pray up* your theology. Learn the art of turning theology into prayer, letting it trigger adoration, confession, and supplication.[15]

"Do those things," he advises, "and your theology will intersect with your experience."[16] Those who are inclined, whether from doctrinal formation or natural temperament, to elevate feelings over theology are planting their feet in midair. But theologically minded believers should likewise beware. "The irony," Keller warns, "is that many conservative Christians, most concerned about conserving true and sound doctrine, neglect the importance of prayer and make no effort to experience God—which can lead to the eventual loss of sound doctrine."[17] Christianity that lacks a real encounter with God will eventually be no Christianity at all.

So there are two ways, not one, to welcome false doctrine into your life or your church. The first is to never value doctrine at all. That's obvious. But the second is far more subtle, and therefore more insidious: Let your heart become sterile over the course of years. Grow numb to the grandeur and splendor of Christ Jesus. Stop listening to his voice in Scripture or letting him hear yours in prayer. Slowly abandon your first love (Rev. 2:4).

The bottom line is we need theology *and* experience—experience that is theological and theology that is experiential. What God has joined together, let no one separate.

Responding to Revelation

One of the most vital takeaways from Keller's teaching is this: Prayer, essentially, is answering God. *He* started the conversation—we did not. This means he sets the agenda and dictates the terms. Our voices are responding to his, not the other way around.

It is therefore impossible to have a rich prayer life apart from careful attention and glad submission to God's word. Otherwise, we will end up talking to a figment of our imagination—in essence, praying to an idol. But if we hope to anchor our life in "the real God," we must pray in accordance with who he's revealed himself to be.[18] Keller puts it frankly: "Without prayer that answers the God of the Bible, we will only be talking to ourselves."[19]

Addressing students at the Oxford Town Hall in England, Keller reflected on the model of prayer that Jesus provides in Gethsemane.

We encounter a Savior who is brutally honest about his desire ("Let this cup pass from me") and yet absolutely submissive to God's plan ("nevertheless, not as I will, but as you will"; Matt. 26:39). Jesus neither represses his feelings nor is ruled by them. What an example for us! "The basic purpose of prayer," Keller observes, "is not to bend God's will to mine but to mold my will into his."[20]

This is why sound biblical interpretation and meditation are indispensable foundations for prayer. Keller commends two questions each time we open our Bibles: First, What did the original author intend to convey to his readers? Second, What role does the passage play in the whole Bible—that is, How does it contribute to the gospel message and move along the main narrative arc of Scripture, which culminates in Jesus Christ? Keller warns us against meditation devoid of such questions, which may unintentionally amount to "listening to your own heart or to the spirit of your own culture"[21] rather than to God's authoritative voice.

Again, this is why theology must inform and fuel experience. Just as you can't grow relationally with a person unless you learn who he or she is, so you can't deepen intimacy with God apart from studying and treasuring his word. Prayer, then, is equal parts response and gift—a response to revelation from God's word and a gift for those secure in his grace.[22]

And this approach to prayer, nourished by biblical meditation, is the pathway to enjoying God.

Praying Your Way to Assured Delight

Biblical meditation is the music of prayer and involves a kind of two-step dance: First, Keller says, we think a truth *out*, and then we think it *in* until its ideas become "big" and "sweet," moving and affecting—until the reality of God is sensed in the heart.[23]

This doesn't mean we are chasing an experience; it means we are pursuing a living God. To ponder his words to the point of delight is to pursue him, the God of delight. Prayer is therefore not merely "a way to get things from God but a way to get more of God himself."[24] This is amazing. Despite our distracted, fidgety, wandering defiance, he beckons us in and—wonder of wonders—offers us himself. And this is precisely what we need, since hearts wired for intimacy were made to be swept up into the life of the Trinity (e.g., John 17:21; 2 Pet. 1:4; 1 John 1:3). As Keller explains, "We can see why a triune God would call us to converse with him, to know and relate to him. It is because he wants to share the joy he has. Prayer is our way of entering into the happiness of God himself."[25]

One key to unlocking this reality is studying and internalizing the doctrine of adoption—the glorious truth that God not only acquits believers in heaven's courtroom but also welcomes us, as it were, into the living room. Because of Jesus we can know our Creator, robed in blazing holiness, not as our Judge but as our Father, who art in heaven. Keller loved to ponder this familial bond and the intimacy it secures. He often returned to an illustration of a man and his young son walking along. Suddenly the father stops, lifts up his boy, and says, "I love you." The boy hugs his dad and says, "I love you too." Then the father puts him down, and they keep walking. Now, here's the question: Legally, was the child more a son in his father's arms than when he was on the street? Of course not. But through the embrace, he vibrantly *experienced* his sonship.[26]

This is what prayer offers us. The most ordinary believer in the world has access to "the most intimate and unbreakable relationship." Just imagine, Keller says, what it takes to visit the president of the United States. Only those who merit his time and attention are granted entry. You must have credentials, accomplishments, and perhaps a power base of your own—*unless*, of course, you're one of his children. That detail changes everything. Likewise, in prayer, we lean experientially—not just theologically—into the Father's loving embrace.[27]

Or as Keller poignantly put it in a sermon: The only person who dares wake up a king at three o'clock in the morning for a glass of water is his child. We have that kind of access.[28]

Upward, Inward, Outward

There are three basic forms of biblical prayer, Keller observes, each oriented in a certain direction.[29] *Upward* prayer focuses on praising and thanking God. *Inward* prayer focuses on self-examination and confession of sin. *Outward* prayer focuses on petition and intercession.

Most of us tend to be best at the outward—and worst at the upward. We pray when we need things or want things, whether for ourselves or others. And praying for such is good! The pages of Scripture brim with summons to boldly approach our Father and lay requests at his feet (e.g., Matt. 7:7–8; Phil. 4:6; Heb. 4:16; James 4:2). Danger arises, though, when adoration becomes a mere afterthought—which reveals more about our self-absorbed hearts than we may care to acknowledge.[30] Reflecting on the parable of the prodigal sons (Luke 15:11–32), Keller warns against an "elder-brother spirit" that robs our ability to enjoy the assurance of fatherly love. How might we detect if we're succumbing to this danger? Keller explains,

> Perhaps the clearest symptom of this lack of assurance is a dry prayer life. Though elder brothers may be diligent in prayer, there is no wonder, awe, intimacy, or delight in their conversations with God. Think of three kinds of people—a business associate you don't really like, a friend you enjoy doing things with, and someone you are in love with, and who is in love with you. Your conversations with the business associate will be quite goal-oriented. You won't be interested in chitchat. With your friend you may open your heart about some of the problems you are having. But with your lover you will sense a strong impulse to speak about what you find beautiful about him or her.
>
> These three kinds of discourse are analogous to forms of prayer that have been called "petition," "confession," and "adoration." The deeper the love relationship, the more the conversation heads toward

the personal, and toward affirmation and praise. Elder brothers may be disciplined in observing regular times of prayer, but their prayers are almost wholly taken up with a recitation of needs and petitions, not spontaneous, joyful praise. In fact, many elder brothers, for all their religiosity, do not have much of a private prayer life at all unless things are not going well in their lives. Then they may devote themselves to a great deal of it, until things get better again. This reveals that their main goal in prayer is to control their environment rather than to delve into an intimate relationship with a God who loves them.[31]

Though it may be unsettling for us to admit, difficult things in life move us to petition far more readily than happy things move us to praise.[32] What does this imbalance reveal about our hearts? One of the most practical "next steps" for your prayer life, then, is simply this: Spend some unhurried time reveling in who God is. If you begin there—contemplating his character, gazing at his glory, praising him for his promises—then your heart will be ready to bring requests to his throne.[33]

Grueling and Glorious

Despite its incredible benefits, prayer is far from easy. Nor is distilling its power into words. When constancy in prayer feels challenging, we shouldn't be shocked. If anything, we should be surprised when it *doesn't* feel challenging. After all, observes Keller, "I can think of nothing great that is also easy. Prayer must be, then, one of the hardest things in the world."[34] He puts it bluntly: "Christianity is not a waltz. It's a fight. . . . You're never going to be any kind of Christian unless you're willing to fight."[35]

Whether on the daily battlefield of distraction or disinterest, prayer is indeed war. But it is the secret to experiencing God—not as some distant commander-in-chief in the skies but as the Father of compassion and the Lord of love. Sadly, though, too few of us persist. "Most of us pursue joy in prayer, don't get it, and then don't stick at it," Keller notes. Instead, we should focus on faithfulness, thinking more of the privilege than the payoff. He offers a straightforward metaphor:

> Imagine that you are rooming with someone and [she] virtually doesn't speak to you. All she does is leave messages. When you mention it, she says, "Well, I don't get much out of talking to you. I find it boring and my mind flitting everywhere, so I just don't try." What will you conclude? Regardless of how scintillating a conversationalist you are, it's rude for her not to talk to you. She owes it to her suitemate to at least interact face-to-face. Of course, *rudeness* is far too weak a word to use for a failure to directly address your Maker, Sustainer, and Redeemer, to whom you owe your every breath.[36]

As children we learned that it's rude not to respond when someone has spoken to us. That's what prayerlessness is.

It is also hypocrisy. A Christian is someone who claims to depend on God for everything; a prayerless Christian, then, is a "contradiction in terms."[37] In the final analysis, prayerlessness reveals pride. It assumes there are certain things in our lives for which, apparently, we don't need God's help. "To fail to pray is not to merely break some religious rule," Keller warns. "It is a failure to treat God as God. It is a sin against his glory."[38]

One of the chief reasons, though, that we fail to enjoy the peace available to us through prayer is that our faith is not yet sight. We struggle to comprehend the staggering magnitude of what awaits us in glory. Again, Keller devised a simple analogy to help us:

> Imagine an eight-year-old boy playing with a toy truck and then it breaks. He is disconsolate and cries out to his parents to fix it. Yet as he's crying, his father says to him, "A distant relative you've never met has just died and left you one hundred million dollars." What will the child's reaction be? He will just cry louder until his truck

is fixed. He does not have enough cognitive capacity to realize his true condition and be consoled. In the same way, Christians lack the spiritual capacity to realize all we have in Jesus.[39]

The good news, though, is that we can grow in grasping our true status and true wealth in Christ. We don't have to remain frozen in a perpetually prayerless state. We can warm ourselves—thaw ourselves—by the fire of God's word and fellowship with his church.[40] We can pray that any dry sense of duty will give way, perhaps first to desperation, but finally to delight.

We also must not overlook prayer's power to soften our hearts toward fellow sinners. In his final published book, Keller observes,

> It is hard to stay angry at someone if you are praying for them. It is also hard to stay angry unless you feel superior, and it is hard to feel superior if you are praying for them, since in prayer you approach God as a forgiven sinner. Praying for them knocks down the superiority, and it turns your heart so you are starting to will them good.[41]

Let's not impoverish our hearts by neglecting time on our knees. The stakes, both vertically and horizontally, are too high: "Prayer—though it is often draining, even an agony—is in the long term the greatest source of power that is possible."[42] We can still hear Keller exhorting us with striking words: "Prayer is awe, intimacy, struggle—yet the way to reality. There is nothing more important, or harder, or richer, or more life-altering. There is absolutely nothing so great as prayer."[43]

When Prayer Seems to Fail

Keller's perspective on prayer will not make sense apart from a high, soaring view of divine sovereignty. It is God's prerogative to answer our prayers (or not) in accordance with his inscrutable will. At first this might seem unsettling, perhaps downright terrifying. And it *is* terrifying—if God is not wise, if he is not good, if he cannot be trusted. But he is, and he can be. He has never made a mistake, never reneged on a promise, never failed one of his children. The witness of his word and believers through the ages converge to wonderfully testify to this truth. We may not comprehend his ways, but we can trust his heart.

When it comes to prayer, a mature Christian weds "shameless assertiveness" with "restful submissiveness"—and neither without the other.[44] We must be patient when our Father's timing differs from ours, which it often will. He is strengthening muscles of trust and fashioning us into people of virtue:

> "The Lord is not slow in keeping his promise, as some understand slowness" (2 Peter 3:9) means, quite simply, that our time frames are not in touch with ultimate reality. Our perspective on timing compared with God's is analogous to a two-year-old's with an adult's. God has good reasons for making us wait a long time to see some prayers answered.[45]

One of Keller's favorite insights into God's sovereign wisdom came from one of his spiritual heroes, John Newton. In a letter to a church member, the eighteenth-century pastor and former slave trader wrote, "Everything is needful that [God] sends; nothing can be needful that he withholds."[46] It is a quote, says Keller, that stuffs "an ocean of biblical theology into a thimble."[47]

What does this mean practically? For starters, God will never give us something if it wouldn't be best for us. This means we should thank him even for unanswered prayers! When Keller was in his early twenties, he prayed for a whole year about a girlfriend he wanted to marry but who wanted out of the relationship. *Lord, don't let her break up with me*, he pleaded. Of course, in hindsight, she wasn't the right girl for him. Later he realized God was saying, "Son, when a child of mine makes a request, I always give that person what he or she would have asked for if they knew everything I know."[48]

That final remark was a favorite of Keller's, and it remains one of the most profound insights on prayer I've ever heard. God will either give you what you ask for or give you what you *would* have asked for if you knew what he knows.[49] Think about that. Let it calm your heart. Every single believer is in the ultimate win-win scenario. It is not possible to be more secure than you already are—in your Father's hands.

God never promises to give his children all good things. What he promises, rather, is to work all things—even the bad—for our ultimate good (Rom. 8:28). And when we don't receive a good thing we want, we can rest in the knowledge that we already have the best thing. We have *him*. As Keller puts it, in God we have the headwaters of all we truly desire—even if a tributary of our joy goes dry.[50]

Again, this is the greatest benefit of prayer—not that we get things but that we get God.

In Jesus's Name, Amen

Another simple but crucial insight from Keller is that we can be verbally praying in Jesus's name while functionally praying in *our* name. This happens whenever we approach God with something to offer him—whether pedigree or performance—rather than coming with empty hands of faith. To make the point, Keller recalled a moment decades earlier:

> I remember how as a student in graduate school, I anxiously approached a well-known speaker after a lecture. He seemed distracted as he greeted other students with perfunctory pleasantries. I, however, was able to mention that I knew a friend of his. When I said the name, he immediately snapped to attention and spoke to me with warmth and interest. I got this kind of access to him not in my own name but in the name of our mutual friend. That is a very dim hint

of how we have access to God the Father. Because we know Jesus, because we are "in Christ," God focuses his almighty love and attention on us when we pray.[51]

Keller is unflinchingly critical of mystical approaches to spirituality that, in essence, advocate emptying our minds or maneuvering around Jesus.[52] This is theologically impossible and practically bankrupt. The reason we can trust that our prayers will be heard is not because we are superspiritual—it is because God is our loving Father, Christ is our mediator giving us access to the throne of the universe, and the Spirit resides within us.

Praying in Jesus's name is therefore far more than mouthing those words. It is acknowledging that we have access to the Father's attention and grace only through the Savior's finished work. It is coming into his holy presence, says Keller, in humility (knowing we don't deserve God's help) and confidence (knowing we're clothed in Christ's righteousness).[53] Think about it, Keller says: When you flip a light switch, a bulb illuminates. But does the power flow from the switch? No, it flows from the electricity. "The switch has no power in itself," Keller reflects, "but rather it connects the bulbs to the power. In the same way, our prayers have no virtue to procure us access to the Father." But they can connect us to the one who *does*.[54] To pray in Jesus's name is to "reground our relationship with God in the saving work of Jesus over and over again."[55] Anything less boils down to praying in our own name.

Unlock the Riches

The ability to converse with the Lord of heaven and earth isn't just an honor—it's the glorious union of two disparate truths: awe before an infinite being and intimacy with a personal friend. Because we're made to know the triune God—a merry, generous, hospitable community of persons—prayer is the furthest thing from a sterile concept or boring duty. It's an invitation into unimaginable joy.[56]

Ultimately, though, the reason we can pursue joy in prayer and know God will hear us is because Jesus received the cosmic silent treatment—for us. Reflecting on both Gethsemane ("Let this cup pass from me"; Matt. 26:39) and Golgotha ("My God, my God, why have you forsaken me?"; Matt. 27:46), Keller observes,

> We know God will answer us when we call because one terrible day he did *not* answer Jesus when *he* called. . . .
>
> . . . God treated Jesus as *we* deserve—he took our penalty—so that, when we believe in him, God can then treat us as Jesus deserved (2 Cor. 5:21). More specifically, Jesus' prayers were given the rejection that we sinners merit so that our prayers could have the reception that he merits. That is why, when Christians pray, [we] have the confidence that [we] will be heard by God and answered in the wisest way.[57]

Framed and fueled by gospel grace, our prayers become a pleasing aroma to God. Without prayer, however, our spiritual lives would become a hazard—we would forget our need for God. This is why he rarely gives us what we want *apart* from prayer.[58] He loves us too much to let us assume his gifts are downstream from something we bring to the equation. Keller summarizes this well:

> Prayer is how God gives us so many of the unimaginable things he has for us. Indeed, prayer makes it safe for God to give us many of the things we most desire. It is the way we know God, the way we finally treat God *as* God. Prayer is simply the key to everything we need to do and be in life.[59]

A vigorous prayer life is often grueling and rarely convenient. It's hard-won. And it's absolutely worth it. Nothing compares to the joy of communing with the King of glory and grace—which is yours through prayer.

8

The Painful Gift

How Suffering Drives Us into God's Heart

SADNESS. LONELINESS. ADDICTION. Anxiety. Poverty. Infertility. Miscarriage. Injury. Wayward children. Abuse. Slander. Betrayal. Persecution. Prejudice. Disease. Disability. Divorce. Depression. Terminal diagnoses. Death.

The most tragic thing about this list is that it's not exhaustive. Not even close.

As a pastor, I have a front-row seat to a dizzying array of human pain. But of course, you don't have to be a minister or a counselor to be familiar with hardship. A single word on that list might send a fresh stab of pain into your heart. Or maybe one day it will.

Ever since the ancient revolt in Eden, suffering has been woven into the fabric of human experience. All of us exist amid the wreckage of life outside the garden. Suffering haunts us, stalks us, plagues us.

Christian teaching on the topic tends to fall into one of three categories. It may be *philosophical*, aimed at the problem of evil and other complex questions from an academic perspective. Or it's *theological*, intended to survey the breadth of God's word to see what it has to say about affliction and evil. Or it's *devotional*, designed to give down-to-earth help to those locked in the grip of pain.[1]

These categories overlap, of course, and some teachers may capably address one or two. It's difficult to think of many, though, who have tackled all three with the surgical finesse of Tim Keller. Though he taught on an extraordinary range of topics related to the Christian life—many of which we've explored in this book—I don't believe his voice was ever more potent than when he focused on the topic of this final chapter.

When the subject matter is darkest, Keller's teaching shines brightest.

Inescapable Intruder

If you haven't experienced much sorrow, it might be because you haven't lived very long. Keller frames the matter frankly: "No matter what precautions we take, no matter how well we have put together a good life, no matter how hard we have worked to be healthy, wealthy, comfortable with friends and family, and successful with our career—something will inevitably ruin it." No amount of "money, power, and planning" can prevent the tentacles of suffering from reaching into our lives. "Life is tragic."[2]

And the reason life is tragic is because suffering isn't natural. It's normal, but it's not natural. It's not the way things were originally designed to be. The first two chapters of the Bible reveal a garden paradise in which humans enjoyed the presence of a holy God—free from slavery to self or fear of death. Until, that is, Satan slithered in and convinced our first parents to turn their backs on God. The fall into sin was not a minor crack; it shattered everything. We do ourselves no favors, then, by living in denial, as if disease and division and affliction are trivial matters. They are massive tragedies.

Just consider death, the chief example of human suffering. To think, *Oh, death is just natural,* warns Keller, is "to harden and perhaps kill a part of your heart's hope that makes you human. We know deep down that we are not like trees or grass. We were created to *last*."[3] Death, therefore, isn't natural; it isn't a friend; it isn't right. No wonder the Bible exhorts us to mourn with those who mourn (Rom. 12:15). In a sin-cursed world, concludes Keller, "we have a lot of crying to do."[4]

Elsewhere, reflecting on Christ's fury toward death outside his friend Lazarus's tomb (John 11:33, 38), Keller asks,

> How could the Creator of the world be angry at something in his world? Only if death is an intruder. Death was not in God's original design for the world and human life. . . . We were meant to get more and more beautiful as time goes on, not more and more enfeebled. We were meant to get stronger, not to weaken and die. . . . So Jesus weeps and is angry at the monstrosity of death. It is a deep distortion of the creation he loves.[5]

Utopian dreams have no place in a cursed world. No amount of scientific advancement or medical progress or artificial intelligence can prevent the stubborn intrusion of suffering into our lives. "Even when you put all your force into stopping it," observes Keller, "it just takes another form and grows in some new way."[6]

Facing suffering well, therefore, requires more than earthly resources.

The Uniqueness of Christianity

When it comes to hardship, earthly means are bankrupt to help—and never more so than in today's secular West. No society in human history, Keller contends, has done a worse job preparing its people to suffer well.

In other cultures, suffering—however unwelcome—was an instrument that could actually help you *achieve* your life's ultimate purpose: "The main thing to live for was something outside this material world and life, some object that suffering and death could not touch. . . . [So] not only [were] tragedy and death unable to destroy your meaning in life, they [could] actually hasten the journey toward it."[7] But the instrument has become an impediment. In a secular framework, suffering can only *spoil* your aim of happiness in this life.[8] "So while other cultures and worldviews see suffering and death as crucial chapters (and not the last) in your coherent life story," notes Keller, "the secular view is completely different."[9] Death *ends* you; it doesn't propel you into another life.

Because Western culture gives people "almost no tools for dealing with tragedy," we are "more shocked and undone by suffering than were our ancestors."[10] Believers, therefore, must "ask for the ancient paths" (Jer. 6:16) by coming to see suffering not as "the interruption of a life story but as a crucial part of a good life."[11]

And yet, the Christian faith doesn't just offer one more vision for "the good life" alongside other decent, legitimate options. It is fundamentally unlike any alternative. Keller summarizes,

> Christianity teaches that, contra fatalism, suffering is overwhelming; contra Buddhism, suffering is real; contra karma, suffering is often unfair; but contra secularism, suffering is meaningful. There is a purpose to it, and if faced rightly, it can drive us like a nail deep into the love of God and into more stability and spiritual power than you can imagine. Suffering—Buddhism says accept it, karma says pay it, fatalism says heroically endure it, secularism says avoid or fix it.[12]

Now consider the difference Christianity makes. Various religions *and* secular people might see trickles of pleasure in everyday life, but it's ultimately a mirage. There's no Fountain of love behind it all. But the Bible sees things differently: "While other worldviews lead us to sit in the midst of life's joys, foreseeing the coming sorrows, Christianity empowers its people to sit in the midst of this world's sorrows, tasting the coming joy."[13]

Our secular neighbors *must* be fixated on the here and now of this world, emotionally beholden to headlines and circumstances, because their worldview has "no other happiness to offer." There is no meaning or hope beyond this world. And so, Keller bluntly warns, "if you can't find it here, there really is no hope for you."[14] No pressure!

The Problem of Suffering

Surely all of us have wondered at times, *Why do we suffer?* When engaging with suffering-based objections to Christianity, Keller regularly returned to a few simple observations.

First, one must reckon with the fact that "before suffering is a philosophical issue, it is [often] a practical crisis—before it is about 'why?' it is about 'how?' "[15] This is a needed caution for those of us who may be tempted to swoop into a suffering friend's presence with ready answers and talking points, rather than loving them enough to simply sit with them in the sadness. God is exceedingly compassionate and patient, and we must be too. Sound theology doesn't necessarily prevent being a miserable comforter.

And yet, second, suffering-based objections and doubts are indeed philosophical at times. In such cases, Keller would simply challenge the logic: if you have a God big enough to be mad at for allowing evil, then you must also have a God big enough to be wiser than you, to have reasons you haven't thought of. You can't have it both ways.[16] In other words, "Just because you can't see or imagine a good reason why God might allow something to happen doesn't mean there can't be one."[17] How could it mean that? If God is God, surely there will be countless things that "fit" into his mind that won't fit into yours. In fact, we should be surprised if he *didn't* have reasons and purposes we haven't thought of. "A seven-year-old cannot question the mathematical calculations of a world-class physicist," notes Keller. "Yet we question how God is running the world. Does that make sense?"[18]

Again, this kind of logical argument may be cold comfort to a person in the throes of pain. We must therefore stress that God is far more than a brilliant mind—he's also a loving Father. He's inscrutably sovereign *and* infinitely good. Keller captures this with an analogy about three-year-olds unable to fathom why Mommy and Daddy disallow certain things:

> Though they aren't capable of comprehending their parents' reasons, they are capable of knowing their parents' love and therefore are capable of trusting them and living securely. That is what they really need. . . . So we should not expect to be able to grasp all God's purposes, but through the cross and gospel of Jesus Christ, we can know his love. And that is what we need most.[19]

The third observation Keller loved to make was doubtless the most important. Here's how he put it in one interview: "I don't know what the reason for your suffering is, but I do know what it *isn't*. It's not that God doesn't love you." Only Christianity, he explained, dares to say that "God actually came to earth and got involved in our suffering." He did it to forgive our sins—and therefore to be able to one day "end suffering without ending us." And over the years "as a pastor and as a sufferer," Keller says, "that has been the thing that has helped my heart."[20]

What, then, is the ultimate answer to the problem of suffering? Convinced that it is not a *what* but a *who*—the Lord Jesus Christ— Keller often returned to the English minister Edward Shillito's poetic words:

> The other gods were strong, but Thou was weak.
> They rode, but Thou didst stumble to a throne.
> But to our wounds only God's wounds can speak,
> And not a god has wounds but Thou alone.[21]

Even when we cannot fathom any good reasons for our pain, we rest in the arms of the only Savior who has scars. For us.

Facing Reality

If nothing else, suffering is a reality check. When it crashes into our lives, we see "not only that we are not in control of our lives but that we never were."[22] It strips away our delusions of grandeur and pitiful self-reliance and catapults us into a confrontation with reality, and often with God.

But the Lord doesn't use pain only to awaken nonbelievers; he also uses it to beautify his beloved, blood-bought people. As a minister, Keller repeatedly got to witness the miracle of pain "[pulling] those who already believed into a deeper experience of God's reality, love, and grace." Why? Because the furnace of affliction is "one of the main ways we move from abstract knowledge about God to a personal encounter with him as a living reality." We wish it weren't so! But affliction is God's well-trodden path to transformation:

> Believers understand many doctrinal truths in the mind, but those truths seldom make the journey down into the heart except through disappointment, failure, and loss. As a man who seemed about to lose both his career and his family once said to me, "I always knew, in principle, that 'Jesus is all you need' to get through. But you don't really know Jesus is all you need until Jesus is all you have."[23]

Over more than forty years of pastoral ministry, Keller watched hardship drive people in one of two directions: further from God or closer to God. The only thing he never saw was pain leaving somebody the same.

In his sermon after September 11, 2001, with smoke still rising from the rubble in lower Manhattan, Keller insisted that God's love and hope must be "rubbed into our grief the way you have to rub salt into meat" in warm climates to keep it from going bad. "Your grief is going to make you bleaker and weaker—or it could make you far more wise and good and tender—depending on what you rub into it."[24]

Theological Ballast for a Therapeutic Age

No matter the prescription, though, our fallen flesh will rage against the medicine. One reason is this: "We are so instinctively and profoundly self-centered that we don't believe we are."[25] And unless we're careful, suffering will only increase our self-absorption, tempting us to fixate on how the circumstance is affecting *me* rather than how it might be leveraged to glorify God.

Interestingly, most modern resources on suffering "no longer talk about *enduring* affliction," as was common in generations past—they instead use "vocabulary drawn from business and psychology to enable people to manage, reduce, and cope with stress, strain, or trauma," Keller notes. "Sufferers are counseled to avoid negative thoughts; to buffer themselves with time off, exercise, and supportive relationships; to problem solve; and to 'learn to accept things we can't change.' But all the focus is on controlling your immediate emotional responses and environment." Now, to be sure, many of these practices represent the way of wisdom. And yet for centuries Christianity has stood distinct by going "both higher and deeper in order to furnish believers with the resources to face tribulation."[26] Much of the solution, frankly, boils down to reckoning seriously with theology:

> Why don't contemporary books on stress and anxiety tell you to respond to it by doing deep thinking about life? It is because our Western secular culture is perhaps the first society that operates without any answers to the big questions. . . . [They] advise you to not think so hard about everything but to relax and to find experiences that give you pleasure.
>
> Paul [in Philippians 4:8–9] is saying Christian peace operates in almost exactly the *opposite* way. Christian peace comes not from thinking less but from thinking more, and more intensely, about the big issues of life.[27]

Simply put, "If you want peace, think hard and long about the core doctrines of the Bible."[28]

Channeling Martyn Lloyd-Jones's insight on Psalm 42, Keller stresses that we must not merely listen to our hearts; we must *address* them: "We should listen for the premises of the heart's reasoning but . . . challenge those premises where they are wrong, and they often are." For example, explains Keller,

We may hear our heart say, "It's hopeless!" but we should argue back. We should say, "Well, that depends on what you were hoping *in*. Was that the right thing to put so much hope in?" Notice how the psalmist [in Psalm 42:5] analyzes his own hopes—"*Why* are you so cast down, O my soul?" Notice that he admonishes himself. "Put your hope in God, for I *will* yet praise him." The psalmist is talking to his heart, telling it to go to God.[29]

The book of Psalms is an unparalleled resource for worshiping God through pain, for pressing divine truths deep into the heart "until they catch fire there."[30] On page after page, the psalmists' language brims with honest lament and tenacious trust. The lesson is plain: We can cling to hope not because life is easy but because God is sovereign and wise and good. "There is no better place to wait for God," advises Keller, "than deep inside the Psalter."[31]

We learn a similar lesson, of course, from the epic story of Job. But have you ever noticed that at the end of the book, with his character vindicated and his fortunes restored, he's *still* not given an answer to all his questions? As Keller puts it, Job "never sees the big picture; he sees only God."[32] And thousands of years later, now that the Messiah has come, we who face the maelstroms of life have more to cling to than words from a whirlwind:

We don't need a voice out of the storm. Rather, we need to know that Jesus Christ bowed his head into the greatest storm—the storm of divine justice—for us, so we can hear a voice of love from the holy God. He took the condemnation we deserve so God can accept us. For Jesus is the ultimate Job, the only truly innocent sufferer.[33]

Compared to other worldviews, then, the Bible's picture of suffering is by far "the most nuanced and multidimensional."[34] Whether it's suffering we bring on ourselves (e.g., Jonah and David), the suffering of betrayal (e.g., Jeremiah and Paul), the suffering of loss (e.g., Mary and Martha), or the suffering of mystery (e.g., Job),[35] God's word contains medicine for every moment.

Prepare Now

One of the most dangerous things you can do is wait until suffering hits before you get serious about God. He never promised us exemption from trouble, as Peter's warning makes plain: "Beloved, do not be surprised at the fiery trial when it comes upon you to test you, as though something strange were happening to you" (1 Pet. 4:12). Suffering is *not* strange. It's actually to be expected for those inhabiting a fallen world and walking in the footsteps of a nail-scarred King.

So when it comes to suffering, as we prepare we need not despair. We are never alone. Pondering Isaiah 43:2, Keller observes,

> God does not say, "*If* you go through the fire" and flood and dark valleys but *when* you go. The promise is not that he will remove us from the experience of suffering. No, the promise is that God will be with us, walking beside us in it. Isaiah takes the metaphor one step further and says that, while God's people will experience the heat, it will not "set them ablaze." That seems to mean that while they will be in the heat, the heat will not be in *them*. That is, it won't enter and poison their souls, harden their hearts, or bring them to despair.[36]

Still, how can we steel ourselves for inevitable seasons of pain? It begins with getting to know God's character and promises and purposes *now*—because in crisis it's often too late. Near the end of his ministry, Keller reflected,

> As a working pastor for nearly four decades, I have often sat beside people who were going through terrible troubles and silently wished they had taken the time to learn more about their faith before the tidal wave of trouble had engulfed them. . . . [There] are profound and rich truths we need to grasp *before* we suffer, or we will be unprepared for it. And many of these lessons are very difficult to learn "on the job" when we are in the midst of adversity.[37]

In other words, suffering can function like "a river that sweeps us into despair." But if we've already developed a firm grasp of God's truth and love, these can function as "anchors that keep us from being sucked into the whirlpool."[38]

In the absence of solid anchors, however, we make ourselves vulnerable to all kinds of lies about God's character and promises. "He walks with us, but the real question is—will we walk with *him*?" asks Keller. "If we have created a false God-of-my-program, then when life falls apart we will simply assume he has abandoned us and we won't seek him."[39] This is why Keller also suggests, interestingly, that the problem of evil today is most problematic not for non-Christians but for *nominal* Christians.[40]

All this points to suffering, however unexpected or excruciating, as an opportunity. Our sorrows must not be squandered.[41] Keller puts it strikingly,

> It is perhaps when we are still in unrelenting darkness that we have the greatest opportunity to defeat the forces of evil. In the darkness

we have a choice that is not really there in better times. We can choose to serve God just because he is God. In the darkest moments we feel we are getting absolutely nothing out of God or out of our relationship to him. But what if *then*—when it does not seem to be paying or benefiting you at all—you continue to obey, pray to, and seek God, as well as continue to do your duties of love to others? If we do that—we are finally learning to love God for himself, and not for his benefits.[42]

And when the darkness does lift, we'll discover that "our dependence on other things besides God for our happiness has shrunk, and that we have new strength and contentment in God himself." And we will find "new fortitude, unflappability, poise, and peace"[43] in the face of future hardships.

As Keller points out, suffering is not just "the way Christ became like and redeemed *us* but is one of the main ways we become like *him* and experience his redemption."[44] Our Savior has removed the only kind of suffering that could really destroy us—God's eternal judgment—so that now our hardships can actually make us radiant. In other words, "Jesus Christ suffered, not so that we would never suffer but so that when we suffer we would be like him."[45]

The mysterious truth of the matter, to which seasoned Christians can testify, is that pain so often unlocks sweeter intimacy with the living God. He brings "fullness of joy not just despite but *through* suffering," Keller observes. Indeed, there is a "peculiar, rich, and poignant joy that seems to come to us only through and in suffering."[46]

Certain Hope

Of all the things sufferers need, nothing is more essential than hope. It's the erosion or loss of hope that, above all, "makes suffering unbearable."[47] Keller highlights the point with a story he read about two men who were captured and imprisoned in a dungeon:

Just before they went into prison, one man discovered that his wife and child were dead, and the other learned that his wife and child were alive and waiting for him. In the first couple years of imprisonment the first man just wasted away, curled up, and died. But the other man endured and stayed strong and walked out a free man ten years later. Notice that these two men experienced the very same circumstances but responded differently because, while they experienced the same present, they had their minds set on different futures. It was the future that determined how they handled the present.[48]

And what is our future destiny as believers? To inherit a remade world, unmarred by suffering or sadness or sin. This is why the Bible portrays our future home in concrete, material terms—"new heavens and a new earth" (Isa. 65:17; cf. 2 Pet. 3:13; Rev. 21:1–4). Our ultimate hope isn't evacuation from this earth but the restoration of it. Contrary to popular belief, we won't be floating around playing golden harps with chubby angels. We'll be running and working and playing and singing and laughing and resting and reveling in the endless wonders of our good and beautiful God.[49]

So it's fine to talk about eternity in heaven so long as we remember the word is shorthand for new heavens and a new earth—our ultimate home of everlasting, ever-increasing joy in the presence of our Redeemer. As Keller often said, the new creation will be not just a *consolation* for the life we lost but a complete *restoration* of the life we always wanted but never had.[50] No, Christianity doesn't offer a full explanation of God's reasons for permitting pain, but it does provide an ultimate answer. And when that answer is unveiled at the end of history, all who "see its fulfillment will find it completely satisfying, infinitely sufficient."[51]

In the meantime, we can face the future with resolute hope, not because our *faith* is so strong but because our *Savior* is. For the joy set before him he endured the cross, bearing in our place the punishment for our sins (Heb. 12:2; 1 Pet. 2:24). Donald Grey Barnhouse was the pastor of Tenth Presbyterian Church in Philadelphia when his wife died of cancer—only in her late thirties—leaving him with four children under the age of twelve. Keller recounted this anecdote:

> When driving with his children to the funeral, a large truck pulled past him in the left lane, casting its shadow over them. Barnhouse asked all in the car, "Would you rather be run over by the truck or the shadow of the truck?" His eleven-year-old answered, "Shadow, of course." Their father concluded, "Well, that's what has happened to your mother. . . . Only the shadow of death has passed over her, because death itself ran over Jesus."[52]

No one in history has ever suffered more than Jesus Christ, for his pain went beyond the physical. As terrible as it was to suffocate on beams of Roman wood, his greatest pain was invisible to mortal eyes. He was draining the cup of God's wrath—so there wouldn't be a drop left for us.[53]

As we think about departed friends and family members who belong to Jesus, we are anticipating our own future. They've simply gone before us. Keller puts it beautifully: "Our loved ones who have died in Christ do not leave us and go into the dark. They leave us and go into the Light."[54]

Four in the Furnace

The third chapter of Daniel recounts the story of Shadrach, Meshach, and Abednego, three young Hebrews commanded to bow to a pagan king—or be thrown into a furnace of white-hot fire. "And who is the god," taunts Nebuchadnezzar, "who will deliver you out of my hands?" (3:15). Remarkably, the trio replies,

> O Nebuchadnezzar, we have no need to answer you in this matter. If this be so, our God whom we serve is able to deliver us from the burning fiery furnace, and he will deliver us out of your hand, O king. But if not, be it known to you, O king, that we will not serve your gods or worship the golden image that you have set up. (3:16–18)

This sends Nebuchadnezzar into a rage, and he orders the men to be hurled into the furnace. But then something unexpected happens. Peering into the flames, Nebuchadnezzar cannot believe his eyes: "I see four men unbound, walking in the midst of the fire, and they are not hurt; and the appearance of the fourth is like a son of the gods" (3:25).

Keller draws two key lessons from this biblical account.

First, the Hebrew men resolved to trust God no matter the outcome. "Their confidence was actually in God, not in their limited understanding of what they thought he would do. They had inner assurance that God would rescue them," notes Keller. And yet "they were not so arrogant as to be sure they were 'reading God right.' They knew he was under no obligation to operate according to their limited wisdom." In other words, their confidence was "in God himself, not in some agenda that they wanted God to promote."[55]

It is so easy, Keller observes, for us to subtly put our hope in "God-plus-my-plan-for-my-life." But these men trusted in "God *period*":

> The "I just know he will rescue us" kind of approach may seem confident on the surface, but underneath, it is filled with anxiety and insecurity. We are scared that maybe he *won't* answer the prayer for deliverance. But Shadrach, Meshach, and Abednego really believed "all the way down" to God. So they were not nervous at all. They were already spiritually fireproofed. They were ready for deliverance or death—either way, they knew God would be glorified and they would be with him. They knew God would deliver them *from* death or *through* death.
>
> Their greatest joy was to honor God, not to use God to get what they wanted in life. And as a result, they were fearless. Nothing could overthrow them.[56]

Second, the fourth man in the flames presents us with an astonishing, flickering picture of another man who, six hundred years later, would come to earth and throw himself into the ultimate furnace. On the cross Jesus Christ was exiled—consumed in the fiery furnace of God's justice—so that we who *bow to him alone* would never have to be. And because Jesus endured that ultimate furnace of suffering for us, we can survive the smaller ones that come our way.

Suffering has a stubborn ability to "[put] its fingers" on good things in our lives that have become ultimate things. Indeed, Keller says, often it's *only* when pain arrives that we begin to discern the difference between the true God and convenient counterfeits. And yet, "only the true God can go with you through that furnace and out to the other side. The other gods will abandon you in the furnace."[57]

So how can we become "spiritually fireproofed"?[58] How can we move from loving-God-as-long-as-he-delivers-me to loving him no matter what—even if I perish in the flames? "I'm afraid the primary way," concludes Keller, "is to have hardship come into your life."[59]

Facing Cancer

I suggested at the outset of the chapter that Keller's teaching shone brightest when the topic was the darkest. But it wasn't just his teaching that glimmered in the dark.

Ultimately it was his life.

In May 2020, two months after the world shut down due to the COVID-19 pandemic, Keller was diagnosed with a particularly invasive and lethal form of cancer. The following year, in an essay for *The Atlantic* titled "Growing My Faith in the Face of Death," he gave powerful voice to his sadness—and his unshakable hope.[60] He began by recalling the immediate aftermath of receiving the news:

> One woman with cancer told me years ago, "I'm not a believer anymore—that doesn't work for me. I can't believe in a personal God who would do something like this to me." Cancer killed her God.
>
> What would happen to me? I felt like a surgeon who was suddenly on the operating table. Would I be able to take my own advice?

Facing such a serious diagnosis, Keller was forced to reexamine not only his "professed beliefs" but his "actual understanding of God." He writes,

> Had [my ideas about God] been shaped by my culture? Had I been slipping unconsciously into the supposition that God lived for me rather than I for him, that life *should* go well for me, that I knew better than God does how things should go? The answer was yes—to some degree. I found that to embrace God's greatness, to say "Thy will be done," was painful at first and then, perhaps counterintuitively, profoundly liberating. To assume that God is as small and finite as we are may *feel* freeing—but it offers no remedy for anger.[61]

Suffering offers a rare kind of gift, ripping away our respectable illusions of piety and forcing the issue in our hearts: "Theoretical ideas about God's love and the future resurrection [have] to become life-gripping truths," Keller contends, "or be discarded as useless." And what he discovered, as he clung to truth and fought for faith, was Jesus's costly love becoming "not just something I believed and filed away, but a hope that sustained me all day."

As he worked through the real prospect of facing death, Keller found he could "sincerely say, without any sentimentality or exaggeration, that I've never been happier in my life, that I've never had more days filled with comfort. But it is equally true that I've never had so many days of grief." Those juxtaposed emotional realities—immense sorrow and irrepressible joy—make sense (and *only* make sense) if the world is fallen and the gospel is true. No wonder the people of Jesus for two thousand years have been "sorrowful, yet always rejoicing" (2 Cor. 6:10).

In his 2021 book *Hope in Times of Fear*, completed in the shadow of his bleak medical prognosis, Keller pondered the implications of the empty tomb:

The resurrection means not merely that Christians have a hope *for* the future but that they have a hope that comes *from* the future. The Bible's startling message is that when Jesus rose, he brought the future kingdom of God into the present.[62]

And this changes everything. "There are the good things of this world, the hard things of this world, and the best things of this world—God's love, glory, holiness, beauty," notes Keller. And Scripture is straightforward: "the road to the best things is not through the good things but usually through the hard things."[63] Keller is emphatic: "Our bad things will turn out for good, our good things cannot be taken away, and the best is yet to come."[64] Such invincible hope! What, then, is there to fear? What can mere humans do to us (Ps. 118:6)? What can *death* do to us (1 Cor. 15:55)? Scripture declares that no power on earth—not even death—can rob us of Christ's love. It can only usher us further in (Rom. 8:38–39).

Despite Keller's terminal diagnosis, the promise of resurrection was powerful enough to keep him and Kathy from grieving "like the rest of mankind, who have no hope" (1 Thess. 4:13 NIV). Consider his response to being asked what he'd say to a young Christian who's nervous about the future:

If Jesus Christ was actually raised from the dead, then you know what? Everything is going to be all right. Whatever you're worried about right now—whatever you're afraid of—everything is actually going to be okay. . . . If Jesus Christ was raised from the dead, then the whole world is going to be, in a sense, resurrected. . . .

Kathy and I cried a lot together last night. Sometimes the reality of the shortness of what we have left just overwhelms us. . . . [But] if Jesus Christ was raised from the dead—and he was—you're going to be okay.[65]

Around the same time, nearly a year after the diagnosis, Keller revealed in another interview what the Lord was teaching him.[66] With a relaxed, even cheerful demeanor, he testified to the disease's purifying effects on his own heart and life. Two comments emerged as particularly poignant.

First, he insisted that he was not primarily fighting cancer but fighting his sin. Why? Because

if it wasn't for my sin, I would be completely resting in Christ, and the resurrection would be spiritually real to me, and I would be absolutely fine—spiritually and emotionally and in every way. . . . [But] it's my sin that keeps me from the spiritual realities that [should] buoy me up. And therefore . . . the way I handle imminent death is by fighting my sin and [pursuing] deeper communion with God.

As for the cancer, Keller hastened to say, "That's not the fight. I'm going to die of something. [But what] I have to do is fight my sin so that I'm actually ready [to die and be with God]."

The second lesson he described as one that he and Kathy were learning together. Instead of trying to "make a heaven out of this earth"—whether through things like vacations (in Kathy's case) or ministry productivity (in Tim's)—they were coming to apprehend a surprising truth: When you stop trying to manufacture heaven, it actually *enhances* earthly joys:

The joys of the earth are more poignant than they used to be. . . . There's a whole lot of things [Kathy and I] never really enjoyed that much. But the more we make *heaven* into the real heaven, the more this world becomes something we are actually enjoying for its own sake—instead of trying to make it give us more than it really can. So oddly enough . . . we've never been happier. We've never enjoyed our days more. We've never enjoyed hugs more. We've never enjoyed food more. We've never enjoyed walks more. We've never enjoyed the actual things we see, touch, taste, hear, and smell more. Why? What's the matter with us? And the answer is, we got our hearts *off* those things and so, weirdly enough, we enjoy them more.[67]

Facing Death

For years Keller loved to paraphrase the seventeenth-century poet George Herbert: "Death used to be an executioner, but the gospel has made him just a gardener."[68] In other words, Keller insisted, "All death can now do to Christians is to make their lives infinitely better."[69] What a consoling thought! Yet while easy to profess and to preach, it's much harder to believe. But Keller clung to this hope to the very end.

And that was possible because, long before, he'd embraced this one preeminent fact: His life didn't belong to himself. This idea is now more countercultural than ever. But it's the essence of Christian living. "If you want to know what it means to live as a Christian," Keller once remarked, "I would probably go to the place in 1 Corinthians 6 where it says, 'You're not your own; you're bought with a price.' *Frankly, every part of being a Christian is a derivative of that one verse.*"[70]

In his final three years on earth, Keller's occasional updates focused on his spiritual condition. This one is representative: "I have Stage IV pancreatic cancer. But it is endlessly comforting to have a God who is both infinitely more wise and more loving than I am. He has plenty of good reasons for everything he does and allows that I cannot know, and therein is my hope and strength."[71]

Eventually, his body weakened until it finally stopped responding to treatment. As Keller lay on his deathbed, his son Michael wrote,

Over the past few days, [Dad] has asked us to pray with him often. He expressed many times through prayer his desire to go home to be with Jesus. His family is very sad because we all wanted more time, but we know he has very little at this point. In prayer, he said two nights ago, "I'm thankful for all the people who've prayed for me over the years. I'm thankful for my family, that loves me. I'm thankful for the time God has given me, but I'm ready to see Jesus. *I can't wait to see Jesus. Send me home.*"[72]

The following day, May 19, 2023, Timothy James Keller was promoted to eternal glory. Michael provided a glimpse into his father's final moments:

Dad waited until he was alone with Mom. She kissed him on the forehead and he breathed his last breath. We take comfort in some of his last words: "There is no downside for me leaving, not in the slightest."[73]

Keller's most eloquent testimony to God's all-sufficient grace in suffering wasn't a sermon or an essay, a seminar or a book. It was his death. He faced it with bravery and hope, and it was the most powerful message he ever delivered.

Better Than Life

Tim Keller is not unique. With the help of the Holy Spirit, you can suffer well too. But something must be settled in your heart: The love of Jesus Christ is even "better than life" (Ps. 63:3). Perhaps it's not surprising that this was one of Keller's favorite verses. After all, suffering "tears us apart if we are uncertain of God's love for us."[74] So we must fight to rest in this truth: We can lose our lives, but we can never lose his love.

When it comes to evil and suffering, we serve a God who is personal and purposeful. Nothing takes him by surprise. Nothing thwarts his plans. And the ultimate proof of his love was unveiled on a hill outside Jerusalem, where Jesus suffered and bled for rebels like us so that we could enjoy everlasting life with him. His tomb is now empty—but the throne of the universe is not. You won't find more galvanizing news than that.

"Either Jesus is on the throne ruling all things for you," Keller once said, "or this is as good as it gets."[75]

Thank God he's on the throne.

Conclusion

THE LINE SNAKED AROUND THE BLOCK as mourners waited, and baked, in the August sun. Saint Patrick's Cathedral, a historic landmark in midtown Manhattan, towered before them. Even in America's biggest metropolis, it was a big event. Thousands had descended on the city that never sleeps to honor a man who, as the biblical writers would say, had simply fallen asleep.[1] They were there to remember, to grieve, to rejoice. They were there because, in one way or another, the Lord had touched their lives through Tim Keller, who had been called home.

The glimmering grandeur of the cathedral, and the man whose life they had gathered to consider, formed quite the juxtaposition. The order of service, which Keller had planned down to humorous detail, was thoroughly Protestant and gospel centered.[2] It was aesthetically simple. It was focused squarely on Jesus Christ.

Keller's body awaits the resurrection in St. Michael's Cemetery, a short drive from LaGuardia Airport. Every day thousands whiz past it to make their flights. The tombstone is not ornate, but the message is straightforward. Beneath the names of Tim (1950–2023) and his closest earthly companion Kathy (1950–), the stone simply and beautifully reads,[3]

Romans 8:1
Therefore, there is now
no condemnation for those
who are in Christ Jesus.

Isaiah 26:12
All that we have accomplished
you have done for us.

Keller didn't seek the spotlight; in fact, he often avoided it. Services at Redeemer were devoid of hype and flash. As Collin Hansen notes,

> When Tim Keller started Redeemer Presbyterian Church in 1989, he deliberately avoided publicizing the church, especially to other Christians. He wanted to meet skeptics of religion on the Upper East Side more than he wanted to sell books in Nashville. . . . So why write about someone so uninterested in publicity? Because it's not really about him.[4]

Fittingly, when Keller knew his time on earth was drawing to a close, he offered a final message to Redeemer—providentially scheduled for video release on the day he died. The exhortation invoked Jeremiah's charge to his scribe, Baruch: "Seekest thou great things for thyself? Seek them not" (Jer. 45:5 KJV). Keller gently reflected,

> Genesis 11 tells us that people tend to go to the city to make a name for themselves. . . . And by the way, ministers very often come to New York City to make a name for themselves. . . . *I'm a minister in New York City. I'm cool. I'm going to do well here.* . . .
>
> Don't make your ministry success your identity—so that if things don't go well, you feel like an utter failure and freak out. Don't make getting a big name in New York City your main thing. Lift up Jesus's name. "Hallowed be *thy* name." Forget yourself. Forget your reputation. Do what you can to lift up God's name.[5]

Tim Keller was far from perfect. But he loved nothing more than pointing people to the Savior who *is*, and to the gospel that can transform your life.

Acknowledgments

FIRST AND FOREMOST, credit goes to my wife, Maghan, to whom the book is dedicated. There is no way I could have completed this—by far the most involved writing project I've ever undertaken—without your consistent encouragement and sacrifice. I still remember learning from Keller with you and our team, via sermon CDs, in our little house church in East Asia circa 2007.

Thanks to my five wonderful children—Norah, Juliet, Benjamin, Hudson, and Henry. Your daddy loves you so much. I pray you each will grow up to, as the subtitle says, experience the transforming power of the gospel.

Thanks to the saints of River City Baptist Church in Richmond, Virginia. I love being your pastor.

Thanks to Justin Taylor at Crossway for pitching this book idea and convincing me to do it. You and Samuel James both made the book better than it otherwise would have been. Thanks also to Kevin Emmert for your diligent copyediting. You are talented, brother.

Thanks to my mother, Lynda Smethurst, for her eagle-eyed proofreading help. She remains my finest editor, having patiently enhanced my work ever since I was a middle schooler (okay, high schooler) writing papers about Michael Jordan. And yes, I'm still waiting for a publisher to ask me to write the definitive case for MJ as the Greatest of All Time.

Thanks to Ben LoPresti, one of my oldest friends, for reading every chapter and providing invaluable feedback. Thanks also to friends like

Sam Allberry, Bethany Jenkins, Trevin Wax, Ivan Mesa, Kevin DeYoung, and Collin Hansen for their advice at various points.

Speaking of Collin, it is immensely gracious for the author of *Timothy Keller: His Spiritual and Intellectual Formation* (Zondervan Reflective, 2023) to get so excited about another book on Keller. That speaks to his humility and character. Besides my mother, no one has influenced me as an editor—and by extension, as a writer—more than Collin.

Thanks to Three Ships Coffee in Virginia Beach for providing an ideal writing atmosphere and a bottomless drip, drip, drip of exquisite coffee. I wrote much of this book (as well as a previous volume, *Before You Share Your Faith*) in this coffee shop.

Thanks to my grandmother, Betty Spring, and to my uncle and aunt, Steve and Liz Ann Parnell, for their generous hospitality while I was on those writing retreats.

Thanks to for my family members who prayed for me throughout this project, including my parents, Doug and Lynda Smethurst, as well as my sisters and their spouses: Laura and Seth Zimmerman, Ellen and Tim Hilliard, and Emily and Bryan Spears.

Thank you, Don Carson, for founding the Gospel Coalition with Tim all those years ago. And thanks to the Gospel Coalition's content team, with whom I labored for years, for translating Keller's theological vision for ministry into helpful material for ordinary Christians.

Thanks to Graham and Laurie Howell, longtime friends of the Kellers, for your wisdom and encouragement along the way. Graham was Tim's "first convert" in 1975. Read his story and be encouraged.[1]

Thank you, Kathy Keller, for Tim. He is a gift from God, but also from you. He was not a self-made man. It is impossible to understand or appreciate his legacy apart from honoring you.

Any oversights or mistakes in these pages are mine. Of course, much more can be written about Keller's life, ministry, and legacy. I simply hope this book provides a helpful on-ramp to his voluminous body of teaching on the Christian life.

Notes

Introduction

1. Collin Hansen, *Timothy Keller: His Intellectual and Spiritual Formation* (Grand Rapids, MI: Zondervan Reflective, 2023), 118. See also the acknowledgments section in Timothy Keller, *Preaching: Communicating Faith in an Age of Skepticism* (New York: Penguin, 2015), 211–12.

2. Timothy Keller, *Walking with God through Pain and Suffering* (New York: Dutton, 2013), 323.

3. Tim Keller, "A Wave Came In: How an Introvert Like Tim Keller Became a Great Preacher," interviewed by Marvin Olasky, *World*, April 23, 2010, https://wng .org/. In the summer of 2000, about fifty members of West Hopewell Presbyterian Church held a reunion for the Keller family. "It's one of the nicest things that has ever happened to me," Keller later said. "What they did at one point was very touching. They went around and said what everybody remembered most from what I had said over the years. . . . Every one of them went around and said something, and it was an utter rebuke to my young self. When I got to Virginia, there was this older pastor in town. He got me alongside and said, 'Now just one thing. Don't just sit in your study and read your books and prepare your sermons. Get out there. Get into the nursing homes. Get into the prisons. Get into the hospitals. Get into their homes. Get out there every day. . . . Talk to people. Be with them.' Here's what I thought. I didn't say this out loud, but I thought it. *Why did I take Greek, Hebrew, and even Aramaic? Why did I get all of these degrees? I am a scholar. I am going to write these incredible sermons, and people are going to come from miles around. They're just going to be dying to get these erudite pearls of wisdom from my lips. I have to work on these things.* . . . He knew exactly what I was thinking. His name was Kennedy [Smart]. I remember what he said. He looked at me (I'll never forget it) and he said: 'The things you say to these people are not going to amount to a hill of beans if they don't know you love them, and you don't love them unless you're out there with them.'" Tim Keller, "Suffering and Glory," open forum at Redeemer Presbyterian Church, November 11, 2001. Unless otherwise noted, all of Keller's sermons cited in this volume were preached at Redeemer Presbyterian Church and are available at https://gospelinlife.com/.

4. Tim Keller, "Contextualization: Radical Hospitality," interviewed by Laurie Sauriat, *To Be Continued . . . with Tim Keller* (podcast), Redeemer City to City, May 1, 2024, https://redeemercitytocity.com/. The episode was recorded in March 2023. Elsewhere, Keller is emphatic: "Contextualization is not—as is often argued—'giving people what they want to hear.' Rather, it is giving people *the Bible's answers*, which they may not at all want to hear, *to questions about life* that people in their particular time and place are asking, *in language and forms* they can comprehend, and *through appeals and arguments* with force they can feel, even if they reject them." Timothy Keller, *Loving the City: Doing Balanced, Gospel-Centered Ministry in Your City* (Grand Rapids, MI: Zondervan, 2016), 26 (emphasis original).

5. Tim Keller, "Pastoring the City: Tim Keller on Coming to Christ and Learning to Love the City," interviewed by Sophia Lee, *World*, December 9, 2021, https://wng.org/. In December 2014, Mark Dever conducted a fascinating interview with Keller about his life. See Dever, "Life, Ministry, and Books with Tim Keller—Part 1: Life," 9Marks, February 9, 2015, https://www.9marks.org/.

6. "[His roommate] Bruce Henderson remembers a decisive moment on his twentieth birthday, April 21, 1970, when he woke up to find Tim sitting on the floor at the foot of his bed, silently waiting for him. Bruce knew something was different, that something significant had changed in Tim. His wrestling was over. Tim had repented of his sin and believed in Jesus. He had put his heart's faith and trust in Christ alone for salvation." Hansen, *Timothy Keller*, 18.

7. Timothy Keller, *Jesus the King: Understanding the Life and Death of the Son of God* (New York: Penguin, 2016), xx.

8. Hansen, *Timothy Keller*, 42.

9. "After graduation, Tim expected to be unemployed for a while so both he and Kathy took the civil service exam and prepared for life as postal carriers! However, at the last minute a call came for Tim to be the three-month interim pastor at West Hopewell Presbyterian Church in Hopewell, Virginia. They stayed for nine years." *Redeemer Guide*, Redeemer Presbyterian Church, http://download.redeemer.com/pdf/welcome_book.pdf.

10. Hansen, *Timothy Keller*, 109–10.

11. Hansen, *Timothy Keller*, 121. As Keller explained in a 2021 interview, "Being in a blue-collar church taught me to be both clear and practical in preaching. . . . I also learned not to build a ministry on leadership charisma (which I didn't have anyway!) or preaching skill (which wasn't so much there early on) but on loving people pastorally and repenting when I was in the wrong." Keller, "Pastoring the City."

12. Keller also regularly visited the city to conduct demographic analysis, meeting people who could direct him to unchurched people groups. See *Redeemer Guide*.

13. Hansen, *Timothy Keller*, 192. Sarah Zylstra writes, "Keller was reading *The Christian in Complete Armor* by Puritan William Gurnall, and came across Gurnall's assertion that it takes more courage to be a Christian than an army captain. 'I realized, ultimately—yes, I didn't have the prayer life I should have, I didn't have the love of God I should have—but ultimately, to not go was just simply

cowardice. And it was not being faithful to the One who had the bravery to come from heaven to earth and go to the cross for me.'" Sarah Eekhoff Zylstra, "The Life and Times of Redeemer Presbyterian Church," The Gospel Coalition, May 22, 2017, https://www.thegospelcoalition.org/.

14. For brief snapshots of how the church got started, see *Redeemer Guide* and Kathy Keller, "Redeemer Begins," Redeemer Report, April 2009, https://www.redeemer.com/.

15. Zylstra, "Life and Times of Redeemer Presbyterian Church." See also Tim Keller and Don Carson, "Keller and Carson on When They Experienced Revival," The Gospel Coalition, June 17, 2014, https://www.thegospelcoalition.org/.

16. Collin Hansen, "The Making of Tim Keller: Overcoming Loneliness, Tim's Teenage Rebellion against Christianity, and Why He Finished Well," interviewed by Carey Nieuwhof, in *Carey Nieuwhof Leadership Podcast*, July 10, 2023, https://careynieuwhof.com/, paraphrased.

17. Zylstra, "Life and Times of Redeemer Presbyterian Church."

18. I am a credobaptist congregationalist, whereas Keller was a paedobaptist Presbyterian.

19. I am indebted to Collin Hansen for this observation (personal conversation with author). On these philosophical categories, see John Frame and Vern Poythress, "What Is Tri-Perspectivalism?," The Works of John Frame and Vern Poythress (website), November 28, 2011, https://frame-poythress.org/.

20. Hansen, *Timothy Keller*, 265–66. Keller likened having multiple positive influences to rings inside a tree: "It's almost like if you cut a person—a good minister, for example—like a tree, there should be a lot of rings. [This] gives that minister his own distinctive voice and . . . helps him listen to what God is calling him to be. . . . Whereas if you only have one or two individuals or even kinds of sources, you really become almost a clone." Tim Keller, Don Carson, and John Piper, "Get More Rings in Your Tree," The Gospel Coalition, July 9, 2014, https://www.thegospelcoalition.org/.

Chapter 1: One Hero

1. One of the beauties of ministry is the breadth of ways a pastor can apply the "whole counsel of God" (Acts 20:27) to the whole course of life. The Bible is timelessly relevant and endlessly rich, so a longtime ministry—especially one devoted to expository preaching—will cover the topical waterfront. Though this book is not primarily for pastors, it's worth noting at the outset that Keller's commitment to exposition is what enabled him to gain wisdom on, and communicate so clearly, the Bible's teaching on various topics. According to Keller, expository preaching—which "grounds the message in the text so that all the sermon's points are points in the text, and it majors in the text's major ideas"—should provide "the main diet of preaching for a Christian community." He argues that it's "the best method for displaying and conveying your conviction that the whole Bible is true. This approach testifies that you believe every part of the Bible to be God's Word, not just particular themes and not just the parts you feel comfortable agreeing with." Timothy Keller, *Preaching: Communicating Faith in an Age of Skepticism* (New York: Penguin, 2015), 32. "Exposition is something of an adventure for the

preacher," he later observes. "You can't completely predetermine what your people will be hearing over the next few weeks and months. As the texts are opened, questions and answers emerge that no one might have seen coming. We tend to think of the Bible as a book of answers to our questions, and it is that. However, if we really let the text speak, we may find that God will show us that we are not even asking the right questions." Keller, 36. For a compelling defense of expository preaching—including how to avoid common pitfalls—see Keller, 29–46.

2. This section and the next are largely adapted from "Approach Your Bible Christocentrically," in Matt Smethurst, *Before You Open Your Bible: Nine Heart Postures for Approaching God's Word* (Leyland, UK: 10Publishing, 2019), 69–76. Used with permission.

3. Keller remarks, "There are, in the end, only two ways to read the Bible: *Is it basically about me or basically about Jesus?* In other words, is it basically about what I must do or basically about what he has done?" Keller, *Preaching*, 60.

4. Keller comments, "The disciples knew the stories of each prophet, each priest, each king, each deliverer from Gideon to David. They knew about the temple and the sacrifices. But while they knew all the substories, they couldn't—until he showed them—see *the* story, about the ultimate prophet, priest, king, deliverer, the final temple and sacrifice. They couldn't see what the Bible was all about." Keller, *Preaching*, 59.

5. See Augustine, *Questions on the Heptateuch* 2.73, quoted in Michael Cameron, *Christ Meets Me Everywhere: Augustine's Early Figurative Exegesis*, Oxford Studies in Historical Theology (New York: Oxford University Press, 2012), 248.

6. Benjamin B. Warfield, *Biblical Doctrines*, The Works of Benjamin B. Warfield, vol. 2 (New York: Oxford University Press, 1932; repr., Grand Rapids, MI: Baker, 2003), 141, quoted in Justin Taylor, "B. B. Warfield's Analogy for the Trinity in the Old Testament," *Between Two Worlds* (blog), The Gospel Coalition, April 18, 2017, https://www.thegospelcoalition.org/.

7. Years ago I heard this rubric from Tommy Nelson, longtime pastor of Denton Bible Church in Denton, Texas. Additional passages that reflect on the Old Testament's role in anticipating Christ include John 1:45; 8:56; 12:16; Acts 13:27, 29; 28:23; 2 Cor. 1:20; 1 Pet. 1:10–12 (cf. Luke 10:24).

8. Keller, *Preaching*, 59. Moreover, "You have to read the Bible as a whole. . . . If you wrote a novel, wouldn't you want people to read the whole novel? Wouldn't it be awful if people only read the middle three chapters and then wrote an Amazon review? You would say, 'Wait a minute. No. It's a story.' Well, the Bible has a narrative arc too." Keller, "Questions About the Bible," Questioning Christianity, address delivered at Redeemer Presbyterian Church on March 6, 2014.

9. Tim Keller, foreword to Alec Motyer, *A Christian's Pocket Guide to Loving the Old Testament* (Fearn, Ross-shire, UK: Christian Focus, 2015), ix.

10. Keller, foreword to Motyer, *Christian's Pocket Guide*, x. Keller continues: "Not long after this I heard a series of lectures by Edmund P. Clowney on the importance of ministers always preaching Christ, even when they are preaching from the Old Testament. Dr. Motyer's little bombshell and Ed Clowney's lectures started

me on a lifetime quest to preach Christ and the gospel every time I expound a biblical text. They are, in a sense, the fathers of my preaching ministry." Keller in Motyer, x–xi. For more on Clowney's singular influence on Keller, see Collin Hansen, *Timothy Keller: His Spiritual and Intellectual Formation* (Grand Rapids, MI: Zondervan Reflective, 2023), 128–46.

11. Keller, *Preaching*, 15. As Keller concludes, "Paul hasn't preached a text unless he has preached about Jesus, not merely as an example to follow but as a savior." Keller, 16.

12. Keller, *Preaching*, 16.

13. Keller didn't always use the language of "union with Christ," but the reality suffused much of what he taught. "Anything that is true of Jesus is true of you," he proclaimed when Redeemer was a year old. "Spiritual Gifts: Part 2," preached on September 30, 1990. Nearly three decades later, he was sounding the same basic note: "We're not just supposed to believe in [Christ] in some abstract way; we're supposed to have intimate communion with him. . . . Do you have that intimacy?" "It Is the Lord," preached on April 23, 2017. The Bible is clear that believers are objectively and positionally "in Christ," united to him through faith. But Christian experience is about *appropriating* the manifold benefits he has won for us, in the context of a dynamic relationship with him, through the power of the Holy Spirit.

14. This statement presupposes, of course, that the Bible is properly interpreted and applied.

15. Timothy Keller, *The Songs of Jesus: A Year of Daily Devotions in the Psalms*, with Kathy Keller (New York: Penguin, 2015), 307.

16. Tim Keller (@timkellernyc), "Unless you have . . . ," Twitter, October 9, 2017, 1:30 p.m., https://x.com/.

17. Keller, *Preaching*, 63–69.

18. Keller, *Preaching*, 66.

19. Keller, *Preaching*, 51.

20. Keller, *Preaching*, 231.

21. Keller, *Preaching*, 233. Elsewhere Keller describes these four movements in terms of plot: (1) the plot winds up; (2) the plot thickens; (3) the plot resolves; (4) the plot winds down. Tim Keller, "Moralism vs. Christ-Centered Exposition," available at https://www.monergism.com/.

22. Keller would likely hasten to point out that this theological conviction informed Paul's own strategy. In 2 Corinthians 8, for example, he wants the Corinthians to give generously. But rather than appealing merely to their emotions ("Look at all those poor starving people in Macedonia!") or to their wills ("Don't you know I'm an apostle? Open your wallets!"), he appeals in 8:9 to the logic of grace ("For you know the grace of our Lord Jesus Christ, that though he was rich, yet for your sake he became poor, so that you by his poverty might become rich"). Generous grace fuels generous giving.

23. Such themes include kingdom, covenant, home and exile, the presence of God and worship, rest and Sabbath, justice and judgment, righteousness and nakedness. See

Keller, *Preaching*, 73–75. For a slightly fuller discussion of kingdom, covenant, and exile, see Keller, *Center Church: Doing Balanced, Gospel-Centered Ministry in Your City* (Grand Rapids, MI: Zondervan Reflective, 2012), 40–43.

24. Keller, *Preaching*, 71–73.

25. Keller, *Preaching*, 83–85.

26. Keller, *Preaching*, 80–82.

27. Keller, *Preaching*, 75–80.

28. Keller, *Preaching*, 77–78 (emphasis added). Different versions of the "true and better" riff are found in numerous sermons Keller gave at Redeemer Presbyterian Church. See also Tim Keller, "What Is Gospel-Centered Ministry?," May 28, 2007, The Gospel Coalition, https://www.thegospelcoalition.org/, delivered at the Gospel Coalition's inaugural conference. Keller paralleled thinkers like John Calvin in this regard. See John Calvin's preface to Pierre-Robert Olivétan's 1535 translation of the New Testament, in *Calvin: Commentaries,* trans. and ed. Joseph Haroutunian (London: S.C.M. Press, 1958), 68–69. Keller quotes Calvin's beautiful passage in "Preaching the Gospel Every Time," Reformed Theological Seminary, John Reed Miller Preaching Series, lecture 3, November 12, 2014, https://rts.edu/.

29. Keller, *Preaching*, 86–87 (emphasis added). Keller credits his friend and Old Testament professor Tremper Longman for this illustration. He shared it in a message titled "Jesus Vindicated," delivered at The Gospel Coalition 2013 National Conference, published October 26, 2017, https://www.thegospelcoalition.org/.

30. Keller, *Preaching*, 48 (emphasis added). Rather than merely "tacking on" Christ ("Oh, and by the way, this also points to him"), we keep our eyes peeled for how a given passage is fulfilled in him. Such interpretation makes all the difference in application. Keller offers two examples: "Without relating it to Christ, the story of Abraham and Isaac means: 'You must be willing to even kill your own son for him.' Without relating it to Christ, the story of Jacob wrestling with the angel means: 'You have to wrestle with God, even when he is inexplicable—even when he is crippling you. You must never give up.' These 'morals-of-the-story' are crushing because they essentially are read as being about us and what we must do." Keller, "Moralism vs. Christ-Centered Exposition."

31. Keller, *Shaped by the Gospel*, 141. Keller elaborates on this example in "Applying Christ: Getting to Christ," a lecture in a Reformed Theological Seminary course (cotaught with Edmund Clowney) titled "Preaching Christ in a Postmodern World." Audio and lecture notes available at https://www.thegospelcoalition.org/.

32. Tim Keller, "Tim Keller on a Fishy Story," interviewed by Matt Smethurst, The Gospel Coalition, October 3, 2018, https://www.thegospelcoalition.org/. See also Timothy Keller, *Rediscovering Jonah: The Secret of God's Mercy* (New York: Penguin, 2018), 237n2.

33. Keller, *Every Good Endeavor*, 123.

34. Keller, *Every Good Endeavor*, 124.

35. Keller, *Every Good Endeavor*, 123.

36. Keller, *Preaching*, 89. See also Tim Keller, "The Norms of the Kingdom," preached on April 15, 2012.

37. Keller, *Preaching*, 90.
38. This paragraph is adapted from Matt Smethurst, *Before You Share Your Faith: Five Ways to Be Evangelism Ready* (Leyland, UK: 10Publishing, 2022), 17. Used with permission.
39. John Stott, *The Cross of Christ*, 20th anniv. ed. (Downers Grove, IL: InterVarsity, 2006), 159. The first time Keller cited a portion of this quote was in "Coming to Christ: Part 2," preached on February 11, 1990. He quoted it at least three more times in Redeemer's first decade; see "Behold, Your King Is Coming" (1991), "Cross: The Way to Forgiveness" (1994), and "Self-Substitution of God" (1998).
40. Timothy Keller, *Rediscovering Jonah: The Secret of God's Mercy* (New York: Penguin, 2018), 156.
41. Tim Keller, "The Good Shepherd," preached on July 14, 1991.
42. Tim Keller, "The Sweetness of the Cross," preached on April 28, 1991.
43. "Because of the guilt and condemnation on us," Keller explains, "a just God can't simply shrug off our sins. Being sorry is not enough. We would never allow an earthly judge to let a wrongdoer off, just because he was contrite—how much less should we expect a perfect heavenly Judge to do so?" Keller then proceeds to show that all sacrificial love is, in a sense, substitutionary: "Even when we forgive personal wrongs against us, we cannot simply forgive without cost. If someone harms us and takes money or happiness or reputation from us, we can either make them pay us back or forgive them—which means *we* absorb the cost ourselves without remuneration. Jesus Christ lived a perfect life—the only human being to ever do so (Heb. 4:15). At the end of *his* life, he deserved blessing and acceptance; at the end of *our* lives, because every one of us lives in sin, we deserve rejection and condemnation (Rom. 3:9–10). Yet when the time had fully come, Jesus received in our place, on the cross, the rejection and condemnation *we* deserve (1 Pet. 3:18), so that, when we believe in him, we can receive the blessing and acceptance *he* deserves (2 Cor. 5:21). There is no more moving thought than that of someone giving his life to save another." Timothy Keller, *Shaped by the Gospel: Doing Balanced, Gospel-Centered Ministry in Your City* (Grand Rapids, MI: Zondervan, 2016), 40–41 (emphasis added).
44. Tim Keller, "The Disciple and the Bible," preached on October 30, 2016.
45. As Keller exhorted his congregation, "You don't know God unless you're paying the price for time alone with him to interact. When you read the Bible, you're hearing from him." Tim Keller, "Our Power: Spirit-Filled Living," preached on June 8, 2014.

Chapter 2: Excavating Sin

1. Timothy Keller, *Counterfeit Gods: The Empty Promises of Money, Sex, and Power, and the Only Hope that Matters* (New York: Penguin, 2016) is Keller's fullest treatment on idolatry.
2. This is a word Keller owned: "The biblical concept of idolatry is an extremely sophisticated idea, integrating intellectual, psychological, social, cultural, and spiritual categories." Keller, *Counterfeit Gods*, xxi.
3. Tim Keller, "Receiving the Fullness: Part 1," preached on August 30, 1992.

4. Tim Keller, "Enslaved to Non-Gods," preached on February 22, 1998.

5. As mentioned in the introduction, Keller pastored West Hopewell Presbyterian Church in Hopewell, Virginia—about twenty-five miles south of Richmond— from 1975 to 1984.

6. Keller, "Enslaved to Non-Gods."

7. Martyn Lloyd-Jones, *Life in Christ: Studies in 1 John* (Wheaton, IL: Crossway, 2002), 728, 731. Keller paraphrases this in "Enslaved to Non-Gods."

8. Keller, "Enslaved to Non-Gods."

9. Tim Keller, "First of All," preached on October 1, 1989.

10. Tim Keller, "Removing Idols of the Heart," preached on October 22, 1989.

11. Tim Keller, "Tim Keller Reflects on David Powlison (1949–2019)," The Gospel Coalition, June 10, 2019, https://www.thegospelcoalition.org/. Here's how Collin Hansen situates it: "While [Edmund] Clowney gave Keller his instincts to search the text for Christ, [David] Powlison gave Keller the tools he needed to apply the gospel as a spiritual surgeon. Powlison's seminal article . . . crystallized much of what Keller read in the Puritans about pastoral counseling. And this counseling worked its way into his preaching as he aimed to expose the idols of the culture and of the heart." Collin Hansen, *Timothy Keller: His Spiritual and Intellectual Formation* (Grand Rapids, MI: Zondervan Reflective, 2023), 144. Powlison's essay appeared in 1991 but was republished in 1995. See "Idols of the Heart and 'Vanity Fair,'" *The Journal of Biblical Counseling* 13, no. 2 (winter 1995), 35–50. Also available at http://ccef.org/.

12. Tim Keller, "Running from God," preached on September 9, 2001. Moreover, "Augustine says basically all of life is about reordering your loves, and all your problems come from disordered loves." Keller, "Suffering and Glory," preached on February 17, 2013.

13. Timothy Keller, *Loving the City: Doing Balanced, Gospel-Centered Ministry in Your City* (Grand Rapids, MI: Zondervan, 2016), 78.

14. Luther says, "Scripture describes man as so curved in upon himself that he uses not only physical but even spiritual goods for his own purposes and in all things seeks only himself." Martin Luther, *Luther's Works*, vol. 25, *Lectures on Romans*, ed. Jaroslav Jan Pelikan, Hilton C. Oswald, and Helmut T. Lehmann (St. Louis, MO: Concordia, 1972), 345.

15. Keller, *Counterfeit Gods*, 166.

16. Timothy Keller, *Shaped by the Gospel: Doing Balanced, Gospel-Centered Ministry in Your City* (Grand Rapids, MI: Zondervan, 2016), 127 (emphasis added).

17. Keller, *Shaped by the Gospel*, 128. For more on the relationship between idolatry and the dynamics of how people change, see the sections "Resurrection and Change" and "Mistakes About Growth and Change" in Timothy Keller, *Hope in Times of Fear: The Resurrection and the Meaning of Easter* (New York: Viking, 2021), 124–28.

18. John Calvin, *Institutes of the Christian Religion*, ed. John T. McNeill, trans. Ford Lewis Battles (Philadelphia: Westminster, 1977), 1.11.8 (108). Idols tend to come in clusters. For example, there are *personal* idols (e.g., romantic love and family; money, power, and achievement; access to particular social circles; emotional dependence of others on you; health, fitness, or physical beauty), there are *cultural*

idols (e.g., military power, technological prowess, and economic prosperity; the idols of traditional societies include family, hard work, duty, and moral virtue, while those of Western cultures are individual freedom, self-discovery, personal affluence, and fulfillment), and there are *intellectual* idols (e.g., various ideologies). See Keller, *Counterfeit Gods*, xxi–xxii.

19. Tim Keller, "Walking in the Spirit," preached on January 7, 1990.

20. Keller, *Counterfeit Gods*, 165.

21. Keller, *Counterfeit Gods*, 165–66 (emphasis original).

22. Keller, *Counterfeit Gods*, xix.

23. Keller, *Counterfeit Gods*, xii–xiii. Here's how Keller puts it elsewhere: "A sure sign of the presence of idolatry is inordinate anxiety, anger, or discouragement when our idols are thwarted. So if we lose a good thing, it makes us sad, but if we lose an idol, it devastates us." Keller, *Shaped by the Gospel*, 127.

24. Keller, *Counterfeit Gods*, 39.

25. "The true god of your heart is what your thoughts effortlessly go to when there is nothing else demanding your attention." Keller, *Counterfeit Gods*, 168.

26. "Your money flows most effortlessly toward your heart's greatest love. In fact, the mark of an idol is that you spend too much money on it, and you must try to exercise self-control constantly." Keller, *Counterfeit Gods*, 168.

27. "If you ask for something that you don't get, you may become sad and disappointed. Then you go on. Hey, life's not over. Those are not your functional masters. But when you pray and work for something and you don't get it and you respond with explosive anger or deep despair, then you may have found your real god." Keller, *Counterfeit Gods*, 169.

28. Keller, *Counterfeit Gods*, 169.

29. Tim Keller, "First of All," preached on October 1, 1989. Keller often employed this particular phrase. See, e.g., Keller, "Only True God: His Supremacy," preached on September 20, 1992.

30. Keller, *Counterfeit Gods*, 170.

31. Timothy Keller, *The Reason for God: Belief in an Age of Skepticism* (New York: Dutton, 2008), 166. See also Tim Keller, "The Fire of God," preached on May 20, 2007.

32. Keller, *Counterfeit Gods*, 149.

33. "If you try to put anything in the middle of the place that was originally made for God, it is going to be too small. It is going to rattle around in there." Timothy Keller, *The Freedom of Self-Forgetfulness: The Path to True Christian Joy* (Leyland, UK: 10Publishing, 2012), 15.

34. "Most books on idolatry," Keller notes, "tend to stress only one of the three models." Keller, *Counterfeit Gods*, 182n11.

35. Keller, *Counterfeit Gods*, xxiv (emphasis added).

36. Keller, *Counterfeit Gods*, xxiv (emphasis added). Further, "One of the signs that an object is functioning as an idol is that fear becomes one of the chief characteristics of life." Keller, 98.

37. Keller, *Counterfeit Gods*, xxiv (emphasis added).

38. Keller, *Counterfeit Gods*, 65.

39. Keller, *Counterfeit Gods*, 65.
40. Keller, *Counterfeit Gods*, 64–65. Elsewhere Keller explains it like this: "Everyone has something about which they say, 'If I get *this*, then I'll know my life counts and that I'm worthy of love.' Those for whom 'this' is power don't mind offending people to get it, but those for whom 'this' is approval would not dare do such a thing. Whatever we set our hearts on as a substitute for Jesus and his salvation will determine how we feel and how we act." Keller, *Hope in Times of Fear*, 126.
41. This paragraph is paraphrased from Keller, *Counterfeit Gods*, 65–66.
42. Tim Keller, "The Freedom of Service," preached on April 17, 1994. This strategy does not appear in any of Keller's books.
43. Keller, "The Freedom of Service." Keller states elsewhere, "What many people call 'psychological problems' are simple issues of idolatry. Perfectionism, workaholism, chronic indecisiveness, the need to control the lives of others—all of these stem from making good things into idols that then drive us into the ground as we try to appease them. Idols dominate our lives." Keller, *Counterfeit Gods*, xxiii.
44. In this sermon, Keller likens idols to slave masters, but I am indebted to John Starke for the abolitionist image. Starke (@john_starke), "Idols are slave-traders . . . ," Twitter, August 1, 2013, 5:11 a.m., https://x.com/.
45. Keller, *Loving the City*, 78. See the whole section, "Sin as Idolatry," 126–28.
46. Charles Taylor, *A Secular Age* (Cambridge, MA: Belknap, 2007), 3.
47. Keller, *Loving the City*, 79 (emphasis original).
48. Keller, *Loving the City*, 80 (first emphasis added; second emphasis original). "Of course, a complete biblical description of sin and grace must recognize our rebellion against the authority of God's law," Keller writes. "But I've found that if people become convicted about their sin as idolatry and misdirected love, it is easier to show them that one of the effects of sin is living in denial about our hostility to God. Why is this? In some ways, idolatry is much like addiction. . . . We become ensnared by our spiritual idols in much the same way that people are snared by drink and drugs. Once we understand this, it is possible to hear the message of Romans 1 and accept that we live in a state of denial—that we repress or 'hold down' the truth that we live in rebellion and bear hostility toward God. Communicating the concept of sin through the biblical teaching of idolatry is an effective way to convey the idea of spiritual blindness and rebellion to postmodern people." Keller, 80. Keller's approach to contextualization is not a strategy for sidestepping confrontation or downplaying truth. He is explicit on this point: "Rejecting [doctrines like substitutionary atonement and forensic justification] does not aid us in [our] encounter with Western culture. In fact, nothing challenges and confronts the modern idolization of the 'expressive autonomous individual' like the simple and ancient gospel message that we are all sinners under God's wrath who need to repent and submit to him." Keller, *Serving a Movement: Doing Balanced, Gospel-Centered Ministry in Your City* (Grand Rapids, MI: Zondervan, 2016), 52.
49. The idolatry approach is also a "natural stepping-stone" to justification by faith alone. Keller, *Loving the City*, 80. Keller invokes Luther's point, which we saw earlier, that violating the first commandment (to have no other gods before Yah-

weh) is "the very same thing as trusting something besides Jesus for our justification." Keller, *Shaped by the Gospel*, 126.

50. Timothy Keller, *Preaching: Communicating Faith in an Age of Skepticism* (New York: Viking, 2015), 159, 160. Elsewhere he writes, "In the Bible the heart is not primarily the seat of the emotions in contrast to the head as the seat of reason. Rather, the heart is the seat of your deepest trusts, commitments, and loves, from which *everything . . . flows* [Prov. 4:23]. What the heart most loves and trusts, the mind finds reasonable, the emotions find desirable, and the will finds doable." Timothy Keller, *God's Wisdom for Navigating Life: A Year of Daily Devotions in the Book of Proverbs*, with Kathy Keller (New York: Viking, 2017), 85 (emphasis original).

51. Thomas Chalmers, *The Expulsive Power of a New Affection* (Wheaton, IL: Crossway, 2020), 34–35 (emphasis added).

52. Keller, *Counterfeit Gods*, 93 (emphasis original). "If you only try to uproot [idols], they grow back; but they can be supplanted . . . by a living encounter with God. . . . Have you heard God's blessing in your inmost being? Are the words *'You are my beloved child, in whom I delight'* an endless source of joy and strength? Have you sensed, through the Holy Spirit, God speaking them to you? That [is] the only remedy against idolatry." Keller, 155, 163–64.

53. Keller, *Hope in Times of Fear*, 125, 126 (emphasis original).

54. Keller, *Counterfeit Gods*, 174.

55. Tim Keller, "No Condemnation," preached on May 28, 1995.

56. Tim Keller, "Self-Control: Part 1," preached on April 8, 1990.

57. Tim Keller, "Counterfeit Gods: When Good Things Aren't Enough," address delivered at Eden Baptist Church in Cambridge, England, on March 7, 2010, https://eden-cambridge.org/. Keller deployed the audio-versus-video analogy from the earliest days at Redeemer. See Keller, "Spirit and Presence of God," preached on December 10, 1989.

58. Tim Keller, "The Grand Demythologizer: The Gospel and Idolatry," address delivered at the Gospel Coalition 2009 National Conference, published October 24, 2017, https://www.thegospelcoalition.org/. Keller commends a little-known sermon by the Puritan David Clarkson (1622–1686) "if you want a far better version of the message you're getting from me right now." In "Soul Idolatry Excludes Men Out of Heaven," Clarkson lists thirteen good things that can, if we're not careful, become "soul idols": esteem, mindfulness, intention, resolution, love, trust, fear, hope, desire, delight, zeal, gratitude, and care and industry. See David Clarkson, *The Works of David Clarkson*, vol. 2 (Carlisle, PA: Banner of Truth, 1988). Clarkson was John Owen's colleague in London and, upon Owen's death in 1682, eulogized him and succeeded him as pastor of the church.

59. Keller, *Shaped by the Gospel*, 57.

60. Keller, *Loving the City*, 74.

61. Keller, *Loving the City*, 74.

62. This term was coined by Daniel Strange. In Keller's foreword to Strange, *Making Faith Magnetic: Five Hidden Themes Our Culture Can't Stop Talking About . . . And How to Connect Them to Christ* (Epsom, UK: The Good Book Company, 2021),

he calls the subversive-fulfillment approach "the essence of good apologetics in a post-Christian, postmodern society." Keller explains elsewhere that in Scripture, "turning from idols always includes a rejection of the culture that the idols produce. God tells Israel that they must not only reject the other nations' gods, but 'you shall not follow their practices' (Exod. 23:24). There is no way to challenge idols without doing cultural criticism, and there is no way to do cultural criticism without discerning and challenging idols." Keller, *Counterfeit Gods*, 167.

63. Keller, *Hope in Times of Fear*, 60. The "rulers and authorities" that Jesus disarmed on Good Friday (Col. 2:15), and vanquished on Easter Sunday, include cultural false gods: "Societies make corporate idols out of military might and war, material prosperity and comfort, sexuality and romance, technology and science, or state power. At the cultural level these become ideologies of nationalism, capitalism, sexual liberation, technocracy, and socialism. Each of these can become a 'power and authority' in our lives. The more we look to them for happiness, significance, and security, the more they enslave us. The cross freed us in principle from these powers, these idols. But the resurrection brings into our lives the power we need to live this freedom in practice. The resurrected Christ sends the Spirit, which makes Jesus real to our hearts so that the old authorities and powers lose their grip on us." Keller, 35.

64. Keller, "Grand Demythologizer."

65. Keller, "Enslaved to Non-Gods."

66. Keller, *Counterfeit Gods*, 149.

67. This paragraph and the next are adapted from Matt Smethurst, *Before You Share Your Faith: Five Ways to Be Evangelism Ready* (Leyland, UK: 10Publishing, 2022), 39–40. Used with permission.

68. Keller, *Encounters with Jesus: Unexpected Answers to Life's Biggest Questions* (New York: Viking, 2013), 37–38. This is one of Keller's favorite turns of phrase. He first said it to Redeemer in "Changed Lives," preached on March 22, 1998. It also appears in Keller's earliest bestsellers: "Jesus is the only Lord who, if you receive him, will fulfill you completely, and, if you fail him, will forgive you eternally." Keller, *Reason for God*, 173. "The only way to free ourselves from the destructive influence of counterfeit gods is to turn back to the true one. The living God, who revealed himself both at Mount Sinai and on the Cross, is the only Lord who, if you find him, can truly fulfill you, and, if you fail him, can truly forgive you." Keller, *Counterfeit Gods*, xxiv.

69. Keller, *Encounters with Jesus*, 30.

70. Keller, *Counterfeit Gods*, 152.

71. In the Bible, turning from dead idols to serve the living God is conversion language. See, e.g., 1 Thess. 1:9.

Chapter 3: Three Ways to Live

1. Phillip Jensen and Tony Payne, "Two Ways to Live," https://twowaystolive.com.

2. Tim Keller, "Discussion with Tim Keller (Part 1)," interviewed by Scott Anderson, Desiring God, December 15, 2010, https://www.desiringgod.org/.

3. C. S. Lewis, *God in the Dock: Essays on Theology and Ethics* (Grand Rapids, MI: Eerdmans, 1970), 101.

4. In a 2009 conference talk, Keller remarked, "[Two ways to live] is how I preached for many years. There's God's way to live and there's man's way. You can submit to God, or you can do your own thing. [But] I think it's actually more clarifying right now to preach the gospel by showing people *three* ways to live." He then jokes, "This is the reason why I waited so long to start writing books—and I'm really glad I did. Because there's like ten years of preaching now that I'm really glad I never put into print." Keller, "Preaching the Gospel," 2009 Newfrontiers Conference at Westminster Chapel in London, available at https://vimeo.com /3484464. Perhaps it's illustrative that he delivered a sermon titled "Two Ways to Live" (April 17, 1994) and then, eighteen years later, "Three Ways to Live" (June 24, 2012). He does hasten to clarify: "I'm not picking on that wonderful Australian little gospel presentation called *Two Ways to Live*." Keller, "Preaching the Gospel."

5. In 1990, when Redeemer was less than a year old, Keller preached, "If you're on the right road, you're going toward life; if you're on the wrong road, every second you're on that wrong road you're going further away from life. . . . According to Jesus, everybody in this room is on one [road] or the other. Everybody. No neutrality. No gray areas. You're not at different places on the mountain. Two roads." Keller, "The Straight and the Narrow," preached on June 10, 1990.

6. In 1993, Keller observed, "This parable comes right after the people who have said, 'Lord, Lord, didn't we do all these things?'—orthodox doctrine, service, teaching, ministry. In other words, both of these men are taking all their moral efforts, all their religious activity (that's what the houses represent), but the difference between the two is the one bases the whole house on the rock, Jesus Christ. The other house is on the sand, which means the other house is its own foundation." Keller, "Authentic Christianity," preached on February 28, 1993.

7. Keller remarks, "That was one of the places where I began to realize that two ways to live in the Sermon on the Mount were not God's way and man's way, but moralism and Christianity." Tim Keller, in personal conversation with the author, November 12, 2015. Lucas was a major influence on Keller. "He was a tremendous expositor, absolutely incredible. . . . I probably listened to a 100 or 150 of his taped sermons. And probably 200 or even more of Lloyd-Jones's sermons. Those are two British guys who both preached to center-city Londoners. Dick was doing that more or less in the 1970s and 1980s; Lloyd-Jones [in] the 1950s and 1960s. But my understanding of New York was that it's more like Europe than it is the rest of the country. It's less traditional; it's more secular. . . . And I could see that Lloyd-Jones preached differently, especially his evening sermons, which were always evangelistic. You brought your non-Christian friends to his evening services. I listened to his evening sermons [and] Dick's lunchtime services, which were also evangelistic. . . . I thought, *Their preaching is more calibrated to the kind of person I'm going to be trying to reach.* And I think they really, really helped me a great deal." Keller, "Discussion with Tim Keller (Part 1)."

8. Timothy Keller, *The Prodigal God: Recovering the Heart of the Christian Faith* (New York: Penguin, 2008), xvii. Clowney's sermon, "Sharing the Father's Welcome," is available in Edmund P. Clowney, *Preaching Christ in All of Scripture* (Wheaton, IL: Crossway, 2003).

9. Keller, *Prodigal God*, xvii.

10. Keller, *Prodigal God*, xix.

11. Keller, *Prodigal God*, 12.

12. Keller, *Prodigal God*, 13.

13. Keller, *Prodigal God*, 9.

14. Keller, *Prodigal God*, 34. See also Tim Keller, "The Prodigal Sons," preached on September 11, 2005, and "The Lord of the Sabbath," preached on February 19, 2006. He writes, "Each acts as a lens coloring how you see all of life, or as a paradigm shaping your understanding of everything. Each is a way of finding personal significance and worth, of addressing the ills of the world, and of determining right from wrong," Keller, *Prodigal God*, 34.

15. Keller, *Prodigal God*, 37.

16. Keller, *Prodigal God*, 37. As Keller explains in a sermon, "Jesus says, 'You're both wrong. You're both lost. You're both making the world a terrible place in different ways.' The elder brothers of the world divide the world in two. They say, 'The good people are in, and the bad people (you) are out.' The younger brothers do as well—the self-discovery people also divide the world in two. They say, 'The open-minded, progressive-minded people are in, and the bigoted and judgmental people (you) are out.' Jesus says neither. He says, 'It's the humble who are in and the proud who are out.'" Keller, "The Prodigal Sons."

17. Keller, *Prodigal God*, 40.

18. Keller, *Prodigal God*, 48. In a 1992 sermon, Keller remarked, "I've seen plenty of people—who have been non-Christians and skeptical and under the influence of the flesh—come on into the Christian faith, and their flesh continues to dominate them, because now they find *religious* ways of avoiding God, whereas before they were finding *irreligious* ways." Tim Keller, "Alive with Christ: Part 2," preached on November 8, 1992.

19. Keller, *Prodigal God*, 44.

20. Keller, *Prodigal God*, 45.

21. Keller, *Prodigal God*, 51.

22. Keller, *Prodigal God*, 53.

23. Keller, *Prodigal God*, 54. Keller explains further, "The younger brother knew he was alienated from the father, but the elder brother did not. That's why elder-brother lostness is so dangerous. Elder brothers don't go to God and beg for healing from their condition. They see nothing wrong with their condition, and that can be fatal. If you know you are sick you may go to a doctor; if you don't know you're sick you won't—you'll just die." Keller, 75.

24. Keller, *Prodigal God*, 43.

25. See, for example, "Preaching the Gospel," 2009 Newfrontiers Conference at Westminster Chapel in London, available at https://vimeo.com/3484464. Elsewhere

Keller illustrates the deceptive nature of our motives: "Once upon a time there was a gardener who grew an enormous carrot. He took it to his king and said, 'My lord, this is the greatest carrot I've ever grown or ever will grow; therefore, I want to present it to you as a token of my love and respect for you.' The king was touched and discerned the man's heart, so as he turned to go, the king said, 'Wait! You are clearly a good steward of the earth. I own a plot of land right next to yours. I want to give it to you freely as a gift, so you can garden it all.' The gardener was amazed and delighted and went home rejoicing. But there was a nobleman at the king's court who overheard all this, and he said, 'My! If that is what you get for a *carrot*, what if you gave the king something better?' The next day the nobleman came before the king, and he was leading a handsome black stallion. He bowed low and said, 'My lord, I breed horses, and this is the greatest horse I've ever bred or ever will; therefore, I want to present it to you as a token of my love and respect for you.' But the king discerned his heart and said, 'Thank you,' and took the horse and simply dismissed him. The nobleman was perplexed, so the king said, 'Let me explain. That gardener was giving *me* the carrot, but you were giving *yourself* the horse.' " Timothy Keller, *The Gospel in Life Study Guide: How Grace Changes Everything* (Grand Rapids, MI: Zondervan, 2010), 17. Keller first shared this illustration at Redeemer on May 5, 1996. Though he attributes it to Charles Spurgeon, I cannot find the original source.

26. Keller, *Prodigal God*, 44–45. See also Keller, 41–42.
27. Tim Keller, foreword to Sinclair Ferguson, *The Whole Christ: Legalism, Antinomianism, and Gospel Assurance—Why the Marrow Controversy Still Matters* (Wheaton, IL: Crossway, 2016), 13.
28. Ferguson, *Whole Christ*, 106.
29. Keller, foreword to Ferguson, *Whole Christ*, 13. He also elaborates on this insight from Ferguson in Timothy Keller, *Preaching: Communicating Faith in an Age of Skepticism* (New York: Viking, 2015), 52–56.
30. Dane Ortlund observes, "When Keller refers to works-righteousness as our default mode, he is not identifying something common to a few Pharisees. He is identifying something that plagues all of humanity. No one escapes this. It is the water we all swim in. It feels normal to us." Dane Ortlund in Tim Keller, *Shaped by the Gospel: Doing Balanced, Gospel-Centered Ministry in Your City* (Grand Rapids, MI: Zondervan, 2016), 153.
31. This paragraph is adapted from Matt Smethurst, *Before You Share Your Faith: Five Ways to Be Evangelism Ready* (Leyland, UK: 10Publishing, 2022), 83–84. Used with permission.
32. In a promotional video for the 2006 Desiring God National Conference, Keller put it like this: "When the average irreligious, secular, postmodern person hears you calling people to Christ—unless you distinguish the gospel from religion and moralism—they assume that you're simply asking them to become better people, nicer, more moral. If you don't distinguish the gospel from religion, they just assume that you're just asking them to be a Pharisee. I think it's absolutely crucial, therefore, to always make a distinction between [three ways to live]." He also credits a lesser-known C. S. Lewis essay, "Three Kinds of Men," and says,

"That really struck me and that's been a cornerstone of my own proclamation of the gospel. Contrast the three ways, not just two, so that the people who are irreligious and secular know what you're actually inviting them into." Keller, "The Gospel, Moralism, and Irreligion," DJ Chuang, September 25, 2006, YouTube video, https://youtube.com/. For an interesting interaction with Lewis's essay, see Dane Ortlund, *How Does God Change Us?* (Wheaton, IL: Crossway, 2021), 80–83. In a 2009 blog comment, Ortlund observes, "Lewis pivots his three kinds of living around desire, and Keller (usually) around acceptance/approval. I.e., Lewis says: some don't want to obey, so don't; some don't want to obey, but do; some want to obey. Keller: some don't care about God's approval, so they live it up; some care about his approval, so they obey; some know they already are accepted. But of course the two paradigms significantly overlap." Ortlund, "Luther: Three Kinds of Obedience," *Strawberry-Rhubarb Theology* (blog), May 27, 2009, https://dogmadoxa.blogspot.com/.

33. John Piper, "John Piper Reflects on Tim Keller's Evangelistic Heart," The Gospel Coalition, May 23, 2023, YouTube video, https://www.youtube.com/.

34. Keller states, "It's off the scales. It's not halfway in the middle. It's something else [entirely]." Keller, "The Prodigal Sons." ·

35. Keller, *Prodigal God*, 94.

36. Hansen, *Timothy Keller*, 218 (emphasis original). As a young man, Keller had, in a sense, embodied both younger-brother and elder-brother tendencies: "Tim was the oldest child who always did the right thing, and yet at the same time when he went off to college he really did rebel, and he rebelled in large part against his [overbearing] mother. He was torn between the dynamics of wanting to do the right thing, but also the pressures of falling far short. . . . Once I saw that [he had demonstrated the proclivities of both sons], all of a sudden Tim's core message of the transforming power of grace—this gift from God that changes everything about our lives—made a lot more sense." Hansen, "Collin Hansen on The Making of Tim Keller, Overcoming Loneliness, Tim's Teenage Rebellion, How He Finished Well, and Why He Wanted People to Know About His Weaknesses," *The Carey Nieuwhof Leadership Podcast*, July 11, 2023, https://careynieuwhof.com/.

In his book, Hansen also shares a poignant story about Tim's literal younger (and only) brother Billy, a gay man who died of complications from AIDS in 1998: "[Over the years] when they visited [Billy and his partner], Tim and Kathy talked to him about the gospel. . . . Tim tried to emphasize the difference between grace and the legalism of their childhood. . . . [Eventually] when Billy entered hospice in December [1997], he said to Tim, 'My Christian family isn't going to come with me when I enter eternity, and neither are my gay friends. So I have to figure out what is on the other side of this life.' . . . [Billy] had thought being a Christian meant cleaning up his life and making himself righteous. But Tim pointed to 2 Corinthians 5:21: 'For our sake he made him to be sin who knew no sin, so that in him we might become the righteousness of God.' Finally, Billy felt God's love. The transformation was immediately evident. He even called his lawyer and told him to give his money [marked for donation to gay causes] to [a local] ministry instead. . . . When all hope seemed lost, God welcomed this prodigal son home." Hansen, *Timothy Keller*, 218–20.

37. Keller, *Prodigal God*, xx.

38. Keller, *Prodigal God*, 136. Keller first shared this story in "Rejecting the Real Jesus," preached on September 22, 1996.

39. Kenneth Macleod, "David Dickson's Sweet Peace," *The Free Presbyterian Magazine* 121, no. 5 (May 2016): 130. Available at https://media.fpchurch.org.uk/2016 /05/FPM-2016-05.pdf.

Chapter 4: Friends on Purpose

1. See US Surgeon General Vivek H. Murthy's essay, "Work and the Loneliness Epidemic," *Harvard Business Review*, September 26, 2017, https://hbr.org/. Loneliness has the same effect on mortality as smoking fifteen cigarettes a day. See Murthy, "Our Epidemic of Loneliness and Isolation: The U.S. Surgeon General's 2023 Advisory on the Healing Effects of Social Connection and Community," Public Health Services, https://www.hhs.gov/sites/default/files/surgeon-general-social -connection-advisory.pdf. According to one survey of twenty thousand Americans, Generation Z (adults eighteen to twenty-two) is the loneliest generation. See "New Cigna Study Reveals Loneliness at Epidemic Levels in America," MultiVu (website), May 1, 2018, https://www.multivu.com/players/English/8294451 -cigna-us-loneliness-survey.

2. See chapter 4, "Kathy the Valiant," in Collin Hansen, *Timothy Keller: His Intellectual and Spiritual Formation* (Grand Rapids, MI: Zondervan Reflective, 2023), 41–51. With the exception of biblical texts, no work on friendship featured more prominently in Keller's sermons than Lewis's *The Four Loves* (1960). In a 1997 address to skeptics, Keller quipped, "I quote C. S. Lewis so much that you say, 'Now, is C. S. Lewis one of the twelve apostles?' [But] I can hardly find [anyone else] who has done any kind of sustained thought on [friendship] for years." Keller, "Friends—What Good Are They?," open forum at Redeemer Presbyterian Church on April 27, 1997. In Lewis's discussion of friendship, he explores the dynamics of *philos* (friendship love), particularly in contrast to *storgē* (familial or tribal love) and *eros* (romantic or sexual love). See Lewis, *The Four Loves* (1960; repr., Norwalk, CT: Easton, 1988).

3. Theological error (even heresy) can creep in when we overemphasize the *social* aspect of the divine life—his threeness at the expense of his oneness—so we must take great care in drawing applications from the Trinity for human relationships. Nonetheless, Jesus himself does so in John 17:20–23, for example.

4. Tim Keller, "You Are My Friends," preached on January 19, 1992.

5. "We have a God-created need that nothing but human love relationships can satisfy. Even Adam's unimpeded relationship with God and his home in paradise could not completely fulfill it. Loneliness, then, is not a sin, and this means two things. First, while it is not necessary to be married (e.g., Paul and Jesus), it *is* necessary for a thriving human life to have great friendships. Second, when God

brings Eve to Adam it is clear she is not merely a sexual or business partner, but the friend for whom he has yearned." Timothy Keller and Kathy Keller, *The Meaning of Marriage: A Couple's Devotional* (New York: Viking, 2019), 2.

6. Keller shared this illustration with Redeemer in 1992, 1997, 2000, 2008, 2010, and 2015. The version I've used here is adapted, with light edits for clarity, from the 1992 sermon "You Are My Friends."

7. Lewis, *The Four Loves*, 58 (emphasis original). Keller shares this quote in two sermons: "Friends—What Good Are They?" (1997) and "Friendship" (2005). Lewis also remarks, "Friendship is unnecessary, like philosophy, like art. . . . It has no survival value; rather it is one of those things which give value to survival." Lewis, *Four Loves*, 71. In Lewis quotes throughout this chapter, I have slightly modernized the punctuation to reflect common usage today. I quote Lewis because it's not possible to grasp Keller's teaching on friendship otherwise.

8. Tim Keller, "Spiritual Friendship," preached on June 1, 2008.

9. Lewis, *Four Loves*, xx. Lewis continues, "We possess each friend not less but more as the number of those with whom we share him increases. In this, friendship exhibits a glorious 'nearness by resemblance' to heaven itself where the very multitude of the blessed (which no man can number) increases the fruition which each has of God. For every soul, seeing him in her own way, doubtless communicates that unique vision to all the rest. That, says an old author, is why the seraphim in Isaiah's vision are crying 'Holy, Holy, Holy' to one another (Isa. 6:3) The more we thus share the Heavenly Bread between us, the more we shall all have." Lewis, 61–62. Keller first shared this story in "Heaven, a World of Love," preached on May 19, 1996.

10. Lewis, *The Four Loves*, 61.

11. Tim Keller, "It Is the Lord," preached on April 23, 2017. Here's an excerpt from an internal brochure for what would become Redeemer: "In order to demonstrate unity within diversity, the Bible requires that local churches be concerned for and connected to one another, so that the strong can support the weak, the comfortable aid the distressed, the vital replenish the bored, and all grow together into the fullness of Jesus Christ. God has given us a vision to build such a network of churches throughout the city of New York." Redeemer Presbyterian Church, 1989 brochure, not available online.

12. Keller, "It Is the Lord." Meaningful membership is essential, not optional, for a follower of Jesus Christ. "You ought to be a member of a church," urged Keller. "You say, 'Well, where does the Bible say anything about membership?' *Everywhere.* Membership just means you make a covenant, a public promise. You make yourself accountable." Keller, "House of God: Part 1," preached on April 18, 1993. "We live in the most individualistic society in the history of the world," Keller observed elsewhere. "Nobody wants anyone to tell them how to live, and yet the Bible says you need to find somebody who is your shepherd. You should not be self-accredited." Keller, "The Gospel Ministry," preached on May 19, 2013. He was emphatic: "To be a disciple means learning the Bible, learning to pray, living with the other disciples, and being accountable. If you just show up at church,

and you're not seriously being instructed in the Bible or in any kind of account-able Christian community . . . you're not a [true] disciple." Keller, "The Great Promise: Rest for Your Soul," preached on September 14, 2014.

13. Keller, "A Movement," preached on April 24, 2016.

14. Keller, "A Movement."

15. Tim Keller (@timkellernyc), ".@josephrdeighton Yes, but you are not . . . ," Twit-ter, July 28, 2014, 1:27 p.m., spelling modified. https://x.com/. Hebrews 13:17 states, "Obey your leaders and submit to them, for they are keeping watch over your souls, as those who will have to give an account. Let them do this with joy and not with groaning, for that would be of no advantage to you."

16. A mature Christian is "accountable to other believers. They don't just come to church like a consumer, but they covenant, and they say, 'I'm accountable . . . I'm responsible here.' In other words, they join the church. . . . Do you understand the gospel? That's one of the implications." Tim Keller, "A Covenant Relationship," preached on September 9, 2007.

17. Tim Keller, "Born into Community," preached on February 25, 2001.

18. Tim Keller, "The Witness of the Kingdom," preached on April 22, 2012. The image of "a city set on a hill" (Matt. 5:14) is delivered in the context of Christ's most famous sermon, to which Keller often returned in order to highlight the countercultural identity of Christ's people: "What the Sermon on the Mount is really about is . . . God's kingdom on earth. In other words, the Sermon on the Mount is talking about an alternate community. It's talking about what a community would look like that's ruled not by the world's values of power and success and acclaim and approval and appearance, but by the kingdom of God's values of sacrifice and service." Keller, "Love in the Neighborhood," preached on April 11, 1999.

19. Tim Keller, "Peace of the King," preached on August 20, 1989.

20. Tim Keller, "Love for the City," preached on March 8, 1998. "The community of people who have experienced the grace of God are a foretaste of that future city," Keller elsewhere explains. "We're citizens of a city, but we're residents of another city. We're citizens of the city to come, but we're residents in the city that is. And there's your tension. We're resident aliens." Keller, "City of God," preached on May 1, 2005.

21. Tim Keller, "The Upper Room," preached on April 6, 2003, and "Community," preached on October 9, 2005.

22. Tim Keller, "The Garden-City of God," preached on April 26, 2009.

23. Tim Keller, "The Community of Jesus," preached on January 19, 2003.

24. Tim Keller, "The Lord Praying for Holiness," August 22, 1999. He elsewhere remarks, "You can't be a city by yourself. I'm sorry, you can't. . . . [But] when the world looks in and sees, inside the church, people [getting] along who outside can't get along, people [loving] each other who outside are fighting each other . . . [people] using sex, money, and power in radically life-giving and different ways, then they'll know who [God] is. . . . Together [and only together] are you the light of the world." Keller, "The New City," preached on October 27, 2002.

See also Timothy Keller, *Center Church: Doing Balanced, Gospel-Centered Ministry in Your City* (Grand Rapids, MI: Zondervan Reflective, 2012), 171, 311. In another sermon, he explains, "What Christianity brought was not simply a spiritual movement but a whole new culture, a counterculture, an alternate way of being a human society. To everybody looking in, except the people at the very top, that counterculture was more attractive than the dominant culture." Keller, "You—Have No Power," preached on February 24, 2008.

25. Keller preaches, "Any city Christians live in, you will be painfully different from your neighbors. You will be in tension and conflict. There will be deep discord between what you believe and what your city believes, no matter what your city is like. . . . No matter where you live, at some point every culture will look at [Christian beliefs] and look at some of the things we do and say, 'Disgrace. I am culturally offended. It's disgraceful those things the Bible says.' We have no enduring city [here on earth]." Keller, "City of God."

26. Keller, "Marriage as Priority and Friendship," preached on September 8, 1991. Or as he states elsewhere, "Friendship is a deep oneness that develops when two people, speaking the truth in love to one another, journey together to the same horizon." Timothy Keller, *The Meaning of Marriage: Facing the Complexities of Commitment with the Wisdom of God*, with Kathy Keller (New York: Dutton, 2011), 116–17.

27. Keller's first major teaching on friendship at Redeemer was in the context of his classic 1991 marriage series. Though much of the content appears in *Meaning of Marriage: Facing the Complexities*, the sermons are well worth listening to. Keller employed some version of "friends let you in but don't let you down" in several messages over the years: 1992 ("You Are My Friends"), 1996 ("David and Jonathan"), 1997 ("Friends—What Good Are They?"), 2000 ("Eating with Jesus" and "God Our Friend"), 2002 ("Befriending Grace"), 2004 ("The Friends"), 2005 ("Friendship"), 2008 ("Spiritual Friendship"), 2010 ("Kindness"), 2013 ("Finishing Well"), and 2015 ("David's Friend").

28. Tim Keller, "David's Friend," preached on May 17, 2015.

29. Lewis, *The Four Loves*, 65.

30. Lewis, *The Four Loves*, 66–67 (emphasis original).

31. Here's the quote from Lewis: "Lovers are always talking to one another about their love; friends hardly ever talk about friendship. Lovers are normally face to face, absorbed in each other; friends, side by side, absorbed in some common interest." Lewis, *The Four Loves*, 61. Keller references this passage in numerous sermons, beginning with "Marriage as Priority and Friendship" (1991) and "Making Peace" (1992).

32. Tim Keller, *God's Wisdom for Navigating Life: A Year of Daily Devotions in the Book of Proverbs*, with Kathy Keller (New York: Viking, 2017), 166. This requires great sensitivity and tact. Elsewhere the Kellers reflect on a cluster of warnings in Proverbs: "Why does someone show inappropriate heartiness when others are just waking up (27:14)? Why do they use humor inappropriately (26:19) or speak lightheartedly to grieving people with a *heavy heart* (25:20)? It is because they are emotionally disconnected and therefore clumsy. They don't know the

other person's inner topography well enough to know what hurts or helps, what inspires or bores, what stimulates or irritates." Keller, 167 (emphasis original).

33. Keller, *God's Wisdom for Navigating Life*, 166 (emphasis added). In a sermon, Keller explains, "Who have you given the green light to blow the whistle on you? To whom are you opening up fairly regularly about everything? About your prayer life? About how you use your money? About your sex life? About your thought life? . . . Superficial fellowship—saying hi to everybody, hugging and kissing at church—is not enough." Keller, "The New Community," preached on May 16, 1999. Moreover, "In this modern individualistic Western culture," Keller observed the following year, "we don't like accountability. We guard our privacy. We don't like to join things. . . . [But] you have to have some people who see you so often, daily or regularly, that they see who you are. They catch you just being yourself. [And] you've authorized these people to tell you what's wrong with you. . . . Outside of community, you [can't really] know who you are." Keller, "Made for Relationship," preached on October 29, 2000.

34. Keller, *God's Wisdom for Navigating Life*, 168.

35. Keller, "Friendship." Elsewhere he writes, "The gospel is this: We are more sinful and flawed in ourselves than we ever dared believe, yet at the very same time we are more loved and accepted in Jesus Christ than we ever dared hope. This is the only kind of relationship that will really transform us. Love without truth is sentimentality; it supports and affirms us but keeps us in denial about our flaws. Truth without love is harshness; it gives us information but in such a way that we cannot really hear it. God's saving love in Christ, however, is marked by both radical truthfulness about who we are and yet also radical, unconditional commitment to us." Keller, *Meaning of Marriage: Facing the Complexities*, 48. And later: "To be loved but not known is comforting but superficial. To be known and not loved is our greatest fear. But to be fully known and truly loved is, well, a lot like being loved by God. It is what we need more than anything. It liberates us from pretense, humbles us out of our self-righteousness, and fortifies us for any difficulty life can throw us." Keller, 95.

36. Tim Keller, *Every Good Endeavor: Connecting Your Work to God's Work*, with Katherine Leary Alsdorf (New York: Penguin, 2012), 256. We will avoid accountability, Keller observes, as long as we fear man more than God. But if we fear and love God even more than we love a given friendship, we will be freed to speak truth in love. He discusses this in "David and Jonathan," preached on May 26, 1996. Keller also discusses the concept of the "hunting license" in various sermons. For example, "The Friends" (February 8, 2004), "Members of One Another" (May 8, 2005), "With Jesus" (February 26, 2006), "David and Bathsheba" (August 23, 2009), "Our Power: Spirit-Filled Living" (June 8, 2014), and "Saul's Rejection" (April 19, 2015).

37. Tim Keller (@timkellernyc), "@JeffersonBethke You are the generation . . . ," Twitter, July 29, 2013, 1:55 p.m., https://x.com/.

38. Keller remarks, "You've made a god out of your independence, and [so] you can't commit to anything." Keller, "Active Discipline," preached on January 14, 1990.

And, "You can't have love and have utter independence. In so many of your cases, dear friends, your autonomy is destroying your freedom." Keller, "Church: Building Blocks," preached on April 4, 1993. Autonomy's corrosive effect on love was a major theme of Keller's teaching.

39. As Keller observes, "[Proverbs 18:24] says that a friend can be better than a sibling—quite a statement in a culture that was far more family-oriented than ours." Keller, *God's Wisdom for Navigating Life*, 164.

40. Keller, "Friendship." The quote has been lightly edited for clarity. Here's how the Kellers put it elsewhere: "[Proverbs 19:6–7] reminds us of the painful truth that most relationships are transactional. That is, people seek out other people to get economic, social, or emotional benefits from the relationship. . . . [But true] friends will be there for you when the chips are down, when you have very little to give them. For a friend, you are not a means to some end but cherished for yourself. And constancy entails availability. . . . However, this means that the best friendships take time, and everyone's time is limited. So while in theory you could have many friends, 20:6 is realistic. Good friends don't grow on trees, nor can you have a large number of them. Give more time to the ones you have." Keller, *God's Wisdom for Navigating Life*, 165.

41. The dedication reads, "To Our Friends for Four Decades: Our journeys have taken us to different places but never away from one another . . . or from our First Love. Doug and Adele Calhoun, Wayne and Jane Frazier, David and Louise Midwood, Gary and Gayle Somers, Jim and Cindy Widmer." Keller, *Meaning of Marriage: Facing the Complexities*; punctuation added and line spacing altered for clarity. On the origins of this friend group, see Hansen, *Timothy Keller*, 83–84.

42. Hansen, *Timothy Keller*, 84. Graham and Laurie Howell represent another decades-spanning friendship with the Kellers. Led to Christ out of a rough, working-class background in 1975, Graham was Tim's "first convert" in pastoral ministry. His testimony is a deeply edifying read. See Graham Howell, "How God Is Making Me into Who I'm Meant to Be," Gospel in Life, Spring 2020, https://gospelinlife.com/. After more than thirty-five years of friendship, including annual summer vacations with the Kellers, Graham delivered a moving remembrance at Tim's memorial service in New York City on August 15, 2023, available at https://timothykeller.com/.

43. Tim Keller, "Befriending Grace," preached on January 27, 2002.

44. Keller explains, "Jesus Christ shows that ultimately the gospel is radical friendship." Tim Keller, "Harvest," preached on February 3, 1991.

45. Keller, "Spiritual Friendship."

46. Tim Keller, "Kindness," preached on May 9, 2010. In their devotional through Proverbs, the Kellers share this brief prayer: "Lord Jesus, you set your face to go up to Jerusalem to die. When you got there all hell was let loose upon you, and still you did not shrink but stood your ground—all for me. How can I, then, not be there for my friends in their times of need? Make me a great friend for others as you were for me. Amen." Keller, *God's Wisdom for Navigating Life*, 165.

47. Keller, *Meaning of Marriage: A Couple's Devotional*, 233.

48. That is, no *invincible* power. Natural barriers often do prevail in a fallen world—but not because the gospel is weaker than those barriers.

49. Keller, *Meaning of Marriage: Facing the Complexities*, 114.

50. Keller, *Meaning of Marriage: Facing the Complexities*, 115.

51. Keller, *Meaning of Marriage: Facing the Complexities*, 121–22 (emphasis original). Additionally, "Any two Christians—with nothing else but common faith in Christ—can have a robust friendship, helping each other on their journey toward the new creation, as well as doing ministry together in the world." Keller, 114–15.

52. Keller, *God's Wisdom for Navigating Life*, 164 (emphasis added). In an age of distraction and hypermobility, friendships are taken from us "faster than we can forge them." We simply "do not have all the friends our hearts need." Keller, "Friendship."

53. C. S. Lewis, *The Weight of Glory and Other Addresses*, rev. ed. (1941; repr., New York: HarperCollins, 1980), 151.

Chapter 5: When Faith Goes to Work

1. Tim Keller, "Why Tim Keller Wants You to Stay in That Job You Hate," interviewed by Andy Crouch, *Christianity Today*, April 22, 2013, https://www.christianitytoday.com/ (emphasis added). The quote has been lightly edited for clarity. Keller also relates the actor anecdote in "The Dream of the Kingdom," preached on April 30, 2000, and in a panel discussion at the 2006 Desiring God National Conference. See John Piper, Mark Driscoll, Tim Keller, and Justin Taylor, "A Conversation with the Pastors," September 29, 2006, https://www.desiringgod.org/.

2. Timothy Keller, *Shaped by the Gospel: Doing Balanced, Gospel-Centered Ministry in Your City* (Grand Rapids, MI: Zondervan, 2016), 34–43, chart on 36. Elsewhere he writes, "Without an understanding of the gospel [story], we will be either naïvely utopian or cynically disillusioned. We will be demonizing something that isn't bad enough to explain the mess we are in; and we will be idolizing something that isn't powerful enough to get us out of it. This is, in the end, what all other worldviews do." Timothy Keller, *Every Good Endeavor: Connecting Your Work to God's Work*, with Katherine Leary Alsdorf (New York: Penguin, 2012), 161. He then sketches some biblical implications for a few fields of work: business (164–68), journalism (169–70), higher education (171–73), the arts (173–75), and medicine (175–80).

3. Keller comments, "The Bible begins talking about work as soon as it begins talking about anything—that is how important and basic it is." Keller, *Every Good Endeavor*, 19.

4. Keller, *Every Good Endeavor*, 22.

5. Keller had little patience for a triumphalist perspective on work: "[We must settle] one sure fact: Nothing will be put perfectly right . . . until the 'day of Christ' at the end of history (Phil. 1:6; 3:12). Until then all creation 'groans' (Rom. 8:22) and is subject to decay and weakness. So work will be put *completely* right only

when heaven is reunited with earth and we find ourselves in our 'true country.' To talk about fully redeeming work is sometimes naïvete, sometimes hubris." Keller, *Every Good Endeavor*, 150–51 (emphasis original).

6. Isaac Watts (1674–1748), "Joy to the World" (1719), Hymnary.org.

7. Keller, *Every Good Endeavor*, 58. He also remarks, "While the Greek thinkers saw ordinary work, especially manual labor, as relegating human beings to the animal level, the Bible sees all work as distinguishing human beings from animals and elevating them to a place of dignity. Old Testament scholar Victor Hamilton notes that in surrounding cultures such as Egypt and Mesopotamia, the king or others of royal blood might be called the 'image of God'; but, he notes, that rarefied term 'was not applied to the canal digger or to the mason who worked on the ziggurat. . . . [But Genesis 1 uses] royal language to describe simply 'man.' In God's eyes all of mankind is royal. The Bible democratizes the royalistic and exclusivistic concepts of the nations that surrounded Israel." Keller, *Every Good Endeavor*, 36. Keller cites V. P. Hamilton, *The Book of Genesis: Chapters 1–17* (Grand Rapids, MI: Eerdmans, 1990), 135.

8. One implication of this, of course, is that we should appreciate many contributions from nonbelievers. Since culture is a complex cocktail of "brilliant truth, marred half-truths, and overt resistance to the truth," in our workplaces we should expect to see real darkness punctuated by flashes of God's common grace. Keller, *Every Good Endeavor*, 198. Moreover, "The doctrine of sin means that believers are never as good as our true worldview should make us. Similarly, the doctrine of grace means that unbelievers are never as messed up as their false worldview should make them. . . . Ultimately, a grasp of the gospel and of biblical teaching on cultural engagement should lead Christians to be the most appreciative of the hands of God behind the work of our colleagues and neighbors." Keller, 195, 197. He also suggests, "Christians who understand biblical doctrine ought to be the ones who appreciate the work of non-Christians the most. We know we are saved by grace alone, and therefore we are not [necessarily] better fathers or mothers, better artists and businesspersons, than those who do not believe as we do. Our gospel-trained eyes can see the world ablaze with the glory of God's work through the people he has created and called—in everything from the simplest actions, such as milking a cow, to the most brilliant artistic or historic achievements." Keller, 64.

9. Keller, *Every Good Endeavor*, 61. The Luther quote is paraphrased from Martin Luther, *Luther's Works*, vol. 21, *Sermon on the Mount and the Magnificat*, ed. J. Pelikan (St. Louis, MO: Concordia, 1958), 237. According to Psalm 147, God "strengthens the bars of your gates" (147:13) and "makes peace in your borders" (147:14). In other words, he provides safety and security for a city *through* lawmakers, law enforcement, military personnel, those working in government and politics, and so on.

10. Tim Keller, "Feeling His Pleasure," preached on October 22, 1989. Keller clarifies, "Slavery in the Greco-Roman world was not the same as the New World institution that developed in the wake of the African slave trade. Slavery in Paul's time was not race-based and was seldom lifelong. It was more like what we would call

indentured servitude. But for our purposes . . . consider this: If *slave owners* are told they must not manage workers in pride and through fear, how much more should this be true of employers today? And if *slaves* are told it is possible to find satisfaction and meaning in their work, how much more should this be true of workers today?" Keller, *Every Good Endeavor*, 219 (emphasis original).

11. Keller, *Every Good Endeavor*, 37.

12. Sebastian Traeger and Greg Gilbert, *The Gospel at Work: How the Gospel Gives New Purpose and Meaning to Our Jobs*, rev. ed. (Grand Rapids, MI: Zondervan: 2018), 18.

13. Keller, "Feeling His Pleasure."

14. Keller, "Feeling His Pleasure."

15. Quoted in Tim Keller, "When the Gospel Invades Your Office: Tim Keller on Faith and Work," interviewed by Matt Smethurst, The Gospel Coalition, November 12, 2012, https://www.thegospelcoalition.org/. See also Iain H. Murray, *David Martyn Lloyd-Jones: The Fight of Faith, 1939–1981* (Carlisle, PA: Banner of Truth), 335.

16. Keller, *Every Good Endeavor*, 108–9. He continues, "Christians agree that when we sell and market, we need to show potential customers that a product 'adds value' to their [life]. [But that] doesn't mean it can *give* them a life. Because Christians have a deeper understanding of human well-being, we will often find ourselves swimming against the very strong currents of the corporate idols of our culture." Keller, 148. Elsewhere Keller notes that the gospel isn't something we *look at* in our work so much as something, like a pair of glasses, we must *look through*. For how such lenses can help you think more wisely about your work, see Keller, *Every Good Endeavor*, 82–83, and *Center Church: Doing Balanced, Gospel-Centered Ministry in Your City* (Grand Rapids, MI: Zondervan, 2012), 332.

17. Keller, *Every Good Endeavor*, 57.

18. Keller, *Every Good Endeavor*, 57–58 (emphasis added). As Keller notes, many young people today "see the process of career selection more as the choice of an identity marker than a consideration of gifting and passions to contribute to the world." Keller, 102. Elsewhere he warns, "While ancient monks may have sought salvation through religious works, many modern people seek a kind of salvation—self-esteem and self-worth—from career success. This leads us to seek only high-paying, high-status jobs, and to 'worship' them in perverse ways. But the gospel frees us from the relentless pressure of having to prove ourselves and secure our identity through work, for we are already proven and secure. It also frees us from a condescending attitude toward less sophisticated labor and from envy over more exalted work. All work now becomes a way to love the God who saved us freely; and by extension, a way to love our neighbor. . . . Since we *already have in Christ* the things other people work for—salvation, self-worth, a good conscience, and peace—now we may work simply to love God and our neighbors." Keller, 63–64 (emphasis added).

19. Tim Keller, "Vocation: Discerning Your Calling," Redeemer City to City white paper, 2007. These three "elements of a call," which Keller first shared with

Redeemer in a 1990 sermon ("Discovering Your Spiritual Gifts: Part 3"), are loosely based on categories from John Newton. See John Newton, *The Works of John Newton*, vol. 2 (London: Hamilton, Adams, 1808), 44–48.

20. In a 2013 panel discussion, Keller invoked the Reformed and Lutheran traditions on work to say (with admitted generalization) that when it comes to discerning one's calling, many Reformed thinkers have essentially said, "Look inside, see what you're good at, and go do that," whereas many Lutherans have essentially said, "Look outside, see the need, and go meet it." Keller's summary: "You can start with the need and get to your ability, [or] you can start with your ability and get to the need. Those are ways of finding your calling." Tim Keller et al., "Redefining Work: Panel Discussion," The Gospel Coalition, March 24, 2014, YouTube video, https://www.youtube.com/.

21. Keller et al., "Redefining Work."

22. Keller, *Every Good Endeavor*, 86–87 (emphasis added). The quote comes from an interview with Sebastian Thrun in Andy Kessler, "Sebastian Thrun: What's Next for Silicon Valley?" *The Wall Street Journal*, June 15, 2012, https://www.wsj.com/.

23. *Chariots of Fire*, directed by Hugh Hudson (Warner Brothers Pictures, 1981). In his preaching, Keller returned to this illustration in 1989 ("Feeling His Pleasure"), 1991 ("Work Wholeheartedly"), 1994 ("Cross: The Way to Know Yourself"), 1996 ("Work"), 2006 ("The Lord of the Sabbath" and "Mortification through Joy"), and 2015 ("A New Sabbath").

24. Tim Keller, "The Lord of the Sabbath," preached on February 19, 2006.

25. Keller, *Every Good Endeavor*, 247. See also Tim Keller, "A New Sabbath," preached on February 8, 2015.

26. Keller, *Every Good Endeavor*, 247.

27. Keller, *Every Good Endeavor*, 70.

28. Tim Keller, "Faith and Work," preached on April 10, 2016. Keller also shared this illustration in "Temptation" (June 15, 2003) and "If I Perish, I Perish" (April 22, 2007), as well as in *Every Good Endeavor*, 115. The illustration is adapted from Dick Lucas, "Genesis 44–45: No Way but Down to Egypt," preached at St. Helens Bishopsgate, London, on July 26, 1989, available at https://www.st-helens.org.uk/resources/talk/3328/audio. (This version is a synthesis of Keller's adaptations, lightly edited for the sake of clarity.) Keller strikes a good balance here: "We must . . . reject approaches to work that counsel withdrawal or indifference regarding the culture. Members . . . send in their tithes so the more committed Christians can please God directly by doing the work of ministry. In these types of churches, there is little to no support or appreciation for the 'secular' work of Christians. On the other hand, we must also reject the approach that stresses social justice and cultural involvement but fails to call us to repentance, conversion, and holiness." Keller, *Serving a Movement: Doing Balanced, Gospel-Centered Ministry in Your City* (Grand Rapids, MI: Zondervan, 2016), 162.

29. Keller, *Every Good Endeavor*, 47.

30. Keller, *Every Good Endeavor*, 67. Moreover, "Even though, as Luther argues, all work is objectively valuable to others, it will not be subjectively fulfilling unless

you consciously see and understand your work as a calling to love your neighbor. . . . When you do that, you can be sure that the splendor of God radiates through any task, whether it is as commonplace as tilling a garden, or as rarefied as working on the global trading floor of a bank. . . . Your daily work is ultimately an act of worship to the God who called and equipped you to do it—no matter what kind of work it is." Keller, 70, 71.

31. Keller, *Every Good Endeavor*, 87. Keller offered a personal reflection (writing in 2012): "I often feel that I have the best job in the world—for me. I am doing what I love to do. We have seen more fruitfulness in our church's ministry than I ever expected to see in a lifetime. But I experience plenty of thorns and thistles. One season I learned I had thyroid cancer and all but the most basic parts of my work were put on hold. My wife has had medical emergencies that thwarted my travel plans or distracted us from new projects. At times staff members have protested that my vision was outpacing my ability to lead it or their ability to implement it. Key leaders in my congregation have moved out of town just as I was ready to entrust some part of the church into their care. I'm grateful to God for the glimpses he's given me of what work was intended to be. But daily I am aware of the maddening encroachment of thorns and thistles in the patch of the world that has been entrusted to me for this season." Keller, 85.

32. Tim Keller et al., "Rethinking Work: Panel Discussion," The Gospel Coalition, May 24, 2014, YouTube video, https://www.youtube.com/. Or as Keller remarks in a sermon, "I've got to tell you, I'm awfully tired of websites that say, 'Come help us change the world.'" Keller, "Holy Father," preached on May 7, 2017.

33. Keller, *Every Good Endeavor*, 187–88. In a 2006 sermon, Keller remarked, "One thing that has always bothered me about secular New Yorkers is when they see how Christian the poor are—when they see the storefront churches and they see the hallelujahs and they see the blood of the Lamb and they see the new birth—they roll their eyes. They say, 'Well, they don't have our education.' It's so paternalistic and, to some degree, racist. If you and I, professional New Yorkers—if the gospel comes into our lives and the kingdom principle comes into our lives, that has to rip the elitist spirit out of our hearts. Of course, we should be involved with the [believing] poor, but the poor have as much for us as we have for them. They know a lot more about suffering. They know a lot more about prayer. They know a lot more about a lot of things. The elitist spirit, the paternalistic spirit, has to be gone. They are our brothers and sisters. They have much to teach us. We need them perhaps more than they need us, contrary to what you might think." Keller, "The Openness of the Kingdom," preached on March 19, 2006.

34. Tim Keller, "Faith and Work," preached on April 10, 2015.

35. Keller, *Every Good Endeavor*, 227. Elsewhere Keller suggests ten ways for ordinary Christians to move toward evangelism in the workplace: (1) Let people around you know you're a Christian. (2) Ask friends about their faith—and just listen. (3) Listen to your friends' problems, and maybe offer to pray for them. (4) Open up about your own problems and share how your Christian faith helps you. (5) Give them a book to read. (6) Share the story of your conversion. (7) Answer

their questions and objections. (8) Invite them to a church event. (9) Offer to read the Bible with them. (10) Take them to an "explore" course. We often jump straight to 8 through 10 because we think that's what counts as true evangelism, Keller says, but with most people we should probably start with 1 through 4. (We may even need to loop through these several times before we can move on to 5 through 10.) Keller, "A Church with an Evangelistic Dynamic," Leader Talk, delivered at Redeemer Presbyterian Church on September 27, 2010.

36. Keller, *Every Good Endeavor*, 224.

37. Keller, *Every Good Endeavor*, 209.

38. Keller, *Every Good Endeavor*, 218.

39. Keller, *Every Good Endeavor*, 224–25.

40. Keller, *Every Good Endeavor*, 236. Ben Salvatore, an ambitious atheist entering Harvard Law School, was converted through Keller's teaching: "A friend and coworker who was exploring Christianity [sent] me a sermon by Tim Keller on idolatry that was trained like a guided missile at the heart of the striving Manhattanite—we who are in desperate, panting pursuit of money, prestige, and power to fill the God-shaped void in our hearts. . . . Hearing the work of Christ on the cross described that way—in the context of my own sudden certainty that all the prestige and power and achievement under the sun could never satisfy my ambition—brought me instantly to my knees. . . . I now work at a high-powered litigation firm in Manhattan. The work is difficult and stressful, but it does not crush me or consume me. I am free to do excellent work and serve my superiors and my clients with zeal because I do not face the more profound and pernicious pressure of having to justify myself to my peers and, ultimately, to God. Christ's work on the cross provides that deep rest—as Pastor Keller called it, that 'REM sleep for the soul'—that frees us to do good work, out of sheer gratitude and for the glory of God. I shudder to think how restless, stressed, and insecure I would be if I had to do this work apart from him." Ben Salvatore, "My Life Is in His Hands," Gospel in Life, Spring 2023, https://gospelinlife.com/.

41. Keller, "When the Gospel Invades Your Office."

42. Keller introduced this image in one of his first sermons in Manhattan, "Entering His Rest," preached on November 5, 1989.

43. According to Keller, the gospel informs our work in at least four ways: (1) It changes our *motivation* for work; (2) it changes our *conception* of work; (3) it provides high *ethics* for Christians in the workplace; and (4) it gives us the basis for rethinking the very *way* in which our kind of work is done. For brief elaboration on each, see Keller, *Serving a Movement*, 161–62. In a wonderful address to students at Samford University, Keller identified five ways Christian faith can transform work: (1) Faith gives you an *identity*, without which work will sink you. (2) Faith gives you a concept of the *dignity* of all work, without which work will bore you. (3) Faith gives you a *moral compass*, without which work could corrupt you. (4) Faith gives you a *world-and-life view*, without which work will enslave you. (5) Faith gives you a *hope*, without which work will frustrate you. Keller, "Every Good Endeavor: Connecting Your Work to God's Work," address delivered at Samford University,

published January 17, 2017, https://www.samford.edu/. He offered similar points in Keller, "Redefining Work," address delivered at The Gospel Coalition 2013 Faith at Work Conference, published August 1, 2013, https://www.thegospelcoalition.org/.

44. The story can be found in J. R. R. Tolkien, "*Tree and Leaf*," "*Mythopoeia*," and "*The Homecoming of Beorhtnoth*" (Harper-Collins, 2001), and J. R. R. Tolkien, The Tolkien Reader (Del Rey, 198b).

45. Keller, *Every Good Endeavor*, 14.

46. Keller, *Every Good Endeavor*, 15 (emphasis original). A similar lesson can be derived from the story of Babette's feast, another favorite illustration of Keller's. See Susannah Black Roberts, "Tim Keller: New York's Pastor," *Plough Quarterly*, May 15, 2024, https://www.plough.com/. At a special event in 1993, Keller spoke to artists about the rational, personal, eternal, and creative aspects of being created in God's image. The ten-minute talk begins at the 3:10 mark and is, by a considerable margin, the earliest video footage of Keller's teaching I have found on the internet. "Timothy Keller, NY Times Bestselling Author & Speaker: Why Do We Need Artists?," Navigating Hollywood, July 10, 2023, YouTube video, https://www.youtube.com/.

47. This statistic is attributed to industrial and organizational psychologist Andrew Naber. See "One third of your life is spent at work," Gettysburg College, https://www.gettysburg.edu/.

48. Keller observes, "A good deal of spiritual nurture in the church is very general and only addresses generic or private-world matters. But we spend most of our week in our vocational field, and we need to hear how other Christians have dealt with the same problems we face every day. Some vocations are so demanding that Christians will drop out of them if they fail to receive specific encouragement and support." Keller, *Serving a Movement*, 163. In a 2013 interview, Andy Crouch asked Keller, "How did you learn how to pastor people well in a city where conversation so often revolves around work?" As part of his reply, Keller commended a couple of pastoral practices: "At one point in my ministry here I regularly visited my members at their workplace—either eating lunch with them in their office or just going by to see them there. Usually these visits had to be brief—20 to 30 minutes. But this made it possible to learn quite a lot about their work issues and the environment in which they spent so much of their time. [You could also] gather some people from your church who work in the same field and ask them to come up with a set of issues or questions they have about how to integrate their Christian faith with their particular kind of work. Then try to answer those questions with biblical theology and pastoral wisdom." Keller, "Why Tim Keller Wants You to Stay in That Job You Hate."

49. Tim Keller, "Tim Keller on Work and Fulfillment," interview on NBC's *Morning Joe*, December 10, 2012, available at crapgametx, YouTube video, https://www.youtube.com/.

50. See, e.g., Tim Keller, "An Identity That Doesn't Crush You or Others," Questioning Christianity, address delivered at Redeemer Presbyterian Church on February 13, 2014. See also Keller, "Mission" and "Faith and Work."

Chapter 6: Do Justice, Love Mercy

1. Harper Lee, *To Kill a Mockingbird* (1960; repr., New York: HarperCollins, 2002), 233.
2. Lee, *To Kill a Mockingbird*, 252.
3. Keller offers a frank reflection: "As a pastor whose church is filled with young adults, I have seen this concern for social justice, but I also see many who do not let their social concern affect their personal lives. It does not influence how they spend money on themselves, how they conduct their careers, the way they choose and live in their neighborhoods, or whom they seek as friends. . . . From their youth culture they have imbibed not only an emotional resonance for social justice but also a consumerism that undermines self-denial and delayed gratification. Popular youth culture in Western countries cannot bring about the broad change of life in us that is required if we are to make a difference for the poor and marginalized." Timothy Keller, *Generous Justice: How God's Grace Makes Us Just* (New York: Penguin, 2010), xiv–xv.
4. Keller, *Generous Justice*, xviii–xix.
5. Keller, *Generous Justice*, xix.
6. Collin Hansen, *Timothy Keller: His Spiritual and Intellectual Formation* (Grand Rapids, MI: Zondervan Reflective, 2023), 120.
7. Keller, *Generous Justice*, xxii.
8. Both are practical manuals for ministry: Timothy J. Keller, *Resources for Deacons: Love Expressed through Mercy Ministries* (Lawrenceville, GA: PCA Committee on Discipleship Ministries, 1985) and Keller, *Ministries of Mercy: The Call of the Jericho Road*, 3rd ed. (1989; repr., Phillipsburg, NJ: P&R, 2015). As Keller put it a decade before planting Redeemer, "Mercy is not just the job of a Christian; mercy is the mark of a Christian." Tim Keller, "Organizing Deacons for Service," address delivered at the 1979 National Presbyterian and Reformed Congress, MP3 audio, 12:50, http://media1.wts.edu/media/audio/np140_copyright.mp3.
9. This ministry, Harvest, eventually became Harvest USA, an independent 501(c)(3). See John Freeman, "Harvest USA: The Early Years," August 22, 2019, https://harvestusa.org/. Kathy recalls, "In 1984, Tim and I attended their one-year anniversary banquet, promising each other that we would not volunteer for anything. We had no time. We ended up serving on the board for five years and supporting them financially to this day." Kathy Keller, personal conversation with author.
10. *Ministries of Mercy* is dedicated "to Kathy, who had a social conscience first."
11. Sarah Zylstra writes, "'[Tim] mentioned [the idea of moving] to his wife, Kathy, who laughed. 'Take our three wild boys (the victims of below-average parenting, as well as indwelling sin) to the center of a big city? . . . Expose them to varieties of sin that I hoped they wouldn't hear about until, say, their mid-30s? My list of answers to "What is wrong with this picture?" was a long, long one.' . . . New York circa 1990 wasn't the ideal place to raise a family. Homicides peaked at 2,245 during Redeemer's first full year, right in line with the rising violence in other American cities, as crack cocaine flooded the streets. . . . 'On a typical day in 1989, New Yorkers reported nine rapes, five murders, 255 robberies, and 194 aggravated

assaults,' the *New York Daily News* reported. Carole Kleinknecht, who counted Redeemer's offering for the first year or so, kept it safe between services by hiding it in paper lunch bags in the heating ducts in the back of the kitchen. . . . In 1980, Manhattan's population fell to 1.4 million, the lowest in 100 years. By the end of the decade, apartment rents across the city were dropping—sometimes as much as 20 percent—for the first time since before World War II. 'Starting a church in New York City was something not just beyond my talent and ability, but pretty much beyond [the] talent or ability [of anybody] that I knew,' Keller said in a Redeemer video. 'Therefore, if God was going to do it, he would not be doing it through the talent of the minister, but through . . . a person who loved and depended on him.' " Sarah Eekhoff Zylstra, "The Life and Times of Redeemer Presbyterian Church," The Gospel Coalition, May 22, 2017, https://www.thegospelcoalition.org/.

12. Keller, *Generous Justice*, xxiii–xxiv (emphasis original).
13. Keller, *Generous Justice*, xxiv. Keller recounts, "He had put it together for himself. When he lost his Phariseeism, his spiritual self-righteousness, he said, he lost his racism." Keller, xxiv. See also Hansen, *Timothy Keller*, 112–13. In a 1977 sermon at West Hopewell, Keller observed, "One of the beauties of expository preaching [is] you are forced to wrestle with passages that normally you would avoid." Keller, "Two Adams," preached at West Hopewell Presbyterian Church on July 27, 1977.
14. "Generous Justice (Lecture)," delivered at a Christ+City event following The Gospel Coalition 2011 National Conference, published April 15, 2011, https://www.thegospelcoalition.org/.
15. Keller, *Generous Justice*, 102. See also Keller, "Generous Justice (Lecture)." A middle-class spirit, Keller says, is a feature of a "right side up" kingdom: " 'I've worked. I've done my best. I've done my duty. God owes me at least a little bit. He shouldn't let bad things happen to me.' If that is your heart, you [may] see Jesus as an example, but you'll never see him as [a substitute]." Tim Keller, "The Upside-Down Kingdom," preached on March 21, 1999.
16. Keller, *Generous Justice*, 103–4.
17. Keller, "Generous Justice (Lecture)."
18. I am indebted to Jonathan Leeman for this general phrasing. See "Identity Politics and the Death of Christian Unity," breakout session at the 2020 Together for the Gospel Conference, https://t4g.org/resources/jonathan-leeman/identity-politics-and-the-death-of-christian-unity.
19. Keller, *Generous Justice*, 139.
20. Keller, *Generous Justice*, 140. He explains further, "Deeds of mercy and justice should be done out of love, not simply as a means to the end of evangelism. And yet there is [often] no better way for Christians to lay a foundation for evangelism than by doing justice." Keller, *Generous Justice*, 142. Is it manipulative to do practical good with a spiritual design—that is, in the hope that someone comes to faith in Christ? Of course not, says Keller—or at least not necessarily. Here's the distinction: "My love isn't *conditional* on you hearing and responding to the gospel, but my love can still be *motivated* by that desire." Keller in "A Conversation:

Tim Keller, John Piper, D. A. Carson (2 of 6)," The Gospel Coalition, October 12, 2008, YouTube video, https://www.youtube.com/.

21. Keller, *Generous Justice*, 139. The priority is clear: "The single most loving thing we can do for anyone is to help them know Christ forever." Tim Keller, "Tim Keller on a Fishy Story," interviewed by Matt Smethurst, The Gospel Coalition, October 3, 2018, https://www.thegospelcoalition.org/. Moreover, "Many today denigrate the importance of [gospel proclamation]. Instead, they say, 'The only true apologetic is a loving community. People cannot be reasoned into the kingdom; they can only be loved. Preach the gospel; use words if necessary.' But while Christian community is indeed a crucial and powerful witness to the truth of the gospel, it cannot replace preaching and proclamation." Tim Keller, "The Gospel and the Poor," *Themelios* 33, no. 3 (December 2008), https://www.the gospelcoalition.org/ (punctuation altered for clarity).

22. Keller, *Generous Justice*, 141 (emphasis added). In a 2008 roundtable discussion, Keller said, "The social gospel collapses evangelism into social improvement and says, 'That *is* the good news. We're going to make the world a better place.' . . . If you're preaching with passion [the real] gospel, it gives you the impetus to do ministry to the poor but also keeps you from the disproportionate emphasis on ministry to the poor." Keller in "A Conversation: Tim Keller, John Piper, D. A. Carson (1 of 6) – Ministries of Mercy," The Gospel Coalition, October 12, 2008, YouTube video, https://www.youtube.com/.

23. Keller writes, "On paper, we may ask, 'Should Christians do evangelism or social justice?' But in real life, these things go together. . . . We must neither confuse evangelism with doing justice, nor separate them from one another." Keller, *Generous Justice*, 143.

24. In a 2021 article, Kathy Keller lamented the mission drift of many modern evangelicals: "It's hard not to notice [in Acts 1:6–8] that when Jesus is asked, 'Is it time to take power and create God's kingdom on earth?' [he] answers that he wants them to preach the gospel, convert people, and grow the number of disciples in the world. . . . Tim and I, and many of our friends and colleagues, have had agonizing conversations with members and leaders in sister churches who are ready to leave because nothing but social justice is preached and prayed about week after week. These are mature Christians who deliberately joined multi-racial congregations in order to advance the gospel by demonstrating its ability to break down barriers, but who now experience every kind of barrier against fellowship and conversation." Kathy Keller, "The Great Commission Must Be Our Guide in These Polarizing Times," Gospel in Life, Spring 2021, https://gospelinlife.com/.

25. Proclamation is the leading partner logically and theologically, but not always chronologically. In his 1989 book, Keller offers a humorous example to make the point: "There is a tornado in your town. The home of an unbeliever near your church has a tree on it. Do you send an evangelism team there first? Of course not! You go and pull off the tree. You offer the family shelter and encouragement. In this extreme example, we see that mercy clearly has the [chronological] priority." Keller, *Ministries of Mercy*, 125. Keller articulated these things with

increasing nuance and care as his ministry matured. *Ministries of Mercy* doesn't sound the "asymmetrical" note as explicitly as his later work. By the time he published *Generous Justice* in 2010, though, he was crystal clear: "I wrote this book to present a very strong case for the Christian's involvement in the work of justice in the world that in no way undermines the *centrality* of the ministry of evangelism." Collin Hansen, "Preview Keller's *Generous Justice: How God's Grace Makes Us Just*," The Gospel Coalition, October 3, 2010, https://www.thegospel coalition.org/ (emphasis added).

26. Hansen, *Timothy Keller*, 158.

27. Hansen, *Timothy Keller*, 158.

28. As John Piper has said, "We Christians care about all suffering, especially eternal suffering." Piper, "Making Known the Manifold Wisdom of God Through Prison and Prayer," address delivered at the 2010 Lausanne Congress for World Evangelization, Desiring God, published October 19, 2010, https://www.desiringgod .org/. In a roundtable discussion with Piper two years earlier, Keller remarked: "For John to say 'eternal suffering especially' is absolutely right, because actually it's common sense." Tim Keller in "A Conversation: Tim Keller, John Piper, D. A. Carson (1 of 6) – Ministries of Mercy." Sadly, one of Keller's most controversial social-media statements was this: "Jesus didn't come primarily to solve the economic, political, and social problems of the world. He came to forgive our sins." Keller (@timkellernyc), "Jesus didn't come . . . ," Twitter, December 18, 2017, 1:30 p.m., https://x.com/. In addition to overlooking the word "primarily," many didn't seem to realize that such a claim is, historically speaking, just basic Christianity.

29. Keller remarks, "The church should help believers shape every area of their lives with the gospel. . . . But that doesn't mean that the church as an institution is [meant] to do everything it equips its members to do." Keller, *Generous Justice*, 144; cf. 145–46, 216n128. As a pastor, much of Keller's own justice work was deliberately indirect. He explained in a 2010 interview, "Many churches who work among the poor establish a 501(c)3—often a 'community development corporation'—to do much of the direct ministry to people in need. That way the elders of the local church can concentrate on building up the flock. That fits in with Abraham Kuyper's insight that it is best for much of Christian work in society to happen through voluntary societies and associations, run by lay people. In the end, then, my main personal contribution to justice in New York City has been to establish and lead my church in a way that makes all this possible." Tim Keller, "Interview with Tim Keller on Generous Justice," interviewed by Kevin DeYoung, The Gospel Coalition, October 26, 2010, https://www.thegospelcoalition.org/.

30. Keller, "Interview with Tim Keller on Generous Justice." Having offered the thumbnail definition of "giving people their due," Keller elaborates: "On the one hand, that means restraining and punishing wrongdoers. On the other hand, it means giving people what we owe them as beings in the image of God. Nick Wolterstorff says that, as a creature in the image of God, each human being comes into your presence with 'claim-rights.' That is, they have the right to not be killed or kidnapped or raped. Of course there is plenty of room for disagreement on the

specifics of these things, but that's my basic definition." Elsewhere Keller observes that the Hebrew word *mishpat*—which appears over two hundred times in the Old Testament and is often translated "justice"—means "giving people what they are due, whether punishment or protection or care. . . . We do justice when we give all human beings their due as creations of God." Keller, *Generous Justice*, 4, 18.

31. Keller, *Generous Justice*, 84.

32. Keller, *Generous Justice*, 84–85. See Nicholas Wolterstorff, *Justice: Rights and Wrongs* (Princeton, NJ: Princeton University Press, 2008), 357–59.

33. Keller, *Generous Justice*, 87. Keller quotes John Calvin's bracing exhortation: "The great part of [men] are most unworthy if they be judged by their own merit. But here Scripture helps in the best way when it teaches that we are not to consider [what] men merit of themselves but to look upon the image of God in all men, to which we owe all honor and love. . . . [You] say, 'He is contemptible and worthless'; but the Lord shows him to be one to whom he has deigned to give the beauty of his image. . . . [You] say that he does not deserve even your least effort . . . but the image of God, which recommends him to you, is worthy of your giving yourself and all your possessions. . . . [You] say, 'He has deserved something far different [from] me.' Yet what has the Lord deserved? . . . Remember not to consider men's evil intention but to look upon the image of God in them, which cancels and effaces their transgressions, and with its beauty and dignity allures us to love and embrace them." John Calvin, *Institutes of the Christian Religion*, ed. John T. McNeill, trans. Ford Lewis Battles (Philadelphia: Westminster, 1960), 3.7.6 (696–97), quoted in "God's Promise to Noah," preached on August 16, 1998.

34. Tim Keller, "Justice in the Bible," Gospel in Life, Fall 2020, https://gospelinlife .com/.

35. Keller, *Generous Justice*, 7 (emphasis added).

36. Keller, *Generous Justice*, 7, 8.

37. Keller, *Generous Justice*, 52; cf. 201n56. Elsewhere he writes, "Our first responsibility is to our own families and relations (1 Tim. 5:8), and our second responsibility is to other members of the community of faith (Gal. 6:10). However, the Bible is clear that Christians' practical love, their generous justice, is not to be confined to only those who believe as we do. Galatians 6:10 strikes the balance when Paul says: 'Do good to all people, especially the family of faith.' Helping 'all people' is not optional; it is a command." Keller, 60–61. See also endnote 53.

38. James is not contradicting Paul or denying justification by faith alone. As the Protestant Reformers put it: faith alone saves, but the faith that saves doesn't remain alone. See, for example, John Calvin, *Institutes*, 3.17.11–12 (814–17).

39. As Keller explains, "Christians are charged to remember the poor (Gal. 2:10) and widows and orphans (James 1:27), to practice hospitality to strangers (Heb. 13:2), and to denounce materialism (1 Tim. 6:17–19). . . . Not only do all believers have these responsibilities, but a special class of officers—deacons—is established to coordinate the church's ministry of mercy. This shows that mercy is a mandated work of the church, just as are the ministry of the Word and discipline (cf. Rom. 15:23–29)." Keller, *Ministries of Mercy*, 43. Pursuing justice for the poor is even

bound up with knowing God: "He judged the cause of the poor and needy; / then it was well. / Is not this to know me? / declares the LORD" (Jer. 22:16). To be clear, this doesn't mean generous justice earns a right relationship with God. But it does reflect one.

40. Keller, *Generous Justice*, 6.
41. Bruce K. Waltke, *The Book of Proverbs: Chapters 1–15*, New International Commentary on the Old Testament (Grand Rapids, MI: Eerdmans, 2004), 97.
42. Timothy Keller, *God's Wisdom for Navigating Life: A Year of Daily Devotions in the Book of Proverbs*, with Kathy Keller (New York: Viking, 2017), 18.
43. Reflecting on Proverbs 15:19 ("The way of a sluggard is like a hedge of thorns, / but the path of the upright is a level highway"), Keller makes an insightful observation: "The slothful person here is contrasted not with the hardworking but with the upright (cf. Matt. 25:26). Laziness is not just a temperament but a moral failing. Sloth is self-centered rather than loving. It is dishonest. . . . And it is extremely foolish." Keller, *God's Wisdom for Navigating Life*, 152.
44. Keller, *Generous Justice*, 89. Keller offers additional explanation and nuance on pp. 88–92.
45. Tim Keller, "Treasure vs. Money," preached on May 2, 1999.
46. Tim Keller, "The Gospel and Wealth," preached on November 6, 2005.
47. Keller, *Generous Justice*, 107. As an example of preaching that "pushes the button," Keller cites nineteenth-century pastor Robert Murray M'Cheyne's reflection on the promise (from Jesus himself) that it is "more blessed to give than to receive" (Acts 20:35). After offering three answers for what Christ might say to our objections to give, M'Cheyne declares, "Oh, my dear Christians! If you would be like Christ, give much, give often, give freely to the vile and poor, the thankless and the undeserving. Christ is glorious and happy and so will you be. It is not your money I want, but your happiness. Remember his own word, 'It is more blessed to give than to receive.'" Robert Murray M'Cheyne, *Sermons of M'Cheyne* (Edinburgh: n.p., 1848), cited in Keller, *Generous Justice*, 108. McCheyne's words are hard-hitting, but they are misapplied if one feels guilty for not giving to every poor person one meets. We must exercise wisdom as we discern what's truly best for the poor—which won't always look like giving them what they, in the moment, think they need. Keller discusses this at length in *Ministries of Mercy*. He writes, "Grace intercepts destructive behavior, protects us from the ravages of sin, sanctifies us so we can be 'holy and happy,' two inseparable qualities. In summary, grace is undeserved caring that intercepts destructive behavior. It is not unconditional acceptance, nor is it a legalism that says, 'Shape up or I will stop loving you.' Rather, it says, 'Your sin cannot separate you from me,' and then, in addition, says, 'I won't let your sin destroy you.' Grace comes to the unlovely person, but refuses to let him remain ugly. . . . Our mercy ministry must help people freely, yet aim to bring their whole lives under the healing lordship of Christ." Keller, *Ministries of Mercy*, 247 (emphasis removed). He further explains, "When the person in need is acting irresponsibly, and your continued aid would only shield him from the consequences of his own behavior, then it is no longer loving or

merciful to continue support. Let mercy limit mercy. You will find, when this is your motive, the termination of aid can have some sobering effects on the recipient of aid. He or she may see your spirit is one of concern and compassion—tough compassion." Keller, 248. He also offers practical suggestions for dealing with vagrants who visit church buildings asking for money. See Keller, 215–16.

48. Keller, *Generous Justice*, 67–68. Keller writes, "Jesus was saying something like this: 'What if your only hope was to get ministry from someone who not only did not owe you any help—but who actually owed you the opposite? What if your only hope was to get free grace from someone who had every justification, based on your relationship with him, to trample you?'" Keller, 76. As evidenced by the subtitle, *The Call of the Jericho Road*, Keller's book *Ministries of Mercy* is an extended practical reflection on the good Samaritan parable.

49. Keller, *Generous Justice*, 76–77.

50. Citing Prov. 12:27 with 13:23, Keller notes: "Poverty cannot be reduced to either a simple lack of initiative or to unjust social structures. Hard work and private property are highly valued, yet property rights are not absolute, because we are only stewards of what God has entrusted to us." In discussing Deut. 23:24, he writes, "In a fully communitarian society, the grapes would belong to the state. In a fully individualistic society, any taking of grapes would be robbery. The Bible's vision for interdependent community, in which private property is important but not an absolute, does not give a full support to any conventional political-economic agenda. It sits in critical judgment on them all." Keller, *God's Wisdom for Navigating Life*, 311. And elsewhere, "Both my sins and my outcomes in life (whether I am well-off or poor) are due to complex factors, both individual and corporate and environmental. Poverty can be due to individual failure and wrongdoing (Prov. 6:6–7; 23:21), or to social injustice and social structures (Prov. 13:23; 18:23; Ex. 22:21–27), or to environmental factors such as floods, disabling injuries, or illnesses. It is because of this complexity that the rendering of justice—both the distribution of rights and punishments—requires the greatest wisdom, deliberation, and prudence." Keller, "Justice in the Bible." "Multiple factors," he writes elsewhere, "are usually interactively present in the life of a poor family. . . . Any large-scale improvement in a society's level of poverty will come through a comprehensive array of public and private, spiritual, personal, and corporate measures." Keller, *Generous Justice*, 34–35.

51. Keller, *Generous Justice*, 18. In a lengthy 2020 essay, Keller exposes the bankruptcy of modern approaches to justice. See Keller, "A Biblical Critique of Secular Justice and Critical Theory," Gospel in Life, August 2020, https://gospelinlife.com/. Regarding postmodern critical theory in particular, he lodges seven major critiques: (1) it is deeply incoherent; (2) it is far too simplistic; (3) it undermines our common humanity; (4) it denies our common sinfulness; (5) it makes forgiveness, peace, and reconciliation between groups impossible; (6) it offers a highly self-righteous "performative" identity; and (7) it is prone to domination. Biblical justice, meanwhile, is superior to every secular alternative—whether libertarian ("freedom"), liberal ("fairness"), utilitarian ("happiness"), or post-

modern ("power"). In addition to being based in trustworthy, sufficient divine revelation, biblical justice (1) addresses all the concerns of justice found across the fragmented alternate views; (2) contradicts each of the alternate views neither by dismissing them nor by compromising with them; (3) has built-in safeguards against domination; and (4) alone offers a radically subversive understanding of power. As Keller concludes, "There is nothing in the world like biblical justice! Christians must not sell their birthright for a mess of pottage. But they must take up their birthright and do justice, love mercy, and walk humbly with their God (Micah 6:8)."

52. Keller writes, "Those Christians who try to avoid all political discussions and engagement are essentially casting a vote for the social status quo. Since no human society reflects God's justice and righteousness perfectly, supposedly apolitical Christians are supporting many things that displease God. So to not be political is to be political." Timothy Keller, *Rediscovering Jonah: The Secret of God's Mercy* (New York: Penguin, 2018), 163.

53. This language primarily refers to fellow Israelites, those within the covenant community. Along with New Testament texts such as Galatians 6:10, this carries implications for how a church's benevolence resources should ordinarily be allocated. In general, Keller writes, "I believe that the local church's 'diaconal' funds should be mainly used to help people with needs who are members or who are involved in the church's worship and community life. In order to reach the poor of the city and the world, it is best—for both practical and theological reasons—to organize Christian nonprofits and other institutions to do that." Keller, *Generous Justice*, 204n62. See also endnote 37.

54. Keller, *God's Wisdom for Navigating Life*, 320.

55. William Billings, "Methinks I See a Heav'nly Host," in *The Singing Master's Assistant* (1778), quoted in Tim Keller, *Hidden Christmas: The Surprising Truth Behind the Birth of Christ* (New York: Penguin, 2016), 74.

56. Keller, "The Gospel and the Poor."

Chapter 7: Answering Heaven

1. Tim Keller, Twitter Q&A, July 28, 2014. Transcript available at https://samluce .com/2014/07/ask-tim-keller-transcript-via-cambassador21.

2. Tim Keller, "Pastoring the City: Tim Keller on Coming to Christ and Learning to Love the City," interviewed by Sophia Lee, *World*, December 9, 2021, https:// wng.org/. He said something similar in a 2014 Twitter Q&A. "What's one piece of advice you would tell your younger self, or something you wish you knew then that you know now about the Lord?" Keller's answer: "I would tell him that prayer is way more important than he thinks." Keller (@timkellernyc), ".@amytamar I would tell him . . . ," Twitter, July 28, 2014, 1:56 p.m., https://x.com/. For more on Keller's personal journey in prayer, there is a twenty-minute conference talk in which he looks back over the decades and identifies three key lessons he learned: prayer as helplessness, prayer as work, and prayer as love. Keller, "A Personal Testimony on Prayer," conference talk delivered at Redeemer Presbyterian

Church, published October 3, 2019, https://podcast.gospelinlife.com/. Portions of this chapter appeared in Matt Smethurst, "Ask God for More of God: Lessons for a Better Prayer Life," Desiring God, January 19, 2024, https://www.desiring god.org/.

3. Tim Keller, *Prayer: Experiencing Awe and Intimacy with God* (New York: Dutton, 2014), 9–10.

4. They commend this practice to others: "Pray together as the last words of the day. One can hardly pray in anger (not very easily, anyway), and even if all you do is spend five minutes petitioning God for his blessing on your family and your lives, you will have to relinquish your anger in order to enter God's presence." Timothy and Kathy Keller, *On Marriage* (New York: Penguin, 2020), 33.

5. Collin Hansen, *Timothy Keller: His Spiritual and Intellectual Formation* (Grand Rapids, MI: Zondervan Reflective, 2023), 190. Hansen elaborates on this anecdote in "Collin Hansen on The Making of Tim Keller, Overcoming Loneliness, Tim's Teenage Rebellion, How He Finished Well, and Why He Wanted People to Know About His Weaknesses," *The Carey Nieuwhof Leadership Podcast*, July 11, 2023, https://careynieuwhof.com/.

6. William Gurnall, *The Christian in Complete Armour* (1655; repr., Carlisle, PA: Banner of Truth, 1964), 12.

7. Hansen, *Timothy Keller*, 193. See also Tim Keller, "Prayer and the Life of Redeemer Presbyterian Church," Redeemer Report, September 2014, https://www.redeemer.com/.

8. For a description of the revival-like conditions of this period, see Hansen, *Timothy Keller*, 202–3.

9. Tim Keller, "How to Pray," preached on May 6, 1990. Similarly, he writes, "The infallible test of spiritual integrity . . . is your private prayer life." Keller, *Prayer*, 23. He also sounds this warning to pastors in Keller, *Preaching: Communicating Faith in an Age of Skepticism* (New York: Viking, 2015), 168–69, and Keller, *Serving a Movement: Doing Balanced, Gospel-Centered Ministry in Your City* (Grand Rapids, MI: Zondervan, 2016), 77.

10. Tim Keller, "Keller on Quiet Times, Mysticism, and the Priceless Payoff of Prayer," interviewed by Matt Smethurst, The Gospel Coalition, October 21, 2014, https://www.thegospelcoalition.org/.

11. Tim Keller, "Beyond the Daily Devotional," Redeemer Report, February 2019, https://www.redeemer.com/. In 1997, Keller introduced a winter sermon series with a personal admission: "What we want to do for several weeks here in the coldest part of the year is to try to get warm. I don't know about you, but [my] spiritual walk with God, my experience with God, [tends to be] warm when it's warm and . . . cold when it's cold. I tend to have more time, or maybe more ability or even more passion, to really get close to God in the warm weather. Then what happens is, during the fall, [ministry and church activity] gears up [and] I find myself right after Christmas looking at Jesus and saying, 'Hi, stranger.' My prayer life has just gotten shorter and shorter every day, every week, and so on. When it gets cold, it's a great time to try to get warm." Keller, "Discipline of Desire:

Part 1," preached on January 19, 1997. Elsewhere he writes, "Every year I look forward to the slower pace of the summer months because of the opportunity it gives me to reinvigorate my prayer life. It's not that I don't pray during the year, but rarely, in the press of hectic scheduling, am I able to consistently devote the hours necessary to reawaken the intimacy with God that not only I crave, but which is my only defense against burnout." Keller, "A Prayer Life That Nourishes Your Relationship with God," Redeemer Churches and Ministries, https://www .redeemer.com/.

12. "The way forward for me came by going back to my own spiritual-theological roots." Keller, *Prayer*, 14.

13. Keller, *Prayer*, 16–17. In the Reformed heritage he discovered "no choice offered between truth *or* Spirit, between doctrine *or* experience." Keller, 15 (emphasis original).

14. Keller, *Prayer*, 80.

15. Keller, "Keller on Quiet Times, Mysticism, and the Priceless Payoff of Prayer."

16. Keller, "Keller on Quiet Times, Mysticism, and the Priceless Payoff of Prayer."

17. Keller, *Prayer*, 180.

18. Keller, *Prayer*, 56. Further, "Our prayers should arise out of immersion in the Scripture. . . . We speak only to the degree we are spoken to." Keller, 55. And, "We would never produce the full range of biblical prayer if we were initiating prayer according to our own inner needs and psychology. It can only be produced if we are responding in prayer according to who God is as revealed in the Scripture. . . . Some prayers in the Bible are like an intimate conversation with a friend, others like an appeal to a great monarch, and others approximate a wrestling match. Why? In every case the nature of the prayer is determined by the character of God, who is at once our friend, father, lover, shepherd, and king. We must not decide how to pray based on what types of prayer are the most effective for producing the experiences and feelings we want. We pray in response to God himself." Keller, 60.

19. Keller, *Prayer*, 62. See also Keller, "Prayer in the Psalms," workshop at The Gospel Coalition 2016 Women's Conference, published October 27, 2017, https://www .thegospelcoalition.org/.

20. Timothy Keller, *Encounters with Jesus: Unexpected Answers to Life's Biggest Questions* (New York: Viking, 2013), 167.

21. Keller, *Prayer*, 149. He later commends reading a biblical passage slowly and answering certain questions: "What does this teach me about God and his character? About human nature, character, and behavior? About Christ and his salvation? About the church, or life in the people of God? . . . Another fruitful approach to meditation is to ask application questions. Look within the passage: for any personal examples to emulate or avoid, for any commands to obey, for any promises to claim, and for any warnings to heed." Keller, 153, 154.

22. Keller, *Prayer*, 57. Elsewhere he explains, "Meditation is not any of the contemplative practices that aim at getting beyond words and rational thought into pure awareness of our oneness with God. Biblical meditation, rather, is filling the mind

with Scripture and then 'loading the heart' with it (to use John Owen's phrase) until it affects not only the emotions but the entire life." Keller, "Keller on Quiet Times, Mysticism, and the Priceless Payoff of Prayer."

23. Keller, *Prayer*, 162. He states simply, "Meditate to the point of delight." Keller, 159. Elsewhere he writes, "Often, as you are meditating, or as you are praying, you may feel your heart warm or even melt with a spiritual sense of the reality of God. Sometimes, of course, nothing happens at all! And very rarely, you can have life-changing experiences of the presence of God that you never forget. The number and power of these encounters are completely out of your control. The Spirit blows wherever he pleases (John 3:8). But it has only been with the practice of meditation that my own experience of God's reality has become at all regular and progressively deeper." Keller, "A Prayer Life That Nourishes Your Relationship to God," Redeemer Churches and Ministries, https://www .redeemer.com/.

24. Keller, *Prayer*, 21.

25. Keller, *Prayer*, 68.

26. Keller derived this from Martyn Lloyd-Jones, who credited the seventeenth-century Puritan Thomas Goodwin. See Martyn Lloyd-Jones, *Joy Unspeakable: Power and Renewal in the Holy Spirit* (1984; repr., New York: Crown, 2000), 95–96. Keller first shared the illustration with Redeemer on April 29, 1990, and returned to it nearly every year.

27. Keller, *Prayer*, 70. Keller also puts it this way: "Prayer is like waking up from a nightmare to reality. We laugh at what we took so seriously inside the dream. We realize that all is truly well. Of course, prayer can have the opposite effect; it can puncture illusions and show us we are in more spiritual danger than we thought." Keller, 130.

28. Tim Keller, "Basis of Prayer: 'Our Father,'" preached on April 23, 1995.

29. Keller, *Prayer*, 189.

30. As Keller explains, "Adoration and thanksgiving—God-centeredness—comes first, because it heals the heart of its self-centeredness, which curves us in on ourselves and distorts all our vision. . . . [Prayer grants] relief from the melancholy burden of self-absorption." Keller, *Prayer*, 114, 139.

31. Timothy Keller, *The Prodigal God: Recovering the Heart of the Christian Faith* (New York: Penguin, 2008), 72–74. On a related note, Keller makes the interesting observation that in all of Paul's writings, his prayers for his friends "contain no appeals for changes in their circumstances." Keller, *Prayer*, 20.

32. Keller, "Call to Worship," preached on August 24, 2008. Or as he writes, "When life is going smoothly, and our truest heart treasures seem safe, it does not occur to us to pray." Keller, *Prayer*, 77.

33. In an autobiographical reflection on his journey in prayer, Keller recalls something he said decades earlier at West Hopewell Presbyterian Church in Virginia that made a difference in one member's life. "Before petition comes adoration. In fact, two-thirds of the Lord's Prayer is adoration. So I guess what this means— I remember preaching this—is, don't . . . start praying *to* God for the thing you

want until you've spent [time] realizing that *in* God you've got everything you want." Keller, "A Personal Testimony on Prayer."

34. Keller, *Prayer*, 24.

35. Tim Keller, "The World and Jesus," preached on December 21, 2014.

36. Keller, *Prayer*, 122.

37. Keller, "Keller on Quiet Times, Mysticism, and the Priceless Payoff of Prayer."

38. Keller, *Prayer*, 26.

39. Keller, *Prayer*, 86. Later he writes, "Imagine you get a notice that someone left you some money, but for various reasons, you assume it is a very modest amount. You get busy and don't get around even to checking on it for quite a while. Finally, you do so and are thunderstruck to discover it was a fortune, and you had not been doing anything with it. *You were actually rich but had been living poor.* This is what Paul wants his Christian friends to avoid, and only through encounter with God in prayer can they avoid it." Keller, 168 (emphasis added).

40. The power of corporate prayer cannot be overestimated. "Giving priority to the inner life doesn't mean an individualistic life," Keller writes. "Knowing the God of the Bible better can't be achieved all by yourself. It entails the community of the church, participation in corporate worship as well as private devotion, and instruction in the Bible as well as silent meditation. At the heart of all the various ways of knowing God is both public and private prayer. . . . [We] cannot know God only on our own but must do so in community with others. Jesus did not teach us to pray '*my* Father' but '*our* Father.'" Keller, *Prayer*, 23, 91 (emphasis original). And invoking a favorite insight from C. S. Lewis's *The Four Loves*, as we saw in chapter 4, Keller observes, "If it takes a community to know an ordinary human being, how much more necessary would it be to get to know Jesus alongside others? By praying with friends, you will be able to hear and see facets of Jesus that you have not yet perceived." Keller, 119. See C. S. Lewis, *The Four Loves* (New York: Harcourt, 1960), 61.

41. Tim Keller, *Forgive: Why Should I and How Can I?* (New York: Viking, 2022), 192.

42. Keller, *Prayer*, 140.

43. Keller, *Prayer*, 32. Moreover, "Though we must always end prayers with 'nevertheless, thy will be done,' our prayers should nonetheless begin with great striving with God. Luther had the temerity to talk of importunate prayer as 'conquering God.' Prayer is not a passive, calm, quiet practice." Keller, 136. Elsewhere he counsels, "I believe prayer should be *more often* than the classic once-daily Quiet Time. . . . I personally find morning and evening prayer the best for me, but I also try to sometimes practice a brief, midday 'stand-up' time of focused prayer to reconnect to my morning prayer insights." Keller, 245–46 (emphasis original).

44. Keller, *Prayer*, 231.

45. Keller, *Prayer*, 236. He preaches, "God's grace virtually never operates on our time frame, never operates on a schedule we consider reasonable, almost never operates according to our time measurements, our calendars, our agendas." Keller, "The Man Who Would Not Be Hurried," preached on December 17, 2000.

46. John Newton, *The Letters of John Newton* (Carlisle, PA: Banner of Truth, 1960), 179–80. Keller first referenced this at Redeemer in a sermon titled "Passive Discipline" on January 21, 1990. Introducing the quote from Newton, he remarked, "This guy was the best pastor I've ever seen in my life." Years later, reflecting on the Joseph story in his book on suffering, Keller enlarged on Newton's insight: "If the story of Joseph and the whole of the Bible is true, then anything that comes into your life is something that, as painful as it is, you need in some way. And anything you pray for that does not come from [God], even if you are sure you cannot live without it, you do not really need." Timothy Keller, *Walking with God through Pain and Suffering* (New York: Penguin, 2013), 267.

47. Keller, *Walking with God*, 267.

48. Keller, *Walking with God*, 302.

49. Keller shared this numerous times at Redeemer, beginning with a sermon on October 4, 1990, titled "Spiritual Gifts: Part 4." Elsewhere he invokes the staggering promise of Romans 8:26, writing, "The Spirit, even when you do not know how to pray, takes your core prayer and prays as you should be praying before the throne (cf. Rom 8:26). When you struggle in prayer, you can come before God with the confidence that he is going to give you what you would have asked for if you knew everything he knows. He does care, and he loves you boundlessly." Keller, *Prayer*, 229.

50. Tim Keller, "Repose: The Power and Glory," preached on November 16, 2014. Why, Keller asks, was Job commended at the end of his long saga of suffering? In part because he never stopped praying: "Yes, he complained, but he complained to *God*. He doubted, but he doubted to *God*. He screamed and yelled, but he did it in God's presence. No matter how much in agony he was, he continued to address God. He kept seeking him. And in the end, God said Job triumphed. How wonderful that our God sees the grief and anger and questioning, and is still willing to say 'you triumphed'—not because it was all fine, not because Job's heart and motives were always right, but because Job's doggedness in seeking the face and presence of God meant that *the suffering did not drive him away from God but toward him*. And that made all the difference. As John Newton said, if we are not getting much out of going to God in prayer, we will certainly get nothing out of staying away." Keller, *Walking with God*, 287–88 (emphasis original); cf. 321.

51. Keller, *Prayer*, 76.

52. Keller was often critical of Eastern meditation in sermons. In addition to his book on prayer, here's an example from 1993: "The goal of Eastern religion and the goal of Eastern meditation is to help you see [that] you and God are the same, whereas the goal of Christian meditation is to show you that you and God are utterly different. The problem you're trying to address in Christian meditation is you really don't realize how holy he is, how loving he is, how wise he is. In Eastern meditation, the whole idea is to find yourself; in Christian meditation, it's to find God. In Eastern meditation, to find the sameness between you and God; in Christian meditation, to find the utter difference in which is the great glory and comfort of the Christian faith." Keller, "Paul's Prayer: Part 2," preached on

August 29, 1993. See also Keller, "The Bridge to Prayer: Practicing the Christian Life," preached on April 27, 2008.

53. Keller, "Keller on Quiet Times, Mysticism, and the Priceless Payoff of Prayer."

54. Keller, *Prayer*, 104.

55. Keller, *Prayer*, 105. Elsewhere Keller names two distortions of prayer that arise from a lack of orientation to the gospel: light without heat and heat without light. He writes, "So, ironically, we see that 'heat without light' prayer and 'light without heat' prayer both stem from the same root. They come from works-righteousness, a conviction that we can earn God's favor, and a loss of orientation with respect to our free justification and adoption." Keller, "Prayer and the Gospel," Redeemer Churches and Ministries, https://www.redeemer.com/.

56. This multifaceted character of prayer can be seen by surveying Keller's "twelve touchstones" for evaluating our prayer lives. He groups them into four clusters of three. For the full discussion, see Keller, *Prayer*, 121–41.

57. Keller, *Prayer*, 237–38 (emphasis original).

58. In a 1996 sermon reflecting on the promise of James 5:16—"The prayer of a righteous person is powerful and effective (NIV)"—Keller told his congregation, "Prayer makes a dent in the world. . . . It really changes things." In the sermon he also quotes fourth-century preacher John Chrysostom: "The potency of prayer has subdued the strength of fire. It has bridled the rage of lions. It has expelled demons. It has broken the chains of death. It has assuaged diseases. It has rescued cities from destruction. It has stopped the sun in its course. It has arrested the progress of the thunderbolt." (All these, of course, are examples from the Bible.) Chrysostom concludes, "There is in prayer an all-sufficient armory, a treasure undiminished, a mine never exhausted, a sky unobscured by clouds, a heaven unruffled by any storm. It's the root, the fountain, the mother of thousands of blessings." Keller, "Healing and Prayer," preached on April 14, 1996. See also Chrysostom, *On the Incomprehensibility of God*, homily 5, quoted in *Ancient Christian Commentary on Scripture*, New Testament 2, *Mark*, ed. Thomas C. Oden and Christopher A. Hall (Downers Grove, IL: IVP Academic, 1998), 162.

59. Keller, *Prayer*, 18 (emphasis original). Further, "A rich, vibrant, consoling, hard-won prayer life is the one good that makes it possible to receive all other kinds of goods rightly and beneficially." Keller, 21. Here's how Keller put it in the afore-mentioned autobiographical talk about his own prayer journey: "The worst thing God can do . . . is to let good things happen to you without prayer, so that you become self-sufficient. . . . The worst thing that can happen to you is that blessings come into your life that you haven't prayed for. Our hearts are not ready for [his] blessings unless we pray for them." Keller, "A Personal Testimony on Prayer."

Chapter 8: The Painful Gift

1. This paragraph is adapted from Tim Keller, "Tim Keller Wants You to Suffer Well," interviewed by Matt Smethurst, The Gospel Coalition, October 1, 2013, https://www.thegospelcoalition.org/.

2. Timothy Keller, *Walking with God through Pain and Suffering* (New York: Dutton, 2013), 3. Tim and Kathy had Psalm 34:1–3 engraved in their wedding rings: "I will bless the LORD at all times; / his praise shall continually be in my mouth. / My soul makes its boast in the Lord; / let the afflicted hear and be glad. / O magnify the LORD with me, / and let us exalt his name together!" "At the time," reflected Keller decades later, "we almost completely ignored the words at the center of the passage. The text's definition of ministry success is that 'the afflicted hear and be glad.' One of the reasons that phrase was lost on us then was because, as Kathy said later, 'at that age neither of us had suffered so much as an ingrown toenail.' We were young, and the hubris of youth does not imagine pain and suffering. Little did we understand how crucial it would be to help people understand and face affliction, and to face it well ourselves." Keller, *Walking with God*, 4.

3. Timothy Keller, *On Death* (New York: Penguin, 2020), 42 (emphasis original). As Kathy Keller explains in the foreword, this short book is based on a sermon Tim delivered at Kathy's sister's funeral.

4. Keller, *On Death*, 43. The sentences in this paragraph without quotation marks are paraphrased for clarity.

5. Keller, *On Death*, 38–39. Keller captures death's multifaceted devastation by identifying it as "the Great Interruption," "the Great Schism," "the Great Insult," and "our Great Enemy." Keller, *On Death*, 1–3.

6. Keller, *Walking with God*, 80.

7. Keller, *On Death*, 9–10.

8. Keller explains, "In the secular view, this material world is all there is. And so the meaning of life is to have the freedom to choose the life that makes you most happy. However, in that view of things, [suffering] is a complete interruption of your life story—it cannot be a meaningful part of the story. [It] should be avoided at almost any cost, or minimized to the greatest degree possible. This means that when facing unavoidable and irreducible suffering, secular people must *smuggle in* resources from other views of life, having recourse to ideas of karma, or Buddhism, or Greek Stoicism, or Christianity, even though their beliefs about the nature of the universe do not line up with those resources. . . . In the strictly secular view, suffering cannot be a good chapter in your life story—only an interruption of it. It can't take you home; it can only keep you from the things you most want in life. In short, in the secular view, suffering always wins." Keller, *Walking with God*, 16–17, 22–23 (emphasis added).

9. Keller, *On Death*, 11.

10. Keller, *On Death*, 15. Also, "Modern culture [is] the worst in history at preparing its members for the only inevitability—death." Keller, 11.

11. Keller, *Walking with God*, 72.

12. Keller, *Walking with God*, 30.

13. Keller, *Walking with God*, 31. Suffering is not a minor theme in God's word; it's at the heart of the story. Indeed, there is a sense in which the Bible is "about suffering as much as it is about anything." Keller, 6.

14. Keller, *Walking with God*, 74.

15. Keller, *Walking with God*, 86.

16. Keller first deployed this argument, I believe, in "Lord of the Whips," preached on November 24, 1996. He quips, "If God is so infinite and great that you're mad at him for not rectifying your situation, then he must be infinite and great enough to have wisdom that is not answerable to yours." See also Keller, *Walking with God*, 99.

17. Timothy Keller, *The Reason for God: Belief in an Age of Skepticism* (New York: Dutton, 2008), 23. Elsewhere he writes, "In earlier times, when suffering occurred, just because we couldn't think within our own mind of good reasons for it didn't mean there couldn't be any. We were humbler about our ability to understand the world." Keller, *Walking with God*, 55; cf. 97. Keller makes a key observation: "Modern discussions of the problem of suffering *start* with an abstract God—a God who, for the sake of argument, is all-powerful and all-good, but who is not glorious, majestic, infinitely wise, beginningless, and the creator and sustainer of all things. No wonder, then, that modern people are far more prone than their ancestors to conclude that, if *they* can see no good reason for a particular instance of suffering, God could not have any justifiable reasons for it either." Keller, 87 (emphasis added).

18. Keller, *Walking with God*, 285.

19. Keller, *Walking with God*, 121–22. Keller also writes, "When one of my sons was around eight years old, he began to exert his will and resist his parents' directions. One time I told him to do something and he said, 'Dad, I'll obey you and do this—but only if first you explain to me why I should do it.' I responded something like this: 'If you obey me only because it makes sense to you, then that's not obedience; it's just agreement. The problem is that you are too young to understand most of the reasons why I want you to do this. Do it because you are eight and I'm thirty-eight—because you are a child and I'm an adult and your father.' We can easily see why children need to trust their parents even when they do not understand them. How much more, then, should we trust God even though *we* do not understand him." Keller, 261–62 (emphasis added). For another bracing reflection on this theme, see the story about Elisabeth Elliot in Keller, 170–74.

20. Tim Keller, "Tim Keller on God and Coronavirus," Premier Christian News, April 9, 2020, YouTube video, https://www.youtube.com/.

21. Edward Shillito, "Jesus of the Scars," in *Masterpieces of Religious Verse*, ed. James Dalton Morrison (New York: Harper Brothers, 1958), 235. Keller first cited the poem in "How to Handle Trouble," preached on September 26, 1993. On this theme, he also sometimes quoted John Stott: "I could never myself believe in God if it were not for the cross. . . . In the real world of pain, how could one worship a God who was immune to it?" John Stott, *Why I Am a Christian* (Downers Grove, IL: InterVarsity, 2003), 63–64. See, for example, Keller, "The Sacrifice," preached on March 20, 2005. Of course, it's significant that Jesus graciously showed his scars to doubting Thomas (John 20:27).

22. Keller, *Walking with God*, 5. He writes later in the book, "Average people in Western society have extremely unrealistic ideas of how much control they have

over how their lives go. Suffering removes the blinders. It does not so much make us helpless and out of control as it shows us we have *always* been vulnerable and dependent on God. Suffering merely helps us wake up to that fact and live in accordance with it." Keller, 190–91 (emphasis original).

23. Keller, *Walking with God*, 5.

24. Tim Keller, "Truth, Tears, Anger, and Grace," preached on September 16, 2001. This was one of Keller's favorite metaphors for handling grief. He first shared it with Redeemer in a 1990 sermon titled "Joy: Overcoming Boredom." In that message he also likened the process to rubbing salt into a flesh wound: "Though it stings, [the salt] keeps [the wound] from [getting infected]. Christians rub their hope into their grief so it keeps it from going bad."

25. Keller, *Walking with God*, 123. Further, "Suffering tends to make you self-absorbed. If it is seen as mainly about you and your own growth, it will strangle you truly. Instead, we must look at suffering—whatever the proximate causes—as primarily a way to know God better, as an opening for serving, resembling, and drawing near to him as never before. It is only if we make God's glory primary in suffering that it will achieve our own." Keller, 188.

26. Keller, *Walking with God*, 225, (emphasis added).

27. Keller, *Walking with God*, 299 (emphasis added).

28. Keller, *Walking with God*, 298.

29. Keller, *Walking with God*, 289 (emphasis original).

30. Timothy Keller, "Growing My Faith in the Face of Death," *The Atlantic*, March 7, 2021, https://www.theatlantic.com/.

31. Keller, *Walking with God*, 291. Two years before his death, Keller wrote, "The first [discipline helping me face pancreatic cancer] was to immerse myself in the Psalms to be sure that I wasn't encountering a God I had made up myself. Any God I make up will be less troubling and offensive, to be sure, but then how can such a God contradict me when my heart says that there's no hope, or that I'm worthless? The Psalms show me a God maddening in his complexity, but this difficult deity comes across as a real being, not one any human would have conjured." Keller, "Growing My Faith."

32. Keller, *Walking with God*, 284.

33. Keller, *Walking with God*, 293. Moreover, "The paradox [of Job] should not be missed. God comes both as a gracious, personal God and as an infinite, overwhelming force—at the very same time. He is both at once. How can this be? Only in Jesus Christ do we see how the untamable, infinite God can become a baby and a loving Savior. On the cross we see how both the love and the holiness of God can be fulfilled at once. God is so holy and just Jesus had to die for sins or we could not be forgiven. But he was so filled with love for us he laid down his life willingly. The gospel, then, explains how God can be both the God of love and of fury that Job meets on that dark and stormy day." Keller, 282.

34. Keller, *Walking with God*, 130.

35. Keller, *Walking with God*, 207–13.

36. Keller, *Walking with God*, 227 (emphasis original).

37. Keller, *Walking with God*, 196–97 (emphasis added).

38. Keller, *Walking with God*, 199.

39. Keller, *Walking with God*, 234 (emphasis original).

40. That is, Christians in name only. Keller explains, "Many people today believe in God, and may go to church, but if you ask them whether they are certain of their salvation and acceptance with God, or whether the idea of Jesus' sacrificial death on the cross is real and profoundly moving to them, or whether they are convinced of the bodily resurrection of Jesus and believers—you are likely to get a negative answer, or just a stare. . . . It is as we get larger in our own eyes, less dependent on God's grace and revelation, and surer that we understand how the universe works and how history should go that the problem of evil becomes so intolerable. And it is only as God becomes more remote—a God who is all-loving only in the abstract, not in the sense of having suffered and died for us to rescue us from evil—that he seems unbearably callous in the face of pain. In short, theism without certainty of salvation or resurrection is far more disillusioning in the midst of pain than is atheism. *When suffering, believing in God thinly or in the abstract is worse than not believing in God at all.*" Keller, *Walking with God*, 59–60 (emphasis added).

41. On May 5, 2020, Keller preached a sermon on Psalm 126 titled "Don't Waste Your Sorrows."

42. Keller, *Walking with God*, 248–49 (emphasis original). Speaking of continuing to "do your duties," Keller further explains, "The strength you need for suffering comes in the *doing* of the responsibilities and duties God requires. Shirk no commands of God. Read, pray, study, fellowship, serve, witness, obey. Do all your duties that you physically can, and the God of peace will be with you." Keller, 288 (emphasis added).

43. Keller, *Walking with God*, 249. Moreover, "It is one thing to have an intellectual explanation for why God allows suffering; it is another thing to actually find a path through suffering so that, instead of becoming more bitter, cynical, despondent, and broken, you become more wise, grounded, humble, strong, and even content." Keller, 202.

44. Keller, *Walking with God*, 163, (emphasis added).

45. Keller, *Walking with God*, 180–81. This quote is a paraphrase of words attributed to George MacDonald.

46. Keller, *Walking with God*, 6 (emphasis original).

47. Keller, *Walking with God*, 313.

48. Keller, *Walking with God*, 314.

49. This paragraph is adapted from Matt Smethurst, "The Gospel Explained," The Gospel Coalition, July 1, 2023, and the next sentence is adapted from Matt Smethurst, "Is There Proof of Heaven?," The Gospel Coalition, April 6, 2016. Both available at https://www.thegospelcoalition.org/.

50. Keller made this consolation-versus-restoration contrast in numerous sermons, beginning with "The Grammar of Hope," preached on March 21, 2004. It also appears in *Reason for God*, 32; *Making Sense of God*, 171–72; *Walking with God*,

46, 59, 117, 159; *On Death*, 54; and *Hope in Times of Fear*, 208. "The Biblical view of things is resurrection—not a future that is just a *consolation* for the life we never had but a *restoration* of the life you always wanted. This means that every horrible thing that ever happened will not only be undone and repaired but will in some way make the eventual glory and joy even greater." Keller offers an analogy: "A few years ago I had a horrible nightmare in which I dreamed that everyone in my family had died. When I awoke my relief was enormous—but there was much more than just relief. My delight in each member of my family was tremendously enriched. I looked at each one and realized how grateful I was for them, how deeply I loved them. Why? My joy had been greatly magnified by the nightmare. . . . [In] the end my love for them was only greater for my having lost them and found them again. This same dynamic is at work when you lose some possession you take for granted. When you find it again (having thought it was gone forever) you cherish and appreciate it in a far deeper way." Keller, *Reason for God*, 32 (emphasis original).

51. Keller, *Walking with God*, 158.

52. Keller, *On Death*, 32–33. Keller shared this illustration in several sermons over the years: "Upside-Down Living" (2003), "Death and the Christian Hope" (2004), "And If Christ Be Not Raised" (2006), "The New Heaven and New Earth" (2009), and "Confident in Hope" (2017).

53. Jesus took the judgment *we* deserved so that, through faith, we could get the blessing *he* deserved. Keller deployed such phrasing numerous times. For example, reflecting on 2 Corinthians 5:21: "The cross means nothing if it's not the hugest reversal ever. God puts himself where we deserve to be so, if we believe . . . we will go where he deserves to be. In other words, the Lord Jesus takes upon himself what we deserve to get so that, when we believe in him, we get what he deserved." Tim Keller, "The World's Sword," preached on April 9, 2000. As Keller prayed before celebrating the Lord's Supper, "When we take the cup, we're thinking about [Christ's] poured-out life and the wrath of God that you poured into his heart—so there's no wrath left for us." Tim Keller, "Holiness," preached on April 23, 1995.

54. Keller, *On Death*, 94.

55. Keller, *Walking with God*, 231.

56. Keller, *Walking with God*, 231 (emphasis original).

57. Keller, *Walking with God*, 308. Also, "[Jesus Christ] did not abandon us despite all his own suffering. Do you think he will abandon you now in the midst of yours?" Keller, 251.

58. See Tim Keller, "The Man in the Furnace" (May 7, 2000) and "The King and the Furnace" (August 21, 2011).

59. Keller, *Walking with God*, 274. Scripture's "profoundly realistic and yet astonishingly hopeful" teaching on suffering keeps us from various pitfalls, such as thinking we can "run *from* the furnace (avoid it) or quickly run through it (deny it) or just lie down hopelessly (despair in it)." Keller, 9.

60. Keller, "Growing My Faith in the Face of Death." This was Keller's second bout with cancer. In 2002, he was diagnosed with thyroid cancer and underwent

surgery to remove it. He recounts in his book on suffering, "There have not been many times in my life when I felt 'the peace that passes understanding' [Phil. 4:7]. But there was one time for which I am very grateful. . . . On the morning of my surgery, after I said my goodbyes to my wife and sons, I was wheeled into a room to be prepped. And in the moments before they gave me the anesthetic, I prayed. To my surprise, I got a sudden, clear, new perspective on everything. It seemed to me that the universe was an enormous realm of joy, mirth, and high beauty. Of course it was—didn't the Triune God make it to be filled with his own boundless joy, wisdom, love, and delight? And within this great globe of glory was only one little speck of darkness—our world—where there was temporarily pain and suffering. But it was only one speck, and soon that speck would fade away and everything would be light. And I thought, 'It doesn't really matter how the surgery goes. Everything will be all right. Me—my wife, my children, my church—will all be all right.' I went to sleep with a bright peace on my heart." Keller, *Walking with God*, 318.

61. Keller, "Growing My Faith in the Face of Death" (first emphasis original; second emphasis added).

62. Timothy Keller, *Hope in Times of Fear: The Resurrection and the Meaning of Easter* (New York: Viking, 2021), 24 (emphasis original). In the acknowledgments at the end of the book, Keller reflects, "Writing in such dark times helped me see in the resurrection new depths of comfort and power. This is not to claim that this is a better book than others I have written. Let readers be the judge of that. *But it is the one in which I felt the most divine guidance and help.*" Keller, 217 (emphasis added).

63. Keller, *Hope in Times of Fear*, 62 (emphasis removed).

64. Keller, *Walking with God*, 301.

65. Tim Keller in, "A Conversation with Pastor Tim Keller About Hope in Times of Fear," Russell Moore, March 31, 2021, YouTube video, https://www.youtube.com/.

66. Tim Keller, "Tim Keller on Reformed Resurgence," interviewed by Kevin DeYoung, Collin Hansen, and Justin Taylor, *Life and Books and Everything* (podcast), Clearly Reformed, February 3, 2021, https://clearlyreformed.org/.

67. Keller made the same point in his 2021 *Atlantic* essay: "Since my diagnosis, Kathy and I have come to see that the more we tried to make a heaven out of this world—the more we grounded our comfort and security in it—the less we were able to enjoy it. . . . [But] to our surprise and encouragement, Kathy and I have discovered that the less we attempt to make this world into a heaven, the more we are able to enjoy it. No longer are we burdening it with demands impossible for it to fulfill. We have found that the simplest things—from sun on the water and flowers in the vase to our own embraces, sex, and conversation—bring more joy than ever. . . . As God's reality dawns more on my heart, slowly and painfully and through many tears, the simplest pleasures of this world have become sources of daily happiness. It is only as I have become, for lack of a better term, more *heavenly minded* that I can see the material world for the astonishingly good divine gift that it is." Keller, "Growing My Faith in the Face of Death."

68. See "George Herbert, "Time" (1633), in *The English Poems of George Herbert*, ed. Helen Wilcock (Cambridge: Cambridge University Press, 2007), 432. The third stanza of Herbert's poem reads, "And in his blessing thou art blest: / For where thou onely wert before / An executioner at best; / Thou art a gard'ner now, and more, / An usher to convey our souls / Beyond the utmost starres and poles." Keller first paraphrased Herbert's quote in "Death of Death," preached on May 16, 1993.

69. Timothy Keller, *Making Sense of God: An Invitation to the Skeptical* (New York: Penguin, 2016), 166.

70. Tim Keller, "Questions About Jesus," Questioning Christianity, Q&A at Redeemer Presbyterian Church on March 13, 2014. Technically he is invoking two verses (1 Cor. 6:19–20). Or as the apostle Paul elsewhere puts it, "For if we live, we live to the Lord, and if we die, we die to the Lord. So then, whether we live or whether we die, we are the Lord's" (Rom. 14:8).

71. Tim Keller (@timkellernyc), "I have Stage IV . . . ," Twitter, December 3, 2021, 1:33 p.m., https://x.com/.

72. Tim Keller (@timkellernyc), "Health Update: Today, Dad is . . . ," Twitter, May 18, 2023, 4:44 p.m., https://x.com/ (emphasis added).

73. Tim Keller (@timkellernyc), "Timothy J. Keller, husband, father . . . ," Twitter, May 19, 2023, 11:17 a.m., https://x.com/.

74. Keller, *Walking with God*, 52. Elsewhere he writes, "Everything in this life is going to be taken away from us, except one thing: God's love, which can go into death with us and take us through it and into his arms. It's the one thing you can't lose. Without God's love to embrace us, we will always feel radically insecure, and we ought to be. . . . It's in death that God says, 'If I'm not your security, then you've got no security, because I'm the only thing that can't be taken away from you. I will hold you in my everlasting arms. Every other set of arms will fail you, but I will never fail you.'" Keller, *On Death*, 26, 27–28.

75. Keller, *Walking with God*, 299.

Conclusion

1. The future resurrection of believers is so certain that the Bible can liken death to a long nap. See the multiple uses of "asleep" in, for example, 1 Cor. 15 and 1 Thess. 4.

2. You can download the program and watch the service at https://timothykeller .com/. Ligon Duncan summed it up well: "Simple, beautiful, Protestant, Evangelical, funeral service. Filled with Gospel hope and great hymns." Duncan (@LigonDuncan), "Simple, beautiful . . . ," X (formerly Twitter), August 15, 2023, 3:30 p.m., https://x.com/.

3. These Scripture quotations are taken from the NIV.

4. Collin Hansen, *Timothy Keller: His Spiritual and Intellectual Formation* (Grand Rapids, MI: Zondervan Reflective, 2023), xi, xii.

5. Tim Keller "Message from Tim Keller," Redeemer Churches and Ministries, https://www.redeemer.com/. Thirty-four years earlier, when Redeemer was just a few months old, Keller had delivered a sober warning. It's worth paraphrasing

in full: "You must not mistake the exercise of gifts for grace. I can be very, very honest about this. It's easy for me to be extremely busy because I'm a professional Christian. I'm talking to people all the time. I'm teaching all the time. But if I'm neglecting my growth in grace—if I'm neglecting to look at my heart and see whether I'm really developing more love for people and for God, if I'm neglecting my prayer life so I'm not really experiencing his presence, if I'm neglecting my inner life—then all my busyness can draw out of me a certain sense of warmth. I have a gift of teaching, so when I begin to teach, I feel a certain warmth that comes out.

What is that? A certain spiritual warmth and passion because it's my spiritual gift—but I can be dying on the inside, and the exercise of my gift is masking that. That's the reason why it's possible for very, very gifted ministers to be doing great deeds and winning people and transforming their lives—and then suddenly collapse, or do some scandalous sin, or just say, 'I've had it' and pick up and leave their wife or something like that. Everybody says, 'How could that be? Was he a hypocrite?'

No. Sometime a long time ago, probably, he began to neglect the actual growth in grace. He began to mistake the exercise of gifts for the exercise of grace—because he was getting so many pats on the back, and he was so busy, and he said, 'Hey! I must be growing. I'm growing because my church is growing. I'm growing because more people are telling me how great I am. More people are buying my tapes. That's why I must be growing.' But all the while, he was shrinking inside." Tim Keller, "How Can We Grow?," preached on October 1, 1989.

Acknowledgments

1. Graham Howell, "How God Is Making Me into Who I'm Meant to Be," Gospel in Life, Spring 2020, https://gospelinlife.com/.

General Index

Abednego, 146–47
Abel, 17
ability, 86
Abraham, 16–17, 164n30
Abrahams, Harold, 87
accountability, 69, 177n16, 179n33, 179n36
achieved identity, 24–25
Adam, 17, 19, 56, 62, 79–80, 176n5
adoption, 124, 201n55
adoration, 121, 125, 198n30
affinity, 86
affliction, 139, 140, 202n2
anger, 167n23
animals, 182n7
antinomianism, 56
anxiety, 44–45, 167n23
apologetics, 170n62
application, 16–17
approval, 36–37
assurance, 147
atheism, 186n40, 205n40
atonement, 13, 21
Augustine, 31, 38–39, 121, 166n12
autonomy, 69, 168n48, 180n38

Babette's feast, 187n46
baptism, 6, 161n18
Barnhouse, Donald Grey, 145
beatitudes, 21–22
betrayal, 142
Bible
  as epic story, 10–12

reduction of, 25
  storyline of, 78–79
  and suffering, 202n13
Bible stories, 9–10
biblical justice, 99, 194–95n51
bigotry, 97
blue-collar work, 3, 83, 84, 90, 91, 160n11
boldness, 92
bravery, 153
The Bride of Frankenstein (film), 62–63
Bucknell University, 2
Buddhism, 136, 202n8
burdens, 71

calling, 83, 84, 184n20
Calvin, John, 32, 39, 85, 121, 164n28,
  192n33
cancer, 118, 145–46, 148–52, 185n31,
  206–7n60
capitalism, 170n63
career, 85–89
career success, 183n18
Carson, D. A., 5
Center for Faith and Work, 5
Chalmers, Thomas, 40, 41
Chariots of Fire (film), 87
charity, 109, 111
Christian
  definition of, 88
  in name only, 205n40
  in the workplace, 91
Christian community, 65

Scripture Index